Microsoft

SOFTWAR

D1543924

REQUIREMENTS

We Try and make Software
a Quantitative Activity
(Process)

Regardless of your Method
the Software Can Only be
as good as the people
developing it. However,
a good implementation
Can Help...

Karl E. Wiegers

PUBLISHED BY
Microsoft Press
A Division of Microsoft Corporation
One Microsoft Way
Redmond, Washington 98052-6399

Library of Congress Cataloging-in-Publication Data
Wiegers, Karl Eugene, 1953–
    Software Requirements / Karl E. Wiegers.
        p.   cm.
    Includes index.
    ISBN 0-7356-0631-5
    1. Computer software--Development.   I. Title.
QA76.76.D47W517 1999
005.1--dc21   99-40447
                                                               CIP

Printed and bound in the United States of America.

7 8 9 10 11 12 13   ML   7 6 5 4 3 2

Distributed in Canada by Penguin Books Canada Limited.

A CIP catalogue record for this book is available from the British Library.

Microsoft Press books are available through booksellers and distributors worldwide. For further information about international editions, contact your local Microsoft Corporation office or contact Microsoft Press International directly at fax (425) 936-7329. Visit our Web site at www.microsoft.com/mspress. Send comments to *mspinput@microsoft.com*.

Acquisitions Editor: Ben Ryan
Project Editor: Mary Kalbach Barnard

For Miss Chris

CONTENTS

PREFACE

D espite some fifty years' collective experience, many software development organizations struggle to gather, document, and manage their product requirements. Lack of user input, incomplete requirements, and changing requirements are the major reasons why information technology projects do not deliver all of their planned functionality on schedule and within budget.[1] Many software developers aren't comfortable or proficient at gathering requirements from customers. Practical requirements engineering techniques aren't widely known to developers, and educational curricula favor technical topics over the softer requirements issues. Project participants often don't even agree on what a "requirement" is.

Software development involves at least as much communication as computing, yet we often emphasize the computing and neglect the communication. This book offers tools to facilitate that communication and help software practitioners, managers, marketers, and customers apply effective requirements engineering methods. It presents many approaches to help the development team and its customers agree on what software must be built to satisfy actual user needs, along with ways to document and manage changes to that agreement. The techniques presented here represent mainstream "good practices" for requirements engineering, not exotic new techniques from the world of academics or an elaborate methodology intended to solve all your requirements problems.

---

1. *The CHAOS Report*, The Standish Group International, Inc., 1995.

Benefits This Book Provides

Of all the software process improvements you could undertake, improved requirements development and management practices will likely provide the greatest benefits. The concepts and methods presented here are independent of specific development methodologies or application domains; you can use them on a wide variety of projects. I focus on describing in a clear fashion a number of practical, proven techniques that can help you to:

- Achieve higher customer satisfaction

- Reduce maintenance and support costs

- Improve the quality of your project's requirements early in the development cycle, which reduces rework and improves productivity

- Meet schedule objectives by controlling scope creep and requirements changes

My objective is to help you improve the processes you use for gathering and analyzing requirements, writing and verifying requirements specifications, and managing the requirements throughout the product development cycle. The goal of process improvement is for people in your organization to work in new ways that yield better results. Therefore, I hope you will actually implement some improved practices, not just read about them.

Case Studies

To help you see how to apply the methods described here, I've provided examples from several case studies based on actual projects. A medium-sized information system called the Chemical Tracking System illustrates many of the techniques. (Don't worry—you don't need to know anything about chemistry to understand this project.) The continuity this sample project provides will help you see how the various practices fit together. Sample dialogues among project participants from the case study projects are sprinkled throughout the book. No matter what kind of software your group builds, I think you'll find these dialogues pertinent.

WHO SHOULD READ THIS BOOK

Anyone involved with defining or understanding the requirements for a new or enhanced software product will find useful information here. One audience includes the analysts, developers, and testers who must understand and satisfy user expectations. A second audience includes users who want to define a product that meets their functional and usability needs. Customers who wish to ensure that the product will satisfy their business needs will better understand the nature and importance of the requirements process. Project managers charged with delivering products on schedule will learn how to manage potentially troublesome requirement changes.

In the course of delivering many training seminars I've found that nontechnical project participants readily understand this material. Anyone who wants to improve his or her understanding of the development process and the critical role that requirements play in software success will find this material helpful.

LOOKING AHEAD

The book is organized into three parts. Part I begins by presenting some basic requirements engineering definitions and describing several characteristics of excellent requirements. I hope you'll share Chapter 2, on the customer–developer partnership, with your key customers. Chapter 3 presents several dozen industry "good practices" for requirements development and management. Chapter 4 helps you plan how to incorporate selected new practices into your group's development process, based on your responses to the current requirements practice self-assessment in the Appendix. Common requirements-related project risks are described in Chapter 5.

Part II presents many techniques for requirements development, beginning with defining the project's business requirements, vision, and scope. Other chapters in Part II address how to find appropriate customer representatives for your project, elicit requirements from the customers, and document functional requirements and quality attributes. Chapter 10 describes several analysis models that represent the requirements from different perspectives, while Chapter 12 addresses the construction and use of software prototypes. Other chapters in Part II explore ways to define requirements priorities and verify that the requirements are correct.

The principles and practices of requirements management are the subject of Part III, particularly techniques for dealing with changing requirements and assessing the impact of each proposed change on the project. Chapter 18 describes how requirements traceability connects individual requirements both to their origins and to downstream development deliverables. Part III concludes with a description of commercial tools that can enhance the way you manage your project's requirements.

FROM PRINCIPLES TO PRACTICE

It's difficult to muster the energy needed to overcome obstacles to change and to put new knowledge into action. You might be tempted to remain in your comfort zone of familiar (if not always effective) practices. To assist you in the journey to improved requirements, each chapter concludes with a section called "Next Steps," detailing specific actions you can take to begin applying the methods presented in that chapter. I have provided annotated templates for requirements documents, inspection checklists, a requirements prioritization spreadsheet, and other items on my Web site, *http://www.processimpact.com*, to jump-start your application of these techniques. Start your requirements improvements small, but start today.

Some project participants will be reluctant to try new requirements techniques. Some people are downright unreasonable, and none of these techniques will work if you're dealing with unreasonable people. Use the material presented here to educate your peers, customers, and managers. Remind them of requirements-related problems that your previous projects encountered, and discuss the potential benefits of some new requirements approaches. Learn together and improve together.

You don't have to launch a new project to begin applying improved requirements engineering practices. An excellent starting point is to put a change control process in place. That way, you can quickly begin to manage requests for requirement changes and enhancements better than you have in the past. As you add new capabilities to an existing application, begin performing systematic impact analysis and creating a traceability matrix to link the new requirements to the corresponding designs, code, and test cases. It's rarely realistic to go back and re-create requirements specifications for an entire existing system. However, you can write the requirements for the next release in a more structured way than before, draw analysis models of the new features, and inspect the new requirements. Implementing requirements practices incrementally is a low-risk process improvement approach that will prepare you for using a suite of new techniques on your next major project.

The goal of requirements engineering is to develop high quality—not perfect—requirements that allow you to proceed with construction at an acceptable level of risk. You need to spend enough time on requirements engineering to minimize the risks of rework, unacceptable products, and blown schedules. This book will help you determine when you've reached the point of suitable requirements quality and suggests some ways to get there.

ACKNOWLEDGMENTS

A number of people took the time to review the manuscript and offer countless recommendations for improvement; they have my deep gratitude. Special thanks go to Kathy Rhode, whose meticulous examination provided many precise and insightful observations that sharpened my thinking and presentation. Chris Fahlbusch, Tammy Hoganson, Deependra Moitra, Mike Rebatzke, Phil Recchio, Johanna Rothman, Joyce Statz, Doris Sturzenberger, Prakash Upadhyayula, and Scott Whitmire commented on nearly every chapter, a time-consuming undertaking for which I'm sincerely grateful. I also appreciate the efforts of those who contributed input on selected chapters, including Steve Adolph, Nikki Bianco, Bill Dagg, Dale Emery, Geoff Flamank, Lynda Fleming, Kathy Getz, Jim Hart, and Mike Malec. These reviewers found many errors in the draft chapters; any that remain are entirely my responsibility.

Thanks also to Steve McConnell, who encouraged me to write a book on software requirements, and to acquisitions editor Ben Ryan of Microsoft Press. Ben helped me explore possible approaches and established a comfortable working relationship from the outset. Mary Kalbach Barnard of Microsoft Press managed the project and, with the assistance of Michelle Goodman, did a fine job of editing the initial manuscript into final form. Artist Rob Nance rendered many preliminary sketches into effective figures and graphics, and compositor Paula Gorelick flowed it all into the pages you see now.

I am grateful to several of my consulting clients, especially Sandy Browning, Matt DeAthos, Kathy Rhode, and Kathy Wallace, who invited me to work with them on their requirements processes, both to teach and to learn. I particularly appreciate Kathy Rhode's willingness to relate her experiences with putting some of the approaches discussed here into action. Thanks also to Robin Goldsmith for offering his perspective on business requirements, and to Matt DeAthos for sharing his delightful term for the last phase of a typical software development project, the "rapid descoping phase." Perhaps some of the techniques presented here will at least alter that to a "controlled descoping phase."

The contributions and feedback from the hundreds of participants in my requirements seminars over the past several years have been most helpful. As a consultant and educator, I learn much from every company I work with and from those seminar participants who share their own experiences. The comments from people who have applied these techniques and found them valuable reassures me that they truly are practical methods for improving project requirements. If you find they work for you—or if you find that they don't—please let me know at kwiegers@acm.org.

My deepest appreciation is reserved for Chris Zambito, the most patient, supportive, and funny wife any author could ever hope to have.

SOFTWARE REQUIREMENTS: WHAT AND WHY

I

1

The Essential Software Requirement

"Hello, Phil? This is Maria in Human Resources. We're having a problem with the employee system you programmed for us. An employee just changed her name to Sparkle Starlight, and we can't get the system to accept the name change. Can you help?"

"She married some guy named Starlight?" asked Phil.

"No, she didn't get married, just changed her name," Maria replied. "That's the problem. It looks like we can change a name only if someone's marital status changes."

"Well, yeah, I never thought someone might just up and change his or her name. I don't remember you telling me about this possibility when we talked about the system. That's why you can get to the Change Name dialog box only from the Change Marital Status dialog box," Phil said.

Maria said, "I figured you knew that people could legally change their name anytime they like. Anyway, we have to get this straightened out by next Friday, or Sparkle won't be able to cash her paycheck. Can you fix the bug by then?"

"It's not a bug! I never knew you needed this capability. I'm busy on the new performance evaluation system. I think I have some other change requests for the employee system here, too." [sound of rustling paper] "Yeah, here's another one. I can probably fix it by the end of the month, but not within a week. Sorry about that. Next time, tell me these things earlier and please write them down."

"What am I supposed to tell Sparkle?" demanded Maria. "She's going to be really ticked if she can't cash her check."

"Hey, Maria, it's not my fault!" Phil protested. "If you'd told me in the first place that you had to be able to change someone's name at any time, this never would have happened. You can't blame me for not reading your mind."

Angry and resigned, Maria snapped, "Yeah, well, this is the kind of thing that makes me hate computer systems. Call me as soon as you get it fixed, will you?"

If you've ever been on the customer side of a conversation like this, you know how frustrating it is to use a software product that doesn't let you perform an essential task. You'd also rather not be at the mercy of a developer who might get to your important change request eventually. From the developer side, you know how frustrating it is to learn of functionality the user expects only after the system has been implemented. It is also annoying to have your current project interrupted by a request to modify a system that is doing precisely what you were told it should do in the first place.

Many of the problems encountered in software development are attributable to shortcomings in the processes and practices used to gather, document, agree on, and alter the product's requirements. As with Phil and Maria, the problem areas might include informal information gathering, unstated or implicit functionality, unfounded or uncommunicated assumptions, inadequately documented requirements, and a casual requirements change process.

Most people wouldn't ask a construction contractor to build a $200,000 house without extensively discussing their needs and desires, understanding that modifications have a cost, and refining the details progressively. However, people blithely gloss over the corresponding issues when it comes to software construction. Between 40 and 60 percent of all defects found in a software project can be traced back to errors made during the requirements stage (Leffingwell 1997). Nonetheless, many organizations still apply ad hoc methods for these essential project functions. The typical outcome is an expectation gap—a difference between what developers think they are supposed to build and what customers think they are going to get.

Nowhere more than in the requirements process do the interests of all the stakeholders in a software project intersect. These stakeholders include customers, users, business or requirements analysts (people who gather and document customer requirements and communicate them to the development community), developers, testers, authors of user documentation, project managers, and customer managers. Handled well, this intersection can lead to great products, happy customers, and fulfilled developers. Handled poorly, this intersection is the source of misunderstanding, frustration, and friction that can undermine the quality and business value of the final product. Because requirements provide the foundation for both the software engineering and project management activities, all the stakeholders must be committed to following an effective requirements process.

This chapter will help you to:

◆ Understand some of the key terms used in software requirements development.

◆ Be aware of some requirements-related problems that can arise on a software project.

◆ Learn about several characteristics that an excellent requirement statement or requirements specification should exhibit.

◆ Recognize the difference between requirements development and requirements management.

Software Requirements Defined

One problem with the software industry is the lack of common definitions for terms we use to describe aspects of our work. A customer's definition of "requirements" might sound like a high-level product concept to the developer. The developer's notion of requirements might sound like detailed design to the user. Actually, there are multiple levels of software requirements, all of them legitimate. They represent different perspectives and varying degrees of detail and precision.

The IEEE Standard Glossary of Software Engineering Terminology (1997) defines a requirement as:

(1) A condition or capability needed by a user to solve a problem or achieve an objective.

(2) A condition or capability that must be met or possessed by a system or system component to satisfy a contract, standard, specification, or other formally imposed document.

(3) A documented representation of a condition or capability as in 1 or 2.

Some Interpretations of "Requirements"

The definition published by the IEEE covers both the user's view of the requirements (the external behavior of the system) and the developer's view (some under-the-hood characteristics).

A key concept is that the requirements must be documented. I was on a project once that had experienced a rotating cast of developers. The primary customer was sick to tears of having each new requirements analyst come along and say, "We have to talk about your requirements." The customer's reaction was "I already gave your predecessors the requirements. Build me a system!" In reality, no requirements had ever been documented, so every new analyst had to start effectively from scratch. To proclaim that you have "the requirements" is self-delusional if what you really have is a pile of e-mail and voice-mail messages, sticky notes, meeting minutes, and vague recollections of hallway conversations.

Another definition suggests that requirements are "the statement of needs by a user that triggers the development of a program or system" (Jones 1994). Requirements authority Alan Davis (1993) broadens this concept to "a user need or a necessary feature, function, or attribute of a system that can be sensed from a position external to that system." These definitions emphasize *what* will go into the product, as distinct from *how* the product will be designed and constructed. The following definition moves further along the spectrum from user needs to system characteristics (Sommerville and Sawyer 1997):

> *Requirements are…a specification of what should be implemented. They are descriptions of how the system should behave, or of a system property or attribute. They may be a constraint on the development process of the system.*

These diverse definitions indicate that no clear, unambiguous understanding of the term "requirements" exists. The real requirements actually reside in people's minds. Any documented form of the requirements (such as a requirements specification) is just a model, or representation (Lawrence 1998). We need to ensure that all project stakeholders arrive at a shared understanding of the terms used to describe these requirements.

LEVELS OF REQUIREMENTS

The following are definitions I will use for some terms commonly encountered in the requirements engineering domain.

Software requirements include three distinct levels—business requirements, user requirements, and functional requirements—as well as various nonfunctional requirements. *Business requirements* represent high-level objectives of the organization or customer requesting the system or product. They are captured in a document describing the project's vision and scope. *User requirements* describe tasks the users must be able to accomplish with the product. These are captured in use cases or scenario descriptions.

Functional requirements define the software functionality the developers must build into the product to enable users to accomplish their tasks, thereby satisfying the business requirements. A *feature* is a set of logically related functional requirements that provides a capability to the user and enables the satisfaction of a business requirement. Figure 1-1 shows some of these components.

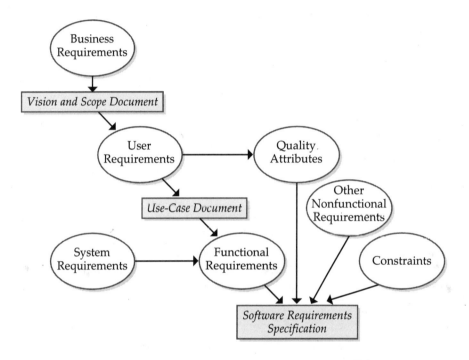

FIGURE 1-1   *Relationship of several components of software requirements.*

Functional requirements are documented in a *software requirements speci-fication* (SRS), which describes as fully as possible the expected external behavior of the software system. The SRS is used in development, testing, quality assurance, project management, and related project functions. For a complex product, the software functional requirements might be a subset of the system requirements, if some have been allocated to software components.

In addition to the functional requirements, which describe the behaviors the system must exhibit and the operations it performs, the SRS contains *nonfunctional requirements*. These might include standards, regulations, and contracts to which the product must conform; descriptions of external interfaces; performance requirements; design and implementation constraints; and quality attributes. *Constraints* are restrictions that are placed on the choices available to the developer for design and construction of the software product. *Quality attributes* augment the description of the product's functionality by describing the product's characteristics in various dimensions that are important either to users or to developers.

As an example of the different kinds of requirements, consider a word processing program. A business requirement might read: "Users will be able to correct spelling errors in a document efficiently." The product's box cover might announce that a spelling checker is included as a feature satisfying this business requirement. Corresponding user requirements might include statements (use cases) such as "Find spelling errors in the document and decide whether to replace each misspelled word with one chosen from a list of suggested replacements." The spelling checker has many individual functional requirements, which deal with operations like finding and highlighting a misspelled word, displaying a dialog box with suggested replacements, and making global replacements.

Managers or marketing might define business requirements for software that will help their company operate more efficiently (for information systems) or successfully compete in the marketplace (for commercial software products). All user requirements must align with the business requirements. The user requirements permit the requirements analyst to derive the bits of functionality that will allow the users to perform their tasks with the product. Developers use the functional requirements to design solutions that implement the necessary functionality.

Note that requirements, according to these definitions, do not include design details, implementation details, project planning information, or testing information. Separate such items from the requirements, so the requirements activities can focus on understanding what you intend to build. Projects can also have other kinds of requirements, such as development environment requirements, or requirements for releasing a product and moving it into the support environment. While these types of requirements can be critical to project success, they do not fall within the scope of this book.

EVERY PROJECT HAS REQUIREMENTS

Frederick Brooks eloquently stated the critical role of the requirements process to a software project in his classic 1987 essay, "No Silver Bullet: Essence and Accidents of Software Engineering":

> *The hardest single part of building a software system is deciding precisely what to build. No other part of the conceptual work is as difficult as establishing the detailed technical requirements, including all the interfaces to people, to machines, and to other software systems. No other part of the work so cripples the resulting system if done wrong. No other part is more difficult to rectify later.*

Every software product has users who rely on it to enhance their life in some way. Consequently, the time spent understanding their needs is a high-leverage investment in project success. This should be obvious for commercial end-user applications, corporate information systems, and products that contain software as part of a larger system. If we, as developers, don't have written requirements that the customers agree on, how will we know when the project is done? How can we satisfy the customers if we don't know what is important to them?

However, even the requirements for software that isn't intended for commercial use must be well understood. Examples include software libraries, components, and tools created for internal use by a development group. Sure, occasionally you can bang out something that's close to what people have in mind without writing down the requirements. But more often than not, iteration and rework are the inevitable consequences, and iterating on code is far more expensive than iterating on a requirements document.

I recently encountered a development group that was using a home-grown computer-aided software engineering tool that included both a flow-charting tool and a source code editor. Unfortunately, after they built the tool they discovered that no one had specified that the tool should permit printing of the source code files, but users of the tool had undoubtedly held this expectation. This group actually had to transcribe the source statements by hand in order to hold a code review. The point is that if we don't write down even our implicit and assumed requirements, we shouldn't be surprised if the software doesn't meet our expectations.

In another situation, I wrote one page of requirements for a simple e-mail interface to be integrated into a commercial defect-tracking system our group was using. The Unix systems administrator who wrote the scripts to handle the e-mail found this simple list of requirements extremely helpful. There was no ambiguity about the intended functionality, and when I tested his implementation against the requirements, there were no errors.

WHEN BAD REQUIREMENTS HAPPEN TO NICE PEOPLE

Project teams that neglect the requirements processes do so at their own peril. Shortcomings in requirements engineering practices pose a variety of risks to project success, where "success" can be defined as delivery of a product that satisfies user expectations of functionality and quality at agreed-on cost and timeliness. A few of these requirements risks are discussed below. Chapter 5 shows how you can apply software risk management to help prevent requirements-related risks from derailing your project.

SOME RISKS FROM INADEQUATE REQUIREMENTS PROCESSES

- Insufficient user involvement leads to unacceptable products.
- Creeping user requirements contribute to overruns and degrade product quality.
- Ambiguous requirements lead to ill-spent time and rework.
- Gold-plating by developers and users adds unnecessary features.
- Minimal specifications lead to missing key requirements.
- Overlooking the needs of certain user classes leads to dissatisfied customers.
- Incompletely defined requirements make accurate project planning and tracking impossible.

Insufficient User Involvement

Customers often don't understand why it is so essential to work hard on gathering requirements and assuring their quality. Developers might not emphasize user involvement, either because working with users isn't as much fun as writing code, or because they think they already know what the users need. In some cases, gaining direct access to people who will actually use the product is difficult, and customer surrogates don't always have an accurate understanding of what the users really need. There is no substitute for involving some representative users directly with the development team early in the project and keeping them engaged throughout the development process.

Creeping User Requirements

As requirements continue to evolve during development, projects become increasingly likely to exceed their planned schedules and budgets. Such plans are not always based on realistic understandings of the size and complexity of the project's requirements, risks, and developer productivity, and creeping requirements make the problem even larger. The problem lies partly in the users' requests for changes in the requirements and partly in the way developers respond to these new requirements and modifications.

To manage scope creep, start with a clear statement of the project's vision, scope, objectives, limitations, and success criteria. Use this statement as the reference frame against which all proposed new features or requirements changes are evaluated. A well-defined (and enforced!) change control process that includes impact analysis of each proposed change will help the stakeholders make informed business decisions about which changes to accept and the associated costs in time, resources, or feature trade-offs.

As changes propagate through the product being developed, its architecture can slowly crumble. Code patches make programs harder to understand and maintain. Insertion of additional code can cause modules to violate the solid design principles of strong cohesion and loose coupling. Backing out of changes and deleting features can also be problematic, particularly if the project's configuration management practices aren't up to snuff. If you can identify early on those features that are likely to involve more changes over time, you can develop a robust architecture for those portions of the system, to better accommodate the evolution. Propagating requirements changes through the design, rather than directly into code patches, can also help control this quality degradation.

Ambiguous Requirements

Ambiguity is the great bugaboo of requirements specifications (Lawrence 1996). Ambiguity is present any time multiple readers of a requirement statement arrive at different understandings of what it means. Another sign of ambiguity is when a single reader can logically interpret a requirement statement in more than one way.

Ambiguity leads to different expectations on the part of different stakeholders, some of whom are then surprised with whatever is delivered. Ambiguous requirements lead to wasted time when developers implement a solution for the wrong problem and when the testers expect the product to behave differently from what the developers built. A system tester once told me that her testing group's interpretation of the requirements often turned out to be wrong, so they had to rewrite many test cases and repeat a lot of the testing.

The inevitable outcome of ambiguity is rework—redoing something you thought was already done. Rework can consume as much as 40 percent of total development costs, and 70 to 85 percent of the total revisions can be attributed to requirements errors (Leffingwell 1997). Imagine how different your life would be if you could cut the rework effort in half! You could build products faster, build more and better products in the same amount of time, or perhaps even go home occasionally.

One way to ferret out ambiguity is to have a team that represents different perspectives inspect the requirements. Simply passing around the requirements document for comments is unlikely to reveal ambiguities. If different reviewers interpret a requirement statement in different ways, but it makes sense to each of those reviewers, the ambiguity probably won't surface until late in the project, when it can cost a great deal to correct. Other techniques for detecting ambiguity are described by Gause and Weinberg (1989) and later in this chapter.

Unnecessary Features

Gold-plating refers to the tendency of some developers to add new functionality that was not in the requirements specification but which "the users are just going to love." Too often, users don't find this functionality useful, and the effort spent on implementing it is wasted. Rather than simply inserting new features, developers should present the customers with ideas, alternatives, and creative approaches for their consideration. Decisions about what functionality to include should represent a balance between what customers want and what developers regard as technically feasible and achievable within the available timeframe. Developers should strive for leanness and simplicity—not going beyond what the customer requests without customer approval.

Similarly, customers might request features that look cool but add little functional value to the product. Everything you build costs time and money. To minimize the threat of gold-plating, make sure you can trace each bit of functionality back to its origin so that you know why it is included. The use-case approach for eliciting requirements helps keep the requirements process focused on defining the specific functionality that permits users to perform their business tasks.

Minimal Specification

Sometimes the customer with the product concept (say, marketing or management) won't understand why emphasizing requirements is important. The temptation is to create a very minimal specification, perhaps nothing more than the product concept sketched on a napkin, and ask the developers to flesh it out as the project progresses. A symptom of this trap is that the developers write the requirements after product construction is well under way. This approach might be appropriate for highly exploratory products, or where the requirements truly are flexible (McConnell 1996). In most cases, though, it leads to frustration for the developers (who might be operating under incorrect assumptions and with limited direction) and annoyance for the customer (who doesn't get the product he or she envisioned).

Overlooked User Classes

Most products are used by different groups of people, who might use different subsets of features, have different frequencies of use, or have different educational and experience levels. If you don't identify all these major types of users—the user classes—for your product early on, someone is likely to be disappointed with what is delivered. For example, menu-driven operations are inefficient for power users, while obscure commands and shortcut keys can confuse infrequent users.

Inaccurate Planning

"Here's my idea for a new product; can you give me a ballpark idea when you'll be done?" Many developers have been confronted with this difficult question. Poorly understood requirements typically lead to overly optimistic estimates, which then come back to haunt us when the inevitable overruns occur. The top five causes reported for poor software cost estimation all relate to requirements engineering: frequent requirements changes, missing requirements, insufficient communication with users, poor specification of requirements, and insufficient requirements analysis (Davis 1995).

The correct response to any request for an estimate is "I'll get back to you on that after I really understand what you are requesting." Premature estimates based on limited information or limited thinking can easily be off by a factor of two or more. When presenting estimates, provide either a range (best case, most likely, worst case) or a confidence level ("I'm 90 percent sure I can have that done within eight weeks"). Offhand single-value estimates are often perceived by the estimator as a guess, but by the listener as a commitment. We should be trying to set achievable expectations and to consistently meet them.

BENEFITS FROM A HIGH-QUALITY REQUIREMENTS PROCESS

Organizations that implement effective requirements engineering processes can enjoy multiple benefits. Perhaps the greatest reward comes from reducing rework during later stages of development and throughout the lengthy maintenance phase. Boehm (1981) found that correcting a requirement error discovered after the product was in operation cost 68 times as much as correcting an erroneous requirement during the requirements phase. More recent studies suggest this defect-cost amplification factor can be as high as 200. The very high leveraging effect of emphasizing quality requirements isn't obvious to many people, who mistakenly believe the time spent on requirements simply delays product delivery by that same amount of time. A holistic cost-of-quality perspective reveals the importance of emphasizing requirements and other early-stage quality practices (Wiegers 1996a).

Sound requirements processes emphasize a collaborative approach to product development, involving multiple stakeholder perspectives in a partnership throughout the project. Collecting requirements enables the development team to better understand its market, a critical success factor for any project. It is far more cost-effective to reach this understanding before building the product than after it is in the hands of dissatisfied customers. Engaging the users in the requirements-gathering process can generate enthusiasm for the product and build customer loyalty. By understanding user tasks, rather than focusing on superficially attractive features, you can avoid implementing functionality that will never be used. The result of this user involvement is to reduce the expectation gap between what the user anticipates receiving and what the developer constructs.

The explicit allocation of selected system requirements to software subsystems emphasizes a systems approach to product engineering. This can simplify hardware-software integration, and it can help make sure the system functions are split most appropriately between the hardware and the software. An effective change control and impact-analysis process will minimize the adverse impact of requirements changes. Finally, documented and unambiguous requirements greatly facilitate system testing, increasing your chances of delivering high-quality products that satisfy all stakeholders.

CHARACTERISTICS OF EXCELLENT REQUIREMENTS

How can you distinguish good requirements specifications from those with problems? Several characteristics that individual requirement statements should exhibit, followed by desirable characteristics of the SRS as a whole, are discussed below (Davis 1993; IEEE 1998). A careful review of the SRS by project stakeholders representing different perspectives is the best way to determine whether each requirement has these desired attributes. If you keep these characteristics in mind as you write and review the requirements, you will produce better (although never perfect) requirements documents and you will build better products. In Chapter 9, we will use these characteristics to find problems with several requirement statements so that we can improve them.

REQUIREMENT STATEMENT CHARACTERISTICS

Complete

Each requirement must fully describe the functionality to be delivered. It contains all the information necessary for the developer to design and implement that functionality.

Correct

Each requirement must accurately describe the functionality to be built. The reference for correctness is the source of the requirement, such as a customer or a higher-level system requirements specification. A software requirement that conflicts with a corresponding system requirement isn't correct. Only user representatives can determine the correctness of user requirements, which is why it is essential to include users, or their surrogates, in requirements reviews. Requirements reviews that don't involve users can lead to reviewers saying, "That doesn't make sense. This is probably what they meant." This is also known as guessing.

Feasible

It must be possible to implement each requirement within the known capabilities and limitations of the system and its environment. To avoid infeasible requirements, have a member of the software engineering team work with marketing or the requirements analysts throughout the elicitation (requirements-gathering) process. This person can provide a reality check on what can and cannot be done technically, and what can be done only at excessive cost.

Necessary

Each requirement should document something that the customers really need or something that is required for conformance to an external system requirement or a standard. Another way to look at "necessary" is that each requirement comes from an origin you recognize as having the authority to specify requirements. Trace each requirement back to specific voice-of-the-customer input, such as a use case, or some other origin.

Prioritized

Assign an implementation priority to each requirement, feature, or use case to indicate how essential it is to a particular product release. If all the requirements are regarded as equally important, the project manager loses a degree of freedom for responding to new requirements added during development, budget cuts, schedule overruns, or the loss of project personnel. Chapter 13 discusses prioritization in further detail.

Unambiguous

All readers of a requirement statement should arrive at a single, consistent interpretation of it. Because natural language is highly prone to ambiguity, write each requirement in simple, succinct, straightforward language of the user domain, not in computerese. Effective ways to reveal ambiguity include holding formal inspections of the requirements documents, writing test cases, developing prototypes, and devising specific usage scenarios.

Verifiable

Examine each requirement to see whether you can devise a small number of tests or use other verification approaches, such as inspection or demonstration, to determine whether the requirement was properly implemented in the product. If a requirement isn't verifiable, determining whether it was correctly implemented becomes a matter of opinion, not objective analysis. Requirements that are inconsistent, infeasible, or ambiguous are also unverifiable.

REQUIREMENTS SPECIFICATION CHARACTERISTICS

Complete

No requirements or necessary information should be missing. Missing requirements are hard to spot, because they are invisible. Focusing on user tasks, rather than on system functions, can help you to prevent incompleteness. If you know you are lacking certain information, use TBD ("to be determined") as a standard flag to highlight these gaps. Resolve all TBDs from a given portion of the requirements before you proceed with construction.

Consistent

Consistent requirements don't conflict with other software requirements or with higher-level (system or business) requirements. Disagreements among requirements must be resolved before development can proceed. You might not know which single requirement (if any) is correct until you do some research.

Modifiable

You must be able to revise the SRS when necessary and maintain a history of changes made to each requirement. This requires that each requirement be uniquely labeled and expressed separately from other requirements so that it can be referred to unambiguously. Each requirement should appear only once in the SRS, as it is easy to generate inconsistencies by changing only one instance of a redundant requirement. A table of contents, an index, and a cross-reference listing will make the SRS easier to modify.

Traceable

You should be able to link each software requirement to its origin and to the design elements, source code, and test cases that implement and verify the correct implementation of the requirement. Traceable requirements are uniquely labeled and are written in a structured, fine-grained way, as opposed to large, narrative paragraphs. Chapter 18 addresses requirements tracing.

REQUIREMENTS DEVELOPMENT AND MANAGEMENT

Confusion about requirements terminology extends even to what to call the whole discipline. Some authors call the entire domain "requirements engineering," while others refer to it as "requirements management." I find it useful to subdivide the entire domain of software requirements engineering into *requirements development* (addressed in Part 2 of this book) and *requirements management* (addressed in Part 3), as shown in Figure 1-2.

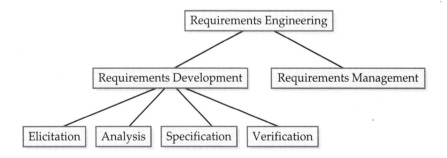

FIGURE 1-2 *Hierarchical decomposition of the requirements engineering domain.*

Requirements development can be further subdivided into *elicitation, analysis, specification,* and *verification* (Thayer and Dorfman 1997). These subdisciplines encompass all the activities involved with gathering, evaluating, and documenting the requirements for a software or software-containing product. Requirements development activities include the following:

- Identifying the expected user classes for the product

- Eliciting needs from individuals who represent each user class

- Understanding actual user tasks and objectives and the business needs supported by those tasks

- Analyzing the information received from users to distinguish their task needs from functional requirements, business rules, quality attributes, suggested solutions, and extraneous information

- Partitioning system-level requirements into major subsystems and allocating a portion of those requirements to software components

- Understanding the relative importance of quality attributes

- Negotiating implementation priorities

- Translating the collected user needs into written specifications and models

- Reviewing the requirements specifications to ensure a common understanding of the users' stated requirements and to correct any problems before the development group accepts them

Requirements management entails "establishing and maintaining an agreement with the customer on the requirements for the software project" (CMU/SEI 1995). That agreement is embodied in the written requirements specifications and models. Customer acceptance is only half the equation for requirements approval. The developers also must agree to accept them and build them into a product. Commonly performed requirements management activities include the following:

- Defining the requirements baseline (a snapshot in time representing the current agreed-on body of requirements)

- Reviewing proposed requirements changes and evaluating the likely impact of each proposed change before deciding whether to approve it

- Incorporating approved requirements changes into the project in a controlled way

- Keeping project plans current with the requirements

- Negotiating new commitments based on the estimated impact of changed requirements

- Tracing individual requirements to their corresponding designs, source code, and test cases

- Tracking requirements status and change activity throughout the project

Figure 1-3 provides another view of the distinction between requirements development and requirements management.

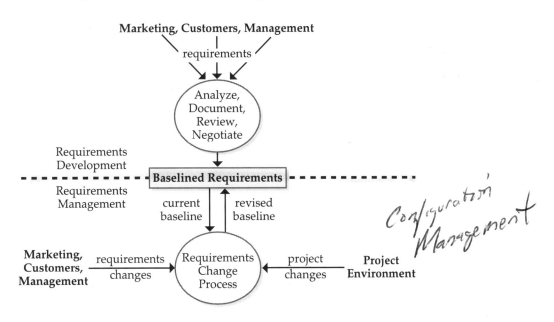

FIGURE 1-3 *The boundary between requirements development and management.*

Next Steps

- Write down any requirements-related problems you have encountered on your current or previous project. Identify each as a requirements development or requirements management problem. Identify the impact caused by each problem and the root cause of each problem.

- Facilitate a discussion with your team members and other stakeholders (customers, marketing, project managers) on requirements-related problems from your current or previous projects, their impacts, and their root causes. Explain to the participants that they have to begin confronting these difficult issues if they ever hope to master them. Are they ready to try?

- Arrange a one-day training class on software requirements for your entire project team. Include key customers, marketing staff, and managers, using whatever it takes to get them into the room. Training is an effective team-building activity. It gives project participants a common vocabulary and a common understanding of techniques, so all can begin addressing their mutual challenges.

2
Requirements from the Customer's Perspective

Gerhard, a senior manager at Contoso Pharmaceuticals, was meeting with Cynthia, the new manager of Contoso's information systems development group. "We need to build a chemical-tracking information system for Contoso," Gerhard began. "The system should let us keep track of all the chemical bottles we already have in the stockroom or in individual laboratories. That way, maybe the chemists can get what they need from someone down the hall instead of buying a new bottle from a vendor. The Health and Safety Office also has to generate some reports on chemical usage for the federal government. Can your group build this in five months, so it's ready when we have the first compliance audit?"

> *"I see why this project is important, Gerhard," said Cynthia. "But before I can commit to a schedule, we'll need to collect some requirements for your system."*
>
> *Gerhard was confused. "What do you mean? I just told you the requirements."*
>
> *"Actually, you described a concept and some objectives for this project," Cynthia explained. "Those high-level business requirements don't give me enough detail to know what software to build or how long it might take. I'd like to have a couple of analysts work with some of the chemists to understand their needs for the system. Then we can figure out what functionality is required to meet both your business objectives and the user needs. You might not even need a new software system to meet your objective of saving money."*
>
> *Gerhard hadn't encountered this reaction before from a systems development person. "The chemists are busy people," he protested. "They don't have time to nail down every detail before you can start programming. Can't your people figure out what to build?"*
>
> *Cynthia tried to explain her rationale for collecting requirements from the people who would use the new system. "If we just make our best guess at what the users need, we can't do a very good job. We're software developers, not chemists. We don't really know what the chemists need to be able to do with the chemical-tracking system. I've learned that if we don't take the time to understand the problem before we start writing code, nobody is happy with the results."*
>
> *"Well, we don't have time for all that," Gerhard insisted. "I gave you the requirements. Now just build the system, please. Keep me posted on your progress."*

Conversations like this take place regularly in the software development business. Customers who request a new information system often do not understand the importance of obtaining input from actual users of the proposed system. Marketing specialists with a great new product concept might feel they adequately represent the interests of prospective buyers. However, there is no substitute for gathering requirements directly from the people who will actually use the product. One study of 8380 projects revealed that the top two reasons why projects failed were lack of user input and incomplete requirements and specifications (Standish 1995).

Part of the requirements problem is caused by confusion over the different levels of requirements: business, user, and functional. Gerhard stated some business requirements, but he cannot describe the user requirements because he is not an intended user of the chemical-tracking system. Actual users can describe the tasks they must be able to accomplish with the system, but they cannot identify all the specific functional requirements that must be implemented to let them accomplish those tasks.

This chapter addresses the customer-developer relationship that is so critical to software project success. I propose a Requirements Bill of Rights for Software Customers, and a corresponding Requirements Bill of Responsibilities for Software Customers, to underscore the importance of customer (and specifically user) involvement in the requirements development process.

WHO IS THE CUSTOMER?

In the broadest sense, a customer is an individual or an organization who derives direct or indirect benefit from a product. Software customers include those project stakeholders who request, pay for, select, specify, or use a software product, or who receive the output generated by that product.

Gerhard represents the kind of customer who is paying for, procuring, or sponsoring a software project. Customers at Gerhard's level are responsible for specifying the business requirements. They provide the high-level concept for the product and the business rationale for launching the project in the first place. As discussed in Chapter 6, business requirements describe the objectives that the customer, company, or other stakeholders want to achieve, or the value they want to receive from the system. Business requirements establish a guiding framework for the rest of the project. Everything else that is specified as a requirement should align with satisfying the business requirements, as should every feature of the software that is constructed. However, business requirements do not provide sufficient detail to tell developers what to build.

The next level of requirements—user requirements—must be collected from people who will actually use the product hands-on. These users (often called end users) therefore constitute another kind of software customer. Users can describe both the tasks they need to perform with the product and the nonfunctional characteristics that are important for the product to be well accepted.

Those customers who provide the business requirements will sometimes purport to speak for the users, but they are usually too far removed from actual user tasks to provide accurate user requirements. For information systems, contract, or custom application development, business requirements should come from the person with the money, while user requirements should come from the person who will press the keys to use the product.

Unfortunately, both kinds of customers might feel they do not have the time to work with requirements analysts, the individuals who gather, analyze, and usually document the requirements. Sometimes customers will expect the analysts or developers to figure out what the users need without a lot of discussion and documentation. If only it were that easy. If your organization is serious about software success, it must accept that the days of sliding some vague requirements and a series of pizzas under the door to the programming department are over.

The situation is somewhat different for commercial (shrink-wrap) software development, where the customer and user often are the same person. Customer surrogates, such as the marketing department, might attempt to determine what the purchasers of the software product will find appealing. Even for commercial software, though, you should get actual users involved in the process of gathering user requirements, as addressed in Chapter 7. If you do not, be prepared to read magazine reviews that describe shortcomings in your product you probably could have avoided with adequate user input.

The Customer–Developer Partnership

Excellent software products are the result of a well-executed design based on excellent requirements. High-quality requirements result from effective communication and collaboration between developers and customers—a partnership. Too often, the relationship between development and customers (or customer surrogates, such as marketing) becomes adversarial. Customer or development managers who override user-supplied requirements to suit their own agenda can also generate friction. No one benefits in these situations.

A collaborative effort can work only when all parties involved know what they need to be successful, and when they understand and respect what their collaborators need to be successful. As project pressures rise, it is easy to forget that all stakeholders share a common objective: to build a successful software product that provides overall business value, user satisfaction, and developer fulfillment.

The Requirements Bill of Rights for Software Customers lists ten expectations that customers can legitimately place on their interactions with analysts and developers during the project's requirements engineering activities. Each of these rights implies a corresponding responsibility on the part of the software developers or analysts. The Requirements Bill of Responsibilities for Software Customers lists ten responsibilities of the customer to the developer during the requirements process. If you prefer, you could phrase these as a developer's bill of rights.

REQUIREMENTS BILL OF RIGHTS FOR SOFTWARE CUSTOMERS

You have the right to:

1. Expect analysts to speak your language.
2. Expect analysts to learn about your business and your objectives for the system.
3. Expect analysts to structure the information you present during requirements elicitation into a written software requirements specification.
4. Have developers explain all work products created from the requirements process.
5. Expect developers to treat you with respect and to maintain a collaborative and professional attitude throughout your interactions.
6. Have developers provide you with ideas and alternatives both for your requirements and for implementation of the product.
7. Describe characteristics of the product that will make it easy and enjoyable to use.
8. Be presented with opportunities to adjust your requirements to permit reuse of existing software components.
9. Be given good-faith estimates of the costs, impacts, and trade-offs when you request a change in the requirements.
10. Receive a system that meets your functional and quality needs, to the extent that those needs have been communicated to the developers and agreed on.

REQUIREMENTS BILL OF RESPONSIBILITIES FOR SOFTWARE CUSTOMERS

You have the responsibility to:

1. Educate analysts about your business and define business jargon.
2. Spend the time it takes to provide requirements, clarify them, and iteratively flesh them out.
3. Be specific and precise when providing input about the system's requirements.
4. Make timely decisions about requirements when requested to do so.
5. Respect a developer's assessment of the cost and feasibility of requirements.
6. Set priorities for individual requirements, system features, or use cases.
7. Review requirements documents and prototypes.
8. Communicate changes to the project requirements as soon as you know about them.
9. Follow the development organization's defined process for requesting requirements changes.
10. Respect the processes the developers use for requirements engineering.

These rights and responsibilities apply directly to customers when the software is being developed for internal corporate use, under contract, or for a known set of major customers. For mass-market product development, the rights and responsibilities are more applicable to customer surrogates such as the marketing department.

As part of project planning, the customer and development participants should review these two lists and reach a meeting of the minds. Busy customers might prefer not to become intimately involved in requirements engineering (that is, they shy away from Responsibility #2). Lack of customer involvement greatly increases the risk of building the wrong product. Make sure the key participants in requirements development understand and accept their responsibilities. If you encounter some sticking points, negotiate to reach a clear understanding regarding your responsibilities to each other. This understanding can reduce friction later, when one party expects something that the other is not willing or able to provide.

REQUIREMENTS BILL OF RIGHTS FOR SOFTWARE CUSTOMERS

Right #1: To expect analysts to speak your language

Requirements discussions should center on your business needs and tasks, using your business vocabulary, which you might have to convey to the analysts. You shouldn't have to wade through computer jargon when talking with analysts.

Right #2: To have analysts learn about your business and objectives

By interacting with users while eliciting requirements, the analysts can better understand your business tasks and how the product fits into your world. This will help developers design software that truly meets your needs and satisfies your expectations. To help educate developers or analysts, consider inviting them to observe what you or your peers do on the job. If the system being built is replacing an existing application, the developers should use the current system as you use it. This will help them see how the current application works, how it fits into your workflow, and where it can be improved.

Right #3: To expect analysts to write a software requirements specification

The analyst will sort through all the information you and other customers provide to separate actual user needs from business requirements and rules, functional requirements, quality goals, solution ideas, and other bits of information. The ultimate product from this analysis is a software requirements specification. The SRS constitutes the agreement between developers and customers on the content of the product that is going to be built. The SRS should be structured and written in a way that you find easy to read and understand. You can review these written specifications to make sure they accurately and completely represent your requirements. A high-quality SRS greatly increases the chance of the developers building what you really need.

Right #4: To receive explanations of requirements work products
The analyst might represent the requirements using various diagrams that complement the textual SRS. These alternative views of the requirements are valuable because sometimes graphics are a clearer medium for expressing some aspects of system behavior, such as workflow. While you probably won't be familiar with these diagrams, they aren't difficult to understand. You can expect analysts to explain the purpose of each diagram or other requirements development work product, what the notations mean, and how to examine the diagram for errors and inconsistencies.

Right #5: To expect developers to treat you with respect
Requirements discussions can be frustrating if users and developers don't understand each other. Working together can open the eyes of both groups to the problems faced by the other. Customers who participate in the requirements development process have the right to have developers treat them with respect and to appreciate the time you are investing in project success. Similarly, demonstrate respect for the developers as they work with you toward your common objective of a successful project.

Right #6: To hear ideas and alternatives for requirements and their implementation
Often, customers present as "requirements" ideas that are actually possible implementation solutions. The analyst will try to probe beneath these solutions to understand the real business issues and needs that must be addressed. Analysts should explore ways your existing systems don't fit well with your current business processes, to make sure the product doesn't automate ineffective or inefficient processes. Analysts who thoroughly understand the business domain can sometimes suggest improvements in your business

processes. An experienced and creative analyst also adds value by proposing ways that new software could provide valuable capabilities the users haven't even envisioned.

Right #7: To describe characteristics that make the product easy to use

You can expect analysts to ask you about characteristics of the software that go beyond your functional needs. These characteristics, or quality attributes, make the software easier or more pleasant to use, allowing you to accomplish your tasks more accurately and efficiently. For example, customers sometimes state that the product must be "user-friendly" or "robust" or "efficient," but this is too subjective to help the developers. Instead, the analysts should inquire about specific characteristics that mean user-friendly, robust, or efficient to the customer (more about this in Chapter 11).

Right #8: To be presented with opportunities to adjust requirements to permit reuse

Requirements are often somewhat flexible. The analyst might be aware of existing software components that come close to addressing some need you described. In such a case, the analyst should present you with the option of modifying your requirements so the developers can reuse some existing software when they construct the new system. If you can adjust your requirements when sensible reuse opportunities are available, this can save time and money that would otherwise be needed to build precisely what the original requirement specified. Some requirements flexibility is essential if you want to incorporate commercial off-the-shelf components into your product, as they will rarely have precisely the characteristics you have in mind.

Right #9: To be given good-faith estimates of the costs of changes

People sometimes make different choices when they know one alternative is more expensive than another. Estimates of the impact and cost of a proposed change in the requirements are necessary to make good business decisions about which requested changes to approve. You have the right to expect developers to present good-faith estimates of impact, cost, and trade-offs, using an analytical process. Developers must not inflate the estimated cost of a change just because they don't want to implement it.

Right #10: To receive a system that meets your functional and quality needs

Everyone desires this outcome for the project. It can happen only if you clearly communicate all the information that will let developers build the product that satisfies your needs and if developers clearly communicate options and constraints. Be sure to state any assumptions or implicit expectations you might hold. Otherwise, the developers probably can't address them to your satisfaction.

REQUIREMENTS BILL OF RESPONSIBILITIES FOR SOFTWARE CUSTOMERS

Responsibility #1: To educate analysts about your business

Analysts depend on you to educate them about your business concepts and terminology. The intent is not to transform analysts into domain experts, but to help them understand your problems and objectives. Don't expect analysts to grasp the nuances and implicit aspects of your business. Analysts aren't likely to be aware of knowledge that you and your peers take for granted.

Responsibility #2: To spend the time to provide and clarify requirements

Customers are busy people, and those of you who are involved in developing requirements are often among the busiest. Nonetheless, you have a responsibility to invest time in workshops, brainstorming sessions, interviews, or other requirements-elicitation activities. Sometimes the analyst might think she understands a point you made, only to realize later that she needs further clarification. Please be patient with this iterative approach to developing and refining the requirements, as it is the nature of complex human communication and a key to software success.

Responsibility #3: To be specific and precise about requirements

Writing clear, precise requirements is difficult. It is tempting to leave the requirements vague and fuzzy because pinning down details is tedious and time-consuming. At some point during development, though, someone will have to resolve the ambiguities and imprecisions. You are most likely the best person to make those decisions. Otherwise, you're relying on the developers to guess correctly.

It's fine to temporarily include TBD (to be determined) markers in the requirements specification, indicating that additional research, analysis, or information is needed. Sometimes, though, TBD is used because a specific requirement is difficult to resolve and no one wants to tackle it. Do your best to clarify the intent of each requirement, so the analyst can express it accurately in the SRS. If you can't be precise, agree to a process to generate the necessary precision. This often involves some form of prototyping, in which you work with the developers in an incremental and iterative approach to requirements definition.

Responsibility #4: To make timely decisions
Just as when a contractor builds a custom home, the analyst will ask you to make many choices and decisions. Such decisions include resolving inconsistent requests received from multiple users, making trade-offs between conflicting quality attributes, and evaluating the accuracy of information. Customers who are authorized to make such decisions must do so promptly when asked. The developers often can't proceed until you render your decision, so time spent waiting for an answer can delay progress.

Responsibility #5: To respect a developer's assessment of cost and feasibility
All software functions have a price, and developers are in the best position to estimate those costs (although many developers are not skilled estimators). Some features you would like included in a product might not be technically feasible, or they might be surprisingly expensive to implement. Certain requirements might demand unattainable performance in the operating environment, or they might require access to data that is simply not available to the system. The developer can be the bearer of bad news about feasibility or cost, and you should respect that judgment.

Sometimes you can rewrite requirements in a way that makes them feasible or cheaper. For example, asking for an action to take place "instantaneously" isn't feasible, but a more specific timing requirement ("within 50 milliseconds") might be achievable.

Responsibility #6: To set requirement priorities

Most projects don't have the time or resources to implement every desirable bit of functionality. Determining which features are essential, which are important, and which are nice to have is an important part of requirements development. You are responsible for setting those priorities, because developers can't usually determine a requirement's priority from your perspective. Developers will provide information about the cost and risk of each requirement to help you define priorities. When you establish priorities, you help ensure that developers deliver the greatest value at the lowest cost and at the right time.

Respect development's judgment as to how much of the requested functionality can actually be completed within the available time and resource constraints. No one likes to hear that something he or she wants can't be completed within the project bounds, but that's just a reality. A business decision has to be made to reduce project scope based on priorities or to extend the schedule, provide additional resources, or compromise on quality.

Responsibility #7: To review requirements documents and prototypes

As we will see in Chapter 14, formal and informal reviews of requirements documents are among the most valuable software quality activities. Having customers participate in reviews is the only way to evaluate whether the requirements demonstrate the desired characteristics of being complete, correct, and necessary. A review also provides an opportunity for customer representatives to provide feedback to the requirements analysts about how well their work is meeting the project's needs. If you aren't confident the documented requirements are accurate, tell the people responsible as early as possible and provide suggestions for improvement.

It's difficult to develop a good mental picture of how the software will actually work by reading a requirements specification. To better understand your needs and explore the best ways to satisfy them, developers often build prototypes of the intended product. Your feedback on these preliminary, partial, or exploratory implementations provides valuable information to the developers and helps ensure that the requirements are well understood. Recognize that a prototype is not a working product and allow the development organization to convert prototypes into fully functioning systems.

Responsibility #8: To promptly communicate changes to the requirements

Continually changing requirements poses a serious risk to the development team's ability to deliver a high-quality product within the planned schedule. Change is inevitable, but the later in the development cycle a change is introduced, the greater its impact. Changes can cause expensive rework and schedules can slip if new functionality is demanded after construction is well under way. Notify the analyst with whom you are working as soon as you become aware of any change needed in the requirements.

Responsibility #9: To follow the development organization's requirements change process

To minimize the negative impact of change, all participants must follow the project's defined change control process. This ensures that requested changes are not lost, the impact of each requested change is analyzed, and all proposed changes are considered in a consistent way. As a result, good business decisions can be made to incorporate certain changes into the product.

Responsibility #10: To respect the requirements engineering processes the developers use

Gathering requirements and making sure they're correct are among the greatest challenges in software development. There is a rationale behind the approaches the analysts use. Although you might become frustrated with the requirements activities, the time spent on developing the requirements is an excellent investment. The process will be less painful if you understand and respect the techniques the analysts use for gathering, documenting, and ensuring the quality of the software requirements. Feel free to ask analysts to explain why they are requesting certain information or asking you to participate in some requirements-related activity.

WHAT ABOUT SIGN-OFF?

Reaching agreement on the requirements for the product to be built is an important part of the customer-developer partnership. Many organizations use the concept of signing off on the requirements document as the act of customer approval of those requirements. It is important that all participants in the requirements approval process know exactly what sign-off means.

One problem is the customer representative who regards signing off on the requirements as a meaningless ritual: "I was presented with a piece of paper that had my name typed on it below a line, so I signed on the line because otherwise the developers wouldn't start coding." This attitude can lead to future conflicts when that customer wants to change the requirements or when he is surprised by what is delivered: "Sure, I signed off on the requirements, but I didn't have time to read them all. I trusted you guys—you let me down!"

Equally problematic is the development manager who views the sign-off process as a way to freeze the requirements. Whenever a change request is presented, he can point to the SRS and protest, "But you signed off on these requirements, so that's what we're building. If you wanted something else, you should have said so."

Both of these attitudes fail to acknowledge the reality that it is impossible to know all the requirements early in the project and that requirements will undoubtedly change over time. Signing off on requirements is an appropriate action that brings closure to the requirements development process. However, the participants have to agree on precisely what they're saying with their signatures.

More important than the sign-off ritual is the concept of establishing a "baseline" of the requirements agreement, a snapshot at some point in time. The subtext of a signature on a requirements specification sign-off page should therefore read something like this: "I agree that this document represents our best understanding of the software requirements for this project today. Future changes in this baseline can be made through the project's defined change process. I realize that approved changes might require us to renegotiate the costs, resources, and schedule commitments for this project."

Some shared understanding along this line might help alleviate the friction that can arise as the project progresses and the requirements oversights are revealed, or as marketplace and business demands evolve. Sealing the initial requirements development activities with such an explicit agreement helps you forge a continuing customer-developer partnership on the way to project success.

Next Steps

◆ Identify the individual customers responsible for providing the business requirements and the user requirements on your project. Which items from the Bill of Rights and the Bill of Responsibilities are accepted, understood, and practiced by these customers? Which are not? ·

◆ Discuss the Bill of Rights and the Bill of Responsibilities with your key customers to reach agreement as to which responsibilities they accept, and whether they feel they are not receiving any of their rights. Agree upon, and implement, actions that will help the customers and developers to better understand each other's contributions to a successful partnership.

◆ If you are a customer participating in a software development project and you don't feel your requirements rights are being adequately respected, discuss the Bill of Rights with the software project leader or business analyst. Offer to do your part to satisfy the Bill of Responsibilities, as you strive to build a more collaborative working relationship.

3

Good Practices for Requirements Engineering

Ten years ago, I was a fan of software development methodologies—packaged sets of models and techniques that purport to provide holistic solutions to our project challenges. Today, though, I am more interested in identifying and applying industry "best practices." Rather than devising or purchasing a whole-cloth solution, the best-practice approach emphasizes stocking your software tool kit with a variety of approaches you can apply to diverse problems. Even if you adopt a commercial methodology, you should augment its recommended techniques with other effective industry practices from your tool kit.

The notion of "best practices" is somewhat debatable: Who gets to decide what is "best" and on what basis does he or she reach this conclusion? One approach is to convene a body of industry experts to analyze the success or failure of projects in many different organizations (Brown 1996). These experts look for practices whose effective performance is associated with successful projects and which might be performed poorly or not at all on failed projects. Through this process, the experts reach consensus on those key activities that consistently yield superior results. Such activities are dubbed "best practices," with the implication that these activities are the most effective known ways for software professionals to increase the chance of project success.

The title of this chapter is "Good Practices for Requirements Engineering," not "Best Practices." More than forty practices in seven categories are presented that can help most development teams do a better job on their requirements activities; these are listed in Table 3-1.

TABLE 3-1   REQUIREMENTS ENGINEERING GOOD PRACTICES

Knowledge	Requirements Management	Project Management
• Train requirements analysts	• Define change control process	• Select appropriate life cycle
• Educate user reps and managers about requirements	• Establish change control board	• Base plans on requirements
• Train developers in application domain	• Perform change impact analysis	• Renegotiate commitments
• Create a glossary	• Trace each change to all affected work products	• Manage requirements risks
	• Baseline and control versions of requirements documents	• Track requirements effort
	• Maintain change history	
	• Track requirements status	
	• Measure requirements stability	
	• Use a requirements management tool	

(continued)

TABLE 3-1   REQUIREMENTS ENGINEERING GOOD PRACTICES *continued*

Requirements Development

Elicitation	Analysis	Specification	Verification
• Write vision and scope	• Draw context diagram	• Adopt SRS template	• Inspect requirements documents
• Define requirements development procedure	• Create prototypes	• Identify sources of requirements	• Write test cases from requirements
• Identify user classes	• Analyze feasibility	• Label each requirement	• Write a user manual
• Select product champions	• Prioritize requirements	• Record business rules	• Define acceptance criteria
• Establish focus groups	• Model the requirements	• Create requirements traceability matrix	
• Identify use cases	• Create a data dictionary		
• Hold JAD sessions	• Apply Quality Function Deployment		
• Analyze user workflow			
• Define quality attributes			
• Examine problem reports			
• Reuse requirements			

Not all of these items have been endorsed as industry best practices; I doubt all of them will ever be systematically evaluated for this purpose. Nonetheless, I and many other practitioners have found these techniques to be effective (Sommerville and Sawyer 1997). Each practice is described briefly and references are provided either to other chapters in this book or to other sources where the technique is addressed in more detail.

Table 3-2 groups these practices by the relative priority of implementing them on a project and their relative difficulty of implementation. While all of the practices can be beneficial, you might begin with the "low-hanging fruit," those practices that have a greater impact on project success and are relatively easy to implement.

TABLE 3-2   IMPLEMENTING REQUIREMENTS ENGINEERING
GOOD PRACTICES

PRIORITY	DIFFICULTY		
	High	*Medium*	*Low*
High	• Define requirements development procedure • Base plans on requirements • Renegotiate commitments	• Identify use cases • Define quality attributes • Prioritize requirements • Adopt SRS template • Define change control process • Establish change control board • Inspect requirements documents	• Train developers in application domain • Write vision and scope • Identify user classes • Draw context diagram • Identify sources of requirements • Label each requirement • Baseline and control versions of requirements documents
Medium	• Educate user reps and managers about requirements • Model the requirements • Manage requirements risks	• Train requirements analysts • Establish focus groups • Create prototypes • Analyze feasibility • Define acceptance criteria	• Create a glossary • Select product champions • Create a data dictionary • Record business rules

(continued)

TABLE 3-2   IMPLEMENTING REQUIREMENTS ENGINEERING
                                  GOOD PRACTICES *continued*

PRIORITY	DIFFICULTY		
	High	*Medium*	*Low*
Medium	• Use a requirements management tool • Create requirements traceability matrix	• Perform change impact analysis • Trace each change to all affected work products • Select appropriate life cycle	• Write test cases from requirements • Track requirements status
Low	• Hold JAD sessions • Reuse requirements • Apply Quality Function Deployment • Measure requirements stability	• Analyze user workflow • Examine problem reports • Write a user manual • Maintain change history • Track requirements effort	

Don't try to apply all these techniques on your next project. Instead, think of the good practices described here as new items to add to your requirements tool kit. You can begin to apply some practices immediately, like those dealing with change management, no matter where your project is in its development cycle. Others, like those for requirements elicitation, will be more useful when you begin the next project. Still others might not be appropriate for your current project or culture.

Chapter 4 presents approaches you can use to evaluate your current requirements-engineering practices and to devise a road map for implementing requirements process improvements selected from the practices described both here and in Chapter 4.

KNOWLEDGE

Few software developers have been formally trained in the techniques and skills required for effective requirements engineering. However, many developers play the role of requirements analyst at some point in their career, working with customers to gather, analyze, and document their requirements. It isn't reasonable to expect developers to be instinctively competent at the communication-intensive tasks of requirements engineering. Some training can help increase the proficiency and comfort level of those who fill the role of requirements analyst.

Because the requirements process is such a key to success, all project stakeholders should have a basic understanding of the rationale, importance, and practices of requirements engineering. Bringing together the project stakeholders (such as developers, marketing personnel, customers, testers, and managers) for a one-day overview of the requirements process can be an effective team-building activity. All parties will gain a better understanding of the challenges their counterparts face and what the participants require from each other for the entire team to succeed. Similarly, developers should receive a grounding in the basic concepts and terminology of the application domain.

Train requirements analysts. All developers should receive basic training in requirements engineering, but those who are primarily responsible for capturing, documenting, and analyzing user requirements should receive a week or more of training in these activities. The skilled requirements analyst is well organized, has effective interpersonal skills and excellent verbal and written communication skills, understands the application domain, and can choose from a robust tool kit of requirements-engineering techniques.

Educate user representatives and managers about software requirements.
User representatives who will participate in the software development activities should receive one day of education about requirements engineering, as should both development managers and customer managers. This will help them understand the importance of emphasizing requirements, the activities and deliverables involved, and the risks of neglecting requirements pro-

cesses. Some users who have attended my requirements seminars have commented that they had more sympathy for the software developers afterward.

Train developers in application domain concepts. To help developers achieve a basic understanding of the application domain, arrange a short seminar on the customer's business activities, terminology, and objectives for the product being created. This can reduce confusion, miscommunication, and rework down the road. You might also match each developer with a "user buddy" for the life of the project to translate jargon and clarify business concepts. The product champion could play this role.

Create a project glossary. To reduce communication problems, compile a glossary that defines specialized terms from the project's application domain. Include terms that have multiple uses or meanings, as well as terms that have both domain-specific and common usage meanings.

REQUIREMENTS ELICITATION

Chapter 1 discussed the three levels of requirements: business, user, and functional. These come from different sources at different times during the project, have different audiences and purposes, and need to be documented in different ways. The business requirements (or product vision and scope) must not exclude any user requirements (or use cases), and all functional requirements should be traceable to user requirements. You also need to elicit nonfunctional requirements, such as quality attributes, from the most appropriate sources. You can find additional information about these topics in the following chapters:

- Chapter 4—Define a requirements development procedure.
- Chapter 6—Write a project vision and scope document.
- Chapter 7—Identify user classes and their characteristics; select product champions for each user class.
- Chapter 8—Have user representatives identify use cases.
- Chapter 11—Determine quality attributes and other nonfunctional requirements.

Define a requirements development procedure. Define and document the steps your organization uses to gather, analyze, specify, and verify requirements. Guidance on performing the key steps will help analysts do a consistently good job, and it will make the requirements-gathering activities and schedules easier to plan.

Write a project vision and scope document. The project's vision and scope document should contain the high-level business objectives for the product. All use cases and functional requirements must align with, and enable achievement of, these business requirements. The vision statement gives all project participants a common understanding of the project objectives. The definition of scope serves as the reference against which potential features or requirements can be evaluated.

Identify user classes and their characteristics. To avoid overlooking the needs of any user community, identify the different groups of customers who are likely to use your product. They might differ in frequency of use, features used, privilege levels, or skill levels. Describe aspects of their job tasks or personal characteristics that might influence product design.

Select product champions for each user class. Identify at least one person who can accurately present the needs of each user class, serve as the voice of the customer for that community, and make decisions on its behalf. This is easiest for internal information systems development, where your users are fellow employees. For commercial development, build on current relationships with major customers or beta test sites to locate appropriate product champions. Product champions must have an ongoing participation in the project and decision-making authority.

Establish focus groups of typical users. Convene small groups of representative users of your previous product releases or similar products. Meet with them to collect their input on both functional and nonfunctional requirements for the current product. Focus groups are particularly valuable for commercial development, where you might have a large and diverse customer base. Unlike product champions, members of focus groups generally do not have decision-making authority.

Have user representatives identify use cases. Collect from your user representatives descriptions of the tasks they need to accomplish with the software—the use cases. Discuss the interactions and dialogues between the users and the system that will allow them to complete each such task. Adopt a standard template for documenting use cases, and derive functional requirements from the use cases.

Hold Joint Application Development sessions. A Joint Application Development (JAD) session is an extended, facilitated workshop that involves a collaboration between analysts and customer representatives to produce draft requirements documents. The JAD session puts the customer-development partnership into practice during an intense period of concentrated and focused effort (Wood and Silver 1995).

Analyze user workflow. Watch users perform their business tasks. Create simple diagrams (data flow diagrams work well) that depict *when* the user has *what* data, and *how* it is used. Documenting the business process flow will help you identify use cases and functional requirements for a product that is intended to support that process. You might even determine that the customers don't really need a new software system to meet their business objectives (McGraw and Harbison 1997).

Determine quality attributes and other nonfunctional requirements. Go beyond the functional requirements to explore nonfunctional quality characteristics that will help your product meet or exceed customer expectations. These characteristics include performance, efficiency, reliability, usability, and many others. Customer input on the relative importance of these quality attributes is essential.

Examine problem reports of current systems for requirement ideas. Problem reports and enhancement requests from customers provide a rich source of ideas for features and improvements to include in a future release or a new product. People who staff the help desk or provide user support can provide valuable input to the requirements-gathering process.

Reuse requirements across projects. If customers request functionality similar to that already implemented in an existing internal or commercially available product, see if they have enough flexibility around the requirements to permit reuse or adaptation of the existing software components.

REQUIREMENTS ANALYSIS

Requirements analysis involves refining, analyzing, and scrutinizing the gathered requirements to make sure all stakeholders understand what they mean and to find errors, omissions, or other deficiencies. Analysis evaluates whether all requirements and the SRS demonstrate the characteristics of excellent requirements described in Chapter 1. The goal is to develop requirements of sufficient quality and detail that you can use them to construct realistic project estimates and to proceed with design, construction, and testing.

Often, it is helpful to represent a portion of the requirements in more than one way, such as in both textual and graphical forms. Analyzing these different views will reveal insights and problems that no single view can provide (Davis 1995). Analysis also involves interacting with customers to clarify points of confusion and to understand which requirements are more important than others. The goal is to ensure that all stakeholders arrive early in the project at a common understanding—a shared vision—of what they will have when the product is delivered. You can find further discussion of the tasks involved in requirements analysis in the following chapters:

◆ Chapter 6—Draw a context diagram of the system.

◆ Chapter 9—Create a data dictionary.

◆ Chapter 10—Model the requirements.

◆ Chapter 12—Create user interface prototypes.

◆ Chapter 13—Prioritize the requirements.

Draw a context diagram of the system. The context diagram is a simple model that defines the boundaries and interfaces between the system being developed and entities external to the system. It also identifies the flows of information and materials across these interfaces.

Create user interface prototypes. When developers or users aren't certain about the requirements, construct a user interface prototype—a partial, possible implementation—to make the concepts and possibilities more tangible. Users can evaluate the prototype to help the project participants achieve a better mutual understanding of the problem being solved. Look for any conflicts between the written requirements and the prototype.

Analyze requirement feasibility. Evaluate the feasibility of implementing each requirement at acceptable cost and performance in the intended delivery environment. Understand the risks associated with implementing each requirement, including conflicts with other requirements, dependencies on external factors, and technical obstacles.

Prioritize the requirements. Apply an analytical approach to determine the relative implementation priority of use cases, product features, or individual requirements. Based on priority, determine which product release will contain each feature or set of requirements. As requirement changes are accepted, allocate each one to a specific future release, and incorporate the effort required to address the change into the planning for that release.

Model the requirements. Graphical analysis models of the requirements can be valuable supplements to the SRS. They will show different information and relationships and will help you find incorrect, inconsistent, missing, and superfluous requirements. Such models include data flow diagrams, entity-relationship diagrams, state-transition diagrams, dialog maps, and object class and interaction diagrams.

Create a data dictionary. The data dictionary is a central repository for definitions of all the data items and structures used by the system. It ensures that developers working on related components use consistent data definitions. At the requirements stage, the data dictionary should at least define customer data items, to ensure that the customer and the development team use the same definitions and terminology. Analysis and design tools often include a data dictionary component.

Apply Quality Function Deployment. Quality Function Deployment (QFD) is a highly systematic technique for relating product features and attributes to customer value. It provides an analytical way to identify those features that will provide the greatest customer satisfaction. QFD addresses three classes of requirements: expected requirements, where the customer might not even state them but will be upset if they are missing; normal requirements; and exciting requirements, which provide high benefit to customers if present but little penalty if not (Zultner 1993; Pardee 1996).

REQUIREMENTS SPECIFICATION

No matter where your requirements come from or how you gather them, you must document them in some consistent, accessible, and reviewable way. The business requirements might appear in a project vision and scope document. The user requirements are documented using a standard use case template. The SRS contains the software functional requirements and non-functional requirements. You must also establish a standard convention to uniquely identify each requirement. Define any conventions that are used in the SRS, to ensure that the SRS is written in a consistent fashion and that readers will know how to interpret it. Specifics of requirements specification are discussed in the following chapters:

◆   Chapter 8—Record business rules.

◆   Chapter 9—Adopt an SRS template; label each requirement.

◆   Chapter 18—Identify sources of requirements; create a requirements traceability matrix.

Adopt an SRS template. Define a standard template for documenting software requirements in your organization. The template provides a consistent structure for recording both the functional requirements and many other important pieces of requirements-related information. Rather than inventing a new template, adapt an existing one to fit the needs and nature of your projects. Many organizations begin with the SRS template described in IEEE Standard 830-1998 (IEEE 1998). Set an expectation that the template will always be used, but that it will be molded to the shape of individual projects as appropriate.

Identify sources of requirements. To ensure that all stakeholders know why every functional requirement belongs in the SRS, trace each one back to its origin. This might be a use case or some other customer input, a higher-level system requirement, a business rule, a government regulation, a standard, or some other external source.

Label each requirement. Define a convention for providing each individual requirement in the SRS with a unique identifying label or tag. The convention must be robust enough to withstand additions, deletions, and changes in requirements over time. Labeling the requirements permits requirements traceability. It also facilitates keeping records of changes made in the requirements and establishing metrics for requirements status and change activity.

Record business rules. Business rules are operating principles about the product, such as who can take what actions and under what circumstances. Document them in a special section of the SRS or in a separate business-rules document. Some business rules will lead to functional requirements that enforce them; these requirements should be traced back to the corresponding business rules.

Create a requirements traceability matrix. Set up a matrix that links each individual requirement to the design and code elements that implement it and the tests that verify it. The requirements traceability matrix can also connect functional requirements to the higher-level requirements from which they were derived and to other related requirements. Populate this matrix during development, not at the end.

REQUIREMENTS VERIFICATION

Verification activities ensure that requirement statements are accurate, complete, and demonstrate the desired quality characteristics. Requirements that seem fine when you read them in the SRS might turn out to have problems when you actually try to work with them. If you write test cases from the requirements, you may discover ambiguities and vagueness in some of the statements. These must be removed if the requirements are to serve as a reliable foundation for design and for final system verification. Customer participation is an essential component of requirements verification, which is discussed further in Chapter 14.

Inspect requirements documents. Formal inspection of requirements documents is one of the highest-value software quality practices available. Assemble a small team of inspectors who represent different perspectives (such as analyst, customer, designer, and tester) and carefully examine the SRS and related models for defects. Informal preliminary reviews during requirements development are also valuable.

Write test cases from the requirements. Derive black-box (functional) test cases from the use cases to document the expected behavior of the product under specified conditions. Walk through the test cases with customers to ensure they reflect the desired behavior. Trace the test cases back to the functional requirements to make sure no requirements have been overlooked and that all have corresponding test cases. Use the test cases to verify the correctness of requirements models, such as dialog maps, and prototypes.

Write a user manual. Draft the user manual early in the requirements development process and use it as the requirements specification or as an aid to requirements analysis. A good user manual will describe all of the user-visible functionality in easily understandable language. Additional requirements, such as quality attributes, performance requirements, and functionality not visible to users, will have to be documented in an SRS.

Define acceptance criteria. Ask users to describe how they will determine whether the product meets their needs and is fit for use. Base acceptance tests on usage scenarios or instances of use cases (Hsia, Kung, and Sell 1997).

REQUIREMENTS MANAGEMENT

Once you have the requirements in hand, you must cope with the inevitable changes that are requested as the project evolves. Effective change management requires a process for proposing changes and evaluating the potential cost and impact of the change on the project. A change control board, comprising key project stakeholders, should make the decisions about which proposed requirements to incorporate. In addition, you should track the status of each requirement as it moves through development and system testing.

Well-established configuration management practices are a prerequisite for effective requirements management. Many development organizations use version control and other configuration management techniques for controlling their code base, but you can also use these practices to manage your requirements documents. Requirements management process improvement can be a way to introduce new configuration management practices into your culture. The techniques involved in requirements management are expanded in the following chapters:

- Chapter 16—Establish a baseline and control versions of requirements documents.

- Chapter 17—Define a requirements change control process; establish a change control board.

- Chapter 18—Perform requirements change impact analysis; trace a requirement change to all affected work products.

- Chapter 19—Use a requirements management tool.

Define a requirements change control process. Establish a process by which requirements changes can be proposed and analyzed and decisions made. All proposed changes must follow the process. Commercial problem-tracking tools can support the change control process.

Establish a change control board. Charter a small group of project stakeholders as a change control board to receive proposed requirements changes, determine whether they are within project scope, evaluate them, make decisions about which to accept and which to reject, and set implementation priorities or target releases.

Perform requirements-change impact analysis. Each proposed requirement change should be evaluated to determine the impact of the change on the project schedule and other requirements. Determine the likely tasks associated with making the change and estimate the effort needed to complete those tasks. This will permit the change control board to make better business decisions about which proposed changes to accept.

Trace a requirement change to all affected work products. When a change in a requirement is accepted, refer to the requirements traceability matrix to identify the other requirements, design components, source code, or test cases that might also have to be changed. This will reduce the chance of overlooking a work product change that must be made in response to a modified requirement.

Establish a baseline and control versions of requirements documents.
Define a requirements baseline, a snapshot of the agreed-on requirements at
a specific point in time. After the requirements have been baselined, changes
can be made only through the defined change-control process. Every version
of the requirements specification must be uniquely identified, to avoid confusion between drafts and baselines and between obsolete and current versions. The most robust solution is to place requirements documents under
version control using appropriate configuration management tools.

Maintain a history of requirements changes. Keep a record of the dates that
versions of the requirements document were changed, the changes that were
made and the reasons for them, who updated the document, and the new
version number. A version control tool can automate these tasks.

Track the status of each requirement. Establish a database with one record
for each discrete functional requirement. Store key attributes about each
requirement, including its status (such as proposed, approved, implemented,
or verified), so that the number of requirements in each status category can
be known at any time.

Measure requirements stability. Record the number of baselined requirements and the number of proposed and approved changes (additions, modifications, deletions) to them per week or month. Excessive requirements
changes are a red flag that suggests the problem is not well understood, the
project scope is not well defined, or politics are running rampant.

Use a requirements management tool. Commercial requirements management tools let you store individual requirements of different types in a database, define attributes for each requirement, track the status of each
requirement, and define traceability links between requirements and other
software development work products.

Project Management

Software project management approaches are intimately related to a project's
requirements processes. Project plans should be based on the functionality
that is to be built, and changes in requirements will affect those plans. The
project plans should therefore anticipate and accommodate expected changes
in requirements and project scope. If the initial requirements are uncertain,

you might select a software development life cycle that accommodates this uncertainty and permits portions of the requirements to be implemented incrementally as they become better understood. More information on project management approaches to requirements engineering is available in the following chapters:

- Chapter 5—Document and manage requirements-related risks.

- Chapter 15—Base project plans on requirements.

- Chapter 16—Track the effort you spend on requirements development and management.

Select an appropriate software development life cycle. The classic waterfall software development life cycle can only succeed if the requirements are fully defined early in the project. Your organization should define several life cycles that are appropriate for different types of projects and different degrees of requirements definition (McConnell 1996). Explicitly include requirements development and management activities in your life-cycle definitions. If the requirements or scope are poorly defined early in the project, plan to develop the product in small increments, beginning with the most clearly understood requirements and a robust, modifiable architecture. Implement sets of features so that partially complete versions of the product can be released periodically (Gilb 1988).

Base project plans on requirements. Develop plans and schedules for your project iteratively as the scope and detailed requirements become more clearly defined. Begin by estimating the effort needed to develop the functional requirements from the initial project vision and scope. Early cost and schedule estimates based on scantily defined requirements will be highly uncertain, but the estimates can be improved as the requirements become better understood.

Renegotiate project commitments when requirements change. As new requirements are incorporated into the project, evaluate whether you can still achieve the current schedule and quality commitments with the available resources. If not, communicate the project realities to management, and negotiate new, realistically achievable commitments (Humphrey 1997). If your negotiations are unsuccessful, communicate the likely outcomes and update the project's risk management plan to reflect any new or revised threats to success.

Document and manage requirements-related risks. Brainstorm and document project risks related to requirements in the project's risk management plan. Think of approaches to mitigate or prevent these risks, implement the mitigation actions, and track their progress and effectiveness.

Track the effort you spend on requirements engineering. Record the effort devoted to requirements development and management activities. Use this data to assess whether the planned requirements activities are being performed as intended and to better plan the resources needed for requirements engineering on future projects.

 Next Steps

◆   Go back to the requirements-related problems you identified from the Next Steps in Chapter 1. Identify good practices from this chapter that might help with each problem you identified. For each practice you suggest, identify any barriers in your organization or culture that might make it difficult to implement.

◆   Make a list of all the requirements good practices you identified in the previous step. For each practice, indicate your project's level of capability: expert, proficient, novice, or unfamiliar. If your team is not at least proficient in any of those practices, ask someone on your project to learn more about the practice and to share what he or she learns with the rest of the team.

4
Improving Your Requirements Processes

Chapter 3 described several dozen requirements engineering good practices you should consider applying in your software organization. Putting better practices into action is the essence of software process improvement. In a nutshell, process improvement consists of using more of the approaches that work well for us and avoiding those that have given us headaches in the past. However, the path to improved performance is paved with false starts, resistance from those who are affected, and the frustration of having too little time to handle current tasks, let alone improvement programs.

Software process improvement has two primary objectives:

1. To correct problems you've encountered on previous or current projects

2. To anticipate and prevent problems you might encounter on future projects

If your current methods seem to work well, you might not see the need to change your approach. However, even successful software organizations can struggle when confronted with larger projects, different customer communities, tighter schedules, or new application domains. At the least, you should be aware of other approaches to requirements engineering that would be valuable additions to your software engineering tool kit.

This chapter describes how requirements relate to other key project processes and stakeholders. Some basic concepts about software process improvement and a suggested process improvement life cycle are presented. I have listed several important requirements "process assets" that your organization should have available. The chapter concludes by describing a process improvement roadmap for implementing improved requirements engineering practices.

HOW REQUIREMENTS RELATE TO OTHER PROJECT PROCESSES

Requirements lie at the heart of a well-run software project, supporting many of the other technical and management activities. Changes you make in your requirements development and management approaches will affect these other processes, and vice versa. Figure 4-1 illustrates some of the connections between requirements and other processes; the process interfaces are described briefly in the sections that follow.

Project planning   Requirements should be the foundation of the project planning process, which develops resource and schedule estimates based on an understanding of what is to be delivered. Often, project planning indicates that the entire desired feature set can't be delivered within the available bounds of resources and time. The planning process can lead to reductions in the project scope or to selection of a staged-release approach to deliver functionality in phases.

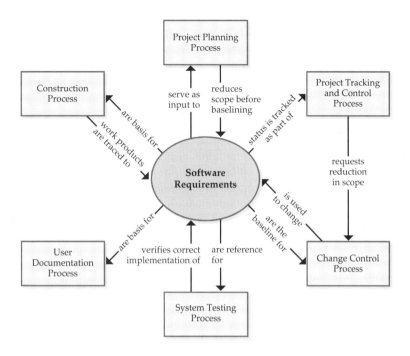

FIGURE 4-1 *Relationship of requirements to other project processes.*

Project tracking and control Monitor the status of each requirement as part of project tracking so that the project manager can see whether construction and verification are proceeding as intended. If not, management might need to request scope reductions through the change control process.

Change control After a set of requirements has been documented and baselined, all subsequent changes should be made through a defined change control process. The change control process helps ensure that:

- The impact of a proposed change is understood.

- All people who are affected by a change are made aware of it.

- The appropriate people make informed decisions to accept changes.

- Resources are adjusted as needed.

- The requirements documents are kept current and accurate.

System testing   User requirements and functional requirements are key inputs to system testing. If the expected behavior of the product under various conditions is not specified, the software testers will be hard-pressed to distinguish the correct behavior from a defect. Conversely, system testing is a means to verify that all planned functionality has been implemented as intended and that the specified user tasks can be properly executed.

User documentation   I once worked in an office that also housed the technical writers who prepared user documentation for commercial products. I asked one of the writers why they worked such long hours. "We're at the end of the food chain," she replied. "We're the ones who have to document the final changes in user interface displays and the features that got dropped or added at the last minute." The product's requirements are an essential input to the documentation process, so low-quality or late requirements will lead to problems with the user documentation.

Construction   Executable software, not requirements documentation, is the primary deliverable of a software project. The requirements are the foundation for all the design and implementation work that follows. The functional requirements lead to design components, which serve as specifications for the code to be written. Use design reviews to ensure that the designs correctly address all of the requirements. Unit testing of the code can determine whether it satisfies the design specification and whether it satisfies the pertinent requirements. Trace every requirement to specific design and code elements of the software.

IMPACT OF SOFTWARE REQUIREMENTS ON OTHER STAKEHOLDERS

When the software development group changes its requirements processes, the interfaces it presents to other project stakeholder communities will also change. Figure 4-2 shows some of the external organizational functions that can interface with a software development group and some of the contributions they make to a project's requirements activities.

To keep these interfaces operating smoothly, communicate your process improvement intentions and justifications to your counterparts in other areas. You'll need to explain the benefits that these other groups will realize from the new process. When seeking collaboration on process improvement, begin from the viewpoint "Here are the problems we've all experienced, and we think these changes will help solve them. This is what we'll do, this is the help we'll need from you, and this is how our work will help you." Resistance to change often indicates fear about the impacts of the change, so address the fears that the people affected by your proposed process changes might have.

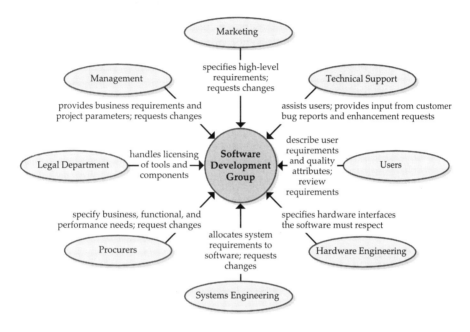

FIGURE 4-2   *Key requirements interfaces between software development and other organizations.*

Explain to people in each functional area the information and contributions you need from them if the entire product development effort is to succeed. Agree on the form and content of key communication interfaces between development and other functional areas, such as a system requirements specification or a marketing requirements document. Too often, important project documents are written strictly from the producer's point of view without fully appreciating the information the consumers of those documents really need.

On the flip side, ask the other organizations what they need from the development group to make their jobs easier. What input about technical feasibility will help marketing plan their product concepts better? What requirements status reports will give management adequate visibility into project progress? What collaboration with systems engineering will ensure that system requirements are properly partitioned among software and hardware subsystems? Strive to build collaborative relationships between development and the other stakeholders of the requirements process so that all can contribute effectively to the project's success.

People do not like to be forced out of their comfort zone, so expect some resistance to your requirements process changes. Strive to understand the origin of the resistance so that you can both respect it and defuse it. Much resistance can be attributed to fear of the unknown, so be prepared to educate people about why the changes are being made, how individuals will be affected, what benefits will be reaped, and why you need their participation in the process improvement initiative. Here are some of the forms of resistance you might encounter:

◆ A requirements change control process might be viewed as a barrier thrown up by development to make it harder to get changes made. In reality, though, it provides structure and order to the change process and permits well-informed people to make good business decisions. Your responsibility is to make sure the change process really does work. If new processes don't yield better results, people will work around them.

◆ Some developers view writing and inspecting requirements documents as bureaucratic time-wasters that prevent them from doing their real work, which they think is writing code. If you can explain the high cost of continually rewriting the code while the team tries to figure out what the code should do, developers and managers will better appreciate the need for good requirements.

◆ If customer-support costs are not connected to the development process in some way, the development team might not be motivated to change how they work because they don't suffer the consequences of poor product quality.

◆ If one objective of improved requirements processes is to reduce support costs by creating higher-quality products, the support manager might feel threatened. Who wants to see his empire shrink?

FUNDAMENTALS OF SOFTWARE PROCESS IMPROVEMENT

You are reading this book presumably because you intend to change some of the current approaches your organization uses for requirements engineering. As you begin your quest for excellent requirements, keep the following four principles of software process improvement in mind (Wiegers 1996a):

1. *Process improvement should be evolutionary, continuous, and cyclical.* Don't expect to improve all of your processes at once, and accept that you won't get everything right the first time you try to make changes. Instead of aiming for perfection, develop a few improved procedures and get started with implementation. You can adjust your approaches as you gain experience with the new techniques.

2. *People and organizations change only when they have an incentive to do so.* The strongest incentive for change is pain. I don't mean artificially induced pain, such as management-imposed schedule pressure intended to make developers work harder, but rather the very real pain you've experienced on previous projects. Such pain is much more motivating than a manager or process zealot who proclaims, "This book says we have to do some new things, so let's get started!" Following are some examples of historical problems that can provide compelling drivers for changing your requirements processes:

    ◆   The project missed deadlines because the requirements turned out to be more complicated than expected.

    ◆   The developers had to work a lot of overtime because misunderstood or ambiguous requirements were addressed late in development.

    ◆   System test effort was wasted because the testers didn't understand what the product was supposed to do.

    ◆   The right functionality was present, but users were dissatisfied because of poor performance, low usability, or other factors.

> ◆ The organization experienced high maintenance costs because customers requested many enhancements that should have been identified during requirements elicitation.
>
> ◆ The development organization acquired a reputation for delivering software that customers don't want.

3. *Process changes should be goal oriented.* Before you begin the journey to superior processes, make sure you know where you're headed. Do you want to reduce the amount of work that is redone because of requirements problems? Do you want better control of the way requirement changes are incorporated into the project? Do you want to make sure no requirements are overlooked during implementation? A roadmap that defines the path you want to take will greatly improve your chances of successful process improvement.

4. *Treat your improvement activities as miniprojects.* Many improvement initiatives founder because they are poorly planned or because the resources committed to them never really materialize. To avoid these problems, treat each improvement activity as a project. Include process improvement resources and tasks in your project's overall plans. Perform the planning, tracking, measurement, and reporting that you'd do for any software development project, scaled down for the size of the improvement project. Write an action plan for each process improvement area you tackle. Track the time the participants spend executing the action plan to see if you're getting the resources you expected and to know how much the improvement work is costing.

THE PROCESS IMPROVEMENT CYCLE

Figure 4-3 illustrates a software process improvement life cycle I have found to be effective. This cycle reflects the importance of knowing where you are before you take off for someplace else, the need to plan your improvement activities, and the importance of learning from your experiences as part of continuous process improvement.

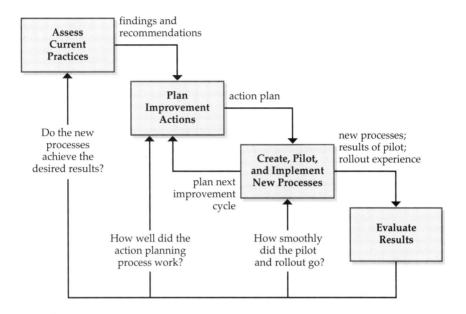

FIGURE 4-3 *The software process improvement cycle.*

ASSESS CURRENT PRACTICES

Step 1 of any process improvement activity is to assess the practices currently being used in an organization and identify their strengths and shortcomings. An assessment does not in itself provide any improvement; it provides information. The assessment lays the foundation for making the right choices about the changes you should make.

You can evaluate your current processes in several ways. If you tried any of the Next Steps at the end of previous chapters, you've already begun an informal evaluation of your requirements practices and their results. Structured self-assessment questionnaires provide a more systematic approach, which can reveal insights about your current processes at low cost.

A more thorough approach is to have an outside consultant evaluate your current software practices objectively. The most comprehensive formal process assessments are based on an established framework for process improvement, such as the Capability Maturity Model for Software (CMM) developed by the Software Engineering Institute (CMU/SEI 1995). Typically, outside assessors will examine many of your software development and management processes, not just the requirements activities. Select an assessment approach that aligns with the business goals you wish to achieve through your process improvement activities, and don't worry too much about satisfying the requirements of the CMM or any other specific model.

The Appendix contains a questionnaire for current requirements practice self-assessment. Use this questionnaire to calibrate your organization's current requirements engineering practices. This self-assessment helps you decide which of your requirements processes are most in need of improvement. Just because you give yourself a low rating on a particular question isn't reason enough to address it immediately, or perhaps at all. Focus your energy on improving those practice areas that are causing your projects the most difficulties and those that pose risks to the success of your future projects. Each question in the self-assessment refers to the chapter of this book that addresses the topic of the question. Motorola developed a similar "Software Requirements Quality Model" for requirements process assessment (Smith 1998).

The deliverables from a formal assessment include a list of findings—statements of both strengths and weaknesses in the current processes—and recommendations for addressing the improvement opportunities. Informal assessments, such as the self-assessment questionnaire, provide insights that can help you select improvement areas to address. You'll find many general recommendations in the chapters of this book to which the self-assessment questions point. Analyze each improvement action you contemplate to make sure it is cost-effective to implement. There is no point in change for its own sake, so select improvement actions that are likely to have a substantial return on investment.

PLAN IMPROVEMENT ACTIONS

In keeping with the philosophy that process improvement activities must be treated as projects, write an action plan after your assessment. Consider writing a strategic plan that describes your organization's overall software process improvement initiative, as well as tactical action plans for specific improvement areas, such as the way you gather requirements. Each tactical action plan should indicate the goals of the improvement activities, the participants, and several individual action items that must be completed to fully implement the plan. Without a plan, it's easy to overlook important tasks. The plan also provides a way to track progress, since you can monitor the completion of individual action items.

Figure 4-4 illustrates a process improvement action plan template I have used many times. Include no more than 10 items in each action plan. This will keep the plan simple and make it easy to achieve some early successes. As an example, I saw a plan for requirements management improvements that included these action items:

1. Draft a requirements change control procedure.

2. Review and revise the change control procedure.

3. Pilot the change control procedure with Project A.

4. Revise the change control procedure based on feedback from the pilot.

5. Evaluate problem-tracking tools, and select one to support the change control procedure.

6. Procure the problem-tracking tool, and customize it to support the change control procedure.

7. Roll out the new change control procedure and tool to the organization.

Assign each action item to a specific individual owner who is responsible for seeing that the item is completed. Don't assign "the team" as an action item owner. Teams don't do work; individuals do.

If you need more than about 10 action items, focus the initial activity cycle on the most important issues and address the rest later in a separate action plan; remember, change is cyclical. The process improvement roadmap described later in this chapter illustrates how you can group multiple improvement actions into an overall software process improvement plan.

Action Plan for Requirements Process Improvement

Project: **Date:**
<your project name here>   *<date plan was written>*

Goals:
<State a few goals you wish to accomplish by successfully executing this plan. State the goals in terms of business results, not in terms of the process changes.>

Measures of Success:
<Describe how you will determine if the process changes have had the desired effects on the project.>

Scope of Organizational Impact:
<Describe the breadth of impact of the process changes described in this plan.>

Staffing and Participants:
<Identify the individuals who will implement this plan, their roles, and their time commitment on an hours/week or percentage basis.>

Tracking and Reporting Process:
<Describe how progress on the action items in this plan will be tracked and to whom status, results, and issues will be reported.>

Dependencies, Risks, and Constraints:
<Identify any external factors that may be required for this plan to succeed or that may prevent successful implementation of the plan.>

Estimated Completion Date for All Activities:
<When do you expect this to be done?>

ACTION ITEMS:
<Write 3 to 10 action items for each action plan.>

Action Item	Owner	Due Date	Purpose	Description of Activities	Deliverables	Resources Needed
<Sequence number>	*<Responsible individual>*	*<Target date>*	*<Objective of this action item>*	*<Activities that will be performed to implement this action item>*	*<Procedures, templates, or other process assets that will be created>*	*<Any external resources needed, including materials, tools, documents, or other people>*

FIGURE 4-4 *Action plan template for software process improvement.*

CREATE, PILOT, AND IMPLEMENT NEW PROCESSES

So far, you've evaluated your current requirements practices and crafted a plan for addressing the process areas you think are most likely to yield benefits. Now comes the hard part: implementing the plan. Many process improvement initiatives stumble when they try to turn action plans into actions.

Implementing an action plan means developing new or better processes that you believe will afford better results than your current processes. However, do not expect to get the new processes perfect the first time. Many approaches that seem like a good idea in the abstract turn out to be less practical or less effective than you hoped. Therefore, plan a process "pilot" for most of the new procedures or document templates you create. Use the knowledge you gain from the pilot to adjust the new technique. This improves the chance that it will be effective and well received when you roll it out to the target community. Keep these suggestions in mind for the process pilots you conduct:

- Select pilot participants who will give the new approaches a fair try and provide helpful feedback. These participants could be either allies or skeptics, but they should not strongly oppose the process improvement effort.

- Quantify the criteria you use to evaluate the pilot, to make the outcome easy to interpret.

- Identify the stakeholders who need to be kept informed of what the pilot is about and why it is being performed.

- Consider piloting portions of the new processes on different projects. This is a way to get more people involved in trying new approaches, thereby increasing awareness, feedback, and buy-in.

- As part of the evaluation, ask pilot participants how they would feel if they had to go back to their old ways of working.

Even motivated and receptive teams have a limited capacity to absorb change, so don't place too many new expectations on a project or group at once. Write a roll-out plan that defines how you'll distribute the new methods and materials to the project team and that describes the training and support you'll provide. Also consider how management will communicate their expectations about the new processes. A formal policy concerning requirements engineering or requirements management is often written to clarify management's commitment and expectations (CMU/SEI 1995).

EVALUATE RESULTS

The final step of a process improvement cycle is to evaluate the activities performed and the results achieved. This evaluation will help you do an even better job on future improvement activities. Assess how smoothly your pilots ran and how effective they were in resolving your uncertainties about the new processes. Would you change anything the next time you conduct a process pilot?

Also consider how well the general rollout of the new processes to the community went. Did you communicate the availability of the new processes or templates to everyone? Did participants understand and successfully apply the new processes? Would you change anything about how you conduct the next rollout?

The critical step is to evaluate whether the newly implemented processes are yielding the desired results. While some new technical and management practices deliver visible improvements quickly, many take time to demonstrate their full value. For example, if you implement a new process for dealing with requirement changes, you should be able to tell quite soon whether changes are being incorporated into the project in a more disciplined way. However, a new SRS template can take some time to prove its worth as analysts and customers get used to the discipline of documenting requirements in a particular format. Give new approaches adequate time to work, and select measures that will demonstrate the success of each process change.

Accept the reality of the learning curve, the productivity drop that takes place as practitioners take time to assimilate new ways of working, as illustrated by Figure 4-5. This short-term productivity drop is part of the investment your organization is making in process improvement. If you don't understand this, you might be tempted to abandon the process improvement effort before it begins to pay off, thereby achieving a zero return on your investment. Educate your managers and peers about the learning curve, and commit to seeing it through: you'll achieve superior project and business results with the help of superior requirements processes.

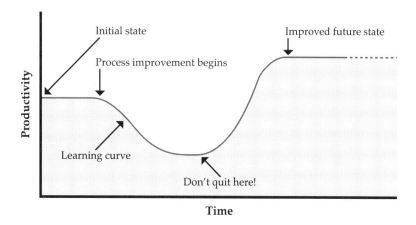

FIGURE 4-5   *The process improvement learning curve.*

REQUIREMENTS PROCESS ASSETS

If you want your projects to consistently achieve superior results, you need effective processes for all the requirements engineering elements: elicitation, analysis, specification, verification, and management. To facilitate these processes, you'll need to develop a collection of *process assets*. A process encompasses the actions you take and the deliverables you produce; process assets help the team members perform processes consistently and effectively. These process assets will help those involved in the project understand the steps they are supposed to follow and the work products they are expected to create. Process assets include the following types of documents:

checklist	A list that enumerates activities, deliverables, or other items to be noted or verified. Checklists are memory joggers. They help ensure that busy people do not overlook important details.
example	A representative of a specific type of work product. Accumulate better examples over time as they become available in your organization.

plan	A document that outlines how an objective will be accomplished and what is needed to accomplish it.
policy	A guiding principle that sets an expectation of behaviors, actions, and deliverables. Processes should align with policies.
procedure	A step-by-step description of the sequence of tasks that accomplishes an activity. Describe the tasks to be performed and identify the project roles that perform them. Avoid including tutorial information in a procedure.
process description	A documented definition of a set of activities performed for some purpose. A process description might include the process objective and key milestones, the participants, appropriate times to perform the activities, communication steps, desired results, and both input and output data associated with the process (Caputo 1998).
template	A pattern to be used as a guide for producing a complete work product. Templates for key project documents remind you to ask yourself questions you might otherwise overlook. A well-structured template provides many "slots" for capturing and organizing information. Guidance text embedded in the template will help the document author use it effectively.

Figure 4-6 identifies some process assets you should accumulate to enable effective and repeatable requirements development and management on your projects. There is no software process rule book that says you have to have all of these items, but they will all assist your requirements-related activities over the long run.

Requirements Development Process Assets	Requirements Management Process Assets
• Project Vision and Scope Template • Requirements Development Procedure • Requirements Allocation Procedure • Use-Case Template • Software Requirements Specification Template • Requirements Prioritization Procedure • SRS and Use-Case Inspection Checklists	• Change Control Procedure • Change Control Board Procedure • Requirements Change Impact Analysis Checklist and Template • Requirements Status Tracking Procedure • Requirements Traceability Matrix Template

FIGURE 4-6 *Key process assets for requirements development and management.*

The procedures listed in Figure 4-6 need not be written as separate documents. For example, an overall requirements management process description could include the change control procedure, status tracking procedure, and impact analysis checklist. For an example of a requirements management process description, see Appendix J of *CMM Implementation Guide* (Caputo 1998).

Following are brief descriptions of each of the process assets listed in Figure 4-6, along with references to the chapters where they are discussed in detail. Keep in mind that each project should tailor the organization's procedures to meet their needs.

REQUIREMENTS DEVELOPMENT PROCESS ASSETS

Project vision and scope template The project's vision and scope document defines the conceptual foundation of the project and provides a reference for making decisions about requirements priorities and changes. The vision and scope document is a concise, high-level description of the new product's business requirements. Writing a project vision and scope document in a consistent way helps ensure that all the right issues have been considered when making business decisions to proceed with the project. Chapter 6 recommends a template for the vision and scope document.

Requirements development procedure   This procedure describes how to identify customers in your domain and techniques for eliciting requirements from them. It also describes the various requirements documents and analysis models your project is expected to create and points toward appropriate templates. The procedure can indicate the kind of information to include for each requirement, such as priority, predicted stability, or planned release number. The procedure should identify the steps the project should perform for requirements analysis and verification of the requirements documents. Also include the steps required to approve the SRS and establish the requirements baseline.

Requirements allocation procedure   The allocation of high-level product requirements to specific subsystems is important when developing systems that include both hardware and software or complex software products that contain multiple subsystems (Nelsen 1990). Allocation takes place after the system-level requirements are specified and the system architecture has been defined. This procedure contains information on how to perform these allocations to ensure the right functionality is assigned to the right system component. It also describes how allocated requirements will be traced back to their parent system requirements and to related requirements in other subsystems.

Use-case template   The use-case template provides a standard way to document each task a user wishes to perform with a software system. A use-case definition includes a brief description of the task, descriptions of alternative behaviors or known exceptions that must be handled, and additional information that characterizes the user task. Use cases can be elaborated into individual functional requirements in the SRS. Alternatively, you can combine the use-case and SRS templates into a single document that contains the product's user requirements and software functional requirements. Chapter 8 suggests a format for a use-case template.

Software requirements specification template   The SRS template provides a structured way to organize the functional and nonfunctional requirements. An organization that adopts a standard SRS template will find that it helps them to create consistently high-quality requirements documents for projects. You might want to adopt more than one template to accommodate the different types or sizes of projects your organization undertakes. This can reduce the frustration that arises when a "one size fits all" template or procedure simply is not suitable for your project. Chapter 9 describes a sample SRS template.

Requirements prioritization procedure   My friend Matt describes the final phase of a typical software project as the "rapid descoping phase," when planned functionality is dropped at the last minute to meet a schedule deadline. To reduce scope at any stage we need to know which features, use cases, or functional requirements have the lowest priority. Chapter 13 describes a prioritization procedure and spreadsheet tool that incorporates the value provided to the customer, the relative technical risk, and the relative cost of implementation for each use case, feature, or requirement.

SRS and use-case inspection checklists   Formal inspection of requirements documents is a powerful software quality technique. An inspection checklist identifies many of the errors commonly found in requirements documents. Use the checklist during preparation for an inspection meeting to focus your attention on common problem areas. Chapter 14 contains sample SRS and use-case inspection checklists.

REQUIREMENTS MANAGEMENT PROCESS ASSETS

Change control procedure   A change control process can reduce the chaos inflicted on many projects by endless and uncontrolled requirements changes. The control change procedure defines the way that a new requirement or a change to an existing requirement is proposed, communicated, evaluated, and decided on. Change control is often supported with a problem-tracking tool, but remember that a tool is not a substitute for a process. Chapter 17 addresses the change control process in detail.

Change control board procedure   The change control board (CCB) is the body of stakeholders that decides which proposed requirements changes to approve, which to reject, and in which product release each approved change will be incorporated. The CCB procedure describes the composition and operating procedures of the change control board. The primary actions of the CCB are to request impact analysis of proposed changes, make a decision about each change, and communicate those decisions to all who are affected by them. Chapter 17 further addresses the composition and function of the CCB.

Requirements change impact analysis checklist and template   Estimating the cost and other impacts of a proposed requirement change is a key step in determining whether a proposed change should be accepted. Impact analysis helps the CCB make smart decisions. As illustrated in Chapter 18, an impact analysis checklist contains many questions to ask yourself as you contemplate the possible tasks, side effects, and potential risks associated with implementing a specific requirement change. An accompanying worksheet provides a simple way to estimate the labor for the tasks so you can better understand the implications of approving the change. A sample template for presenting the results of the impact analysis performed for a proposed new or changed requirement can also be found in Chapter 18.

Requirements status tracking procedure   Requirements management includes monitoring and reporting the status of each functional requirement and the conditions under which the status can change. You'll need to use a database or a commercial requirements management tool to track the status of a large number of requirements in a complex system. This procedure also describes the reports you can generate to view the status of the collected requirements at any time. See Chapter 16 for more about requirements status tracking.

Requirements traceability matrix template   The requirements traceability matrix lists all the functional requirements from the SRS, along with the design components that address each requirement, the source files and procedures that implement the requirement, and the test cases that verify the proper implementation of the requirement. The traceability matrix should also identify the parent user or system requirement from which each functional requirement was derived. Chapter 18 addresses requirements traceability.

REQUIREMENTS PROCESS IMPROVEMENT ROADMAP

Improving your organization's requirements engineering processes is not trivial. Haphazard approaches to process improvement do not often lead to sustainable success. Instead, you should develop a roadmap for implementing improved requirements practices. This roadmap should be part of your strategic software process improvement plan. If you tried one of the requirements process assessment approaches described earlier, you have some ideas about the techniques or process assets that might address the shortcomings this assessment revealed. Now you need to sequence these improvement actions in a way that will yield the greatest benefits with the smallest investment. A process improvement roadmap depicts just such a sequencing.

Because every situation is different, I cannot give you a one-size-fits-all roadmap. Formulaic approaches to process improvement cannot replace thought and common sense. Figure 4-7 illustrates one organization's roadmap for improving their requirements processes. The desired business results are shown in the boxes on the right side of the figure. The major improvement activities are shown in the other boxes, and some intermediate milestones (circles) are indicated along the paths to achieving the desired business objectives. Implement each set of improvement activities from left to right. Once you've created a similar roadmap, give ownership of each milestone to an individual, who can then write an action plan for achieving that milestone. Then turn those action plans into actions!

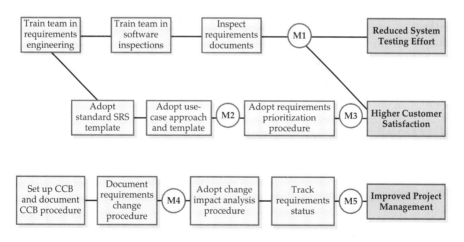

FIGURE 4-7 *Sample requirements process improvement roadmap.*

Next Steps

◆   Complete the Current Requirements Practice Self-Assessment in the Appendix. Identify your top three improvement opportunities for requirements practices, based on the severity of the impact from shortcomings in your current practices.

◆   Determine which of the requirements engineering process assets listed in Figure 4-6 are not presently available in your organization but which you think would be useful.

◆   Based on the two preceding steps, develop a requirements process improvement roadmap patterned after that shown in Figure 4-7. Persuade someone in your organization to take responsibility for each milestone. Have each milestone owner write an action plan for implementing the recommendations leading up to his or her milestone, using the action plan template in Figure 4-4. Track the progress of the action items in the plan as they are implemented.

5

Software Requirements and Risk Management

Dave, the project manager for the Chemical Tracking System at Contoso Pharma-ceuticals, is meeting with his lead programmer, Helen, and the lead tester, Ramesh. All are excited about the new project, but they remember some of the problems they ran into on an earlier project called the Pharm-Simulator.

"Remember how we didn't find out the users hated the Simulator user inter-face until beta testing?" Helen asked. "It took us five weeks to rebuild it and retest it. I sure don't want to go through that death march again."

"That wasn't fun," Dave agreed. "It was also annoying that the users we talked to swore they needed a lot of features that no one has used so far. That drug interaction modeling feature took three times as long to code as we expected, and we wound up throwing it out anyway. What a waste!"

"We really had to rush on the Simulator and didn't have time to write detailed requirements," Ramesh remembered. "Half the time the testers had to ask a programmer how some feature was supposed to work so they could test it. Then it turned out that some of the functions the programmers designed didn't do what the users requested anyway."

"I was really annoyed that the manager who requested the Pharm-Simulator signed off on the requirements without even reading them," Dave added. "Then we got this constant stream of requests for new features and changes from everybody in her department. It's no surprise the project came in four months late and cost almost twice what they budgeted. If that happens again, I'll probably get fired."

Ramesh had a suggestion. "Maybe we should make a list of these problems from the Simulator so we can try to avoid them on the Chemical Tracking System. I read an article on software risk management that said we should identify risks and figure out how to prevent them from hurting the project."

"I don't know about that," Dave protested. "We learned a lot from the Simulator, so we probably won't have those problems again. This project isn't big enough to need risk management. If we write down things that could go wrong on the Chemical Tracking System, it will look like I don't know how to run a software project. I don't want any negative thinkers on this project. We have to plan for success!"

As Dave's final comments suggest, software engineers are eternal optimists. We often expect our next project to run smoothly, despite the history of problems on earlier projects. The reality is that dozens of potential pitfalls can prevent projects from proceeding as planned. Contrary to Dave's beliefs, it's imperative that software project managers identify and control their project risks, beginning with requirements engineering risks.

A risk is a condition that could cause some loss or otherwise threaten the success of a project. This condition has not actually caused a problem yet, and you'd like to keep it that way. These potential problems might have an adverse impact on the project's cost, schedule, or technical success, the product's quality, or team effectiveness. Risk management—a software industry best practice—is the process of identifying, evaluating, and controlling risks before they damage your project. If something untoward has already happened on your project, it is not a risk: It is an issue. Deal with current problems and issues through your project's ongoing status tracking and corrective action processes.

While no one can predict the future with certainty, risk management lets you take actions to minimize the likelihood or impact of potential problems. Risk management means dealing with a concern *before* it turns into a problem or crisis. This improves the chance of project success and reduces the consequences, financial or otherwise, of those risks that you can't avoid. Risks that lie outside your personal sphere of control should be addressed to the appropriate level of management.

Because requirements play such a central role in software projects, the prudent project manager will identify requirements-related risks early and control them aggressively. Typical requirements risks include misunderstanding the requirements, inadequate user involvement, uncertain or changing project scope and objectives, and continually changing requirements. Project managers can control requirements risks only through collaboration with customers or their representatives, such as marketing personnel. Jointly documenting requirements risks and planning mitigation actions reinforces the customer-developer partnership discussed in Chapter 2.

Simply knowing about the risks doesn't make them go away, so this chapter presents a brief tutorial on software risk management. A number of risk factors that can raise their ugly heads during requirements engineering activities are described later in the chapter. Use this information to launch an attack on your requirements risks before they attack your project.

FUNDAMENTALS OF SOFTWARE RISK MANAGEMENT

Projects face many kinds of risks besides those related to project scope and requirements. Dependency on an external entity, such as a subcontractor or another project that is producing components to be reused, is a common source of risk. Project management is fraught with risks caused by poor estimation, rejection of accurate estimates by managers, insufficient visibility into project status, and staff turnover. Technology risks threaten highly complex or leading-edge development projects. Lack of knowledge is another source of risk, as with practitioners who have insufficient experience with the technologies being used or with the application domain. Imposed and ever-changing government regulations can disrupt the best-laid project plans.

Scary! This is why all projects should take risk management seriously. Risk management involves peeking over the horizon periodically to look for the icebergs, rather than proceeding full speed ahead with great confidence that your ship cannot sink. As with other processes, scale your risk management activities to your project's size. Small projects can get by with a simple risk list, although formal risk management planning is a key element of a successful large-scale project.

ELEMENTS OF RISK MANAGEMENT

Risk management is the application of tools and procedures to contain project risk within acceptable limits. Risk management provides a standard approach to identify and document risk factors, evaluate their potential severity, and propose strategies for mitigating those risks (Williams, Walker, and Dorofee 1997). Risk management includes the activities shown in Figure 5-1.

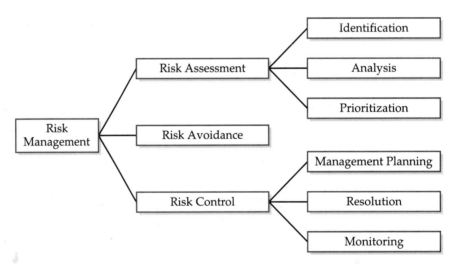

FIGURE 5-1   *Elements of risk management.*[1]

Risk assessment is the process of examining a project to identify areas of potential risk. You can facilitate *risk identification* with lists of common risk factors for software projects, including the requirements risk factors described

---

1. Adapted from McConnell, Steve. *Rapid Development: Taming Wild Software Schedules.* Redmond, Wash.: Microsoft Press, 1996.

later in this chapter (Carr et al. 1993; McConnell 1996). During *risk analysis,* you will examine the potential consequences of specific risks to your project. *Risk prioritization* helps you focus on the most severe risks by assessing the potential *risk exposure* from each. Risk exposure is a function of both the probability of incurring a loss due to the risk and the potential magnitude of that loss.

Risk avoidance is one way to deal with a risk: don't do the risky thing. You can avoid risks by not undertaking certain projects, by relying on proven rather than cutting-edge technologies when possible, or by excluding features that will be especially difficult to implement correctly.

More often, you will have to perform *risk control* activities to manage the top-priority risk factors you identified. *Risk management planning* produces a plan for dealing with each significant risk, including mitigation approaches, contingency plans, owners, and timelines. You can try to prevent the risk from becoming a problem at all, or you can try to reduce the adverse impact if it does. The risks will not control themselves, so *risk resolution* involves executing the plans for mitigating each risk. Finally, track your progress toward resolving each risk item through *risk monitoring,* which should become part of your routine project status tracking. Monitor how well your risk mitigation actions are working, and revise the contents and priorities of your risk list periodically.

DOCUMENTING PROJECT RISKS

It's not enough to simply recognize the risks that face your project. You need to document and manage them in a way that lets you communicate risk issues and status to stakeholders throughout the project's duration. Figure 5-2 shows a template for documenting an individual risk statement. You might find it more convenient to store this information in tabular form in a spreadsheet, which makes it easy to sort the list of individual risks. Keep the risk list as a stand-alone document to make it easy to update and maintain throughout the project's duration.

Risk Item Tracking Template

ID:
<sequence number>

Date Opened:
<date risk was identified>

Date Closed:
<date risk was closed out>

Description:
<description of the risk in the form "condition–consequence"> .

Probability:
<the likelihood of this risk becoming a problem>

Impact:
<the potential damage if the risk does become a problem>

Exposure:
<probability times impact>

Mitigation Plan:
< one or more approaches to control, avoid, minimize, or otherwise mitigate the risk>

Owner:
< individual responsible for resolving the risk>

Date Due:
<date by which the mitigation approach is to be completed>

FIGURE 5-2   *Risk item tracking template.*

Use a *condition–consequence* format when you document risk statements. That is, state the condition that you are concerned about, followed by the potential adverse outcome—the consequence—if that risk should turn into a problem. Often, people who suggest risks state only the condition ("the customers don't agree on the product requirements") or the consequence ("we can only satisfy one of our major customers"). Pull these statements together into the condition–consequence structure: "The customers don't agree on the product requirements, so we will only be able to satisfy one of our major customers." One condition might lead to several consequences, and several conditions can contribute to the same consequence.

The template provides locations to record the probability of a risk materializing into a problem, the negative impact on the project as a result of that problem, and the overall risk exposure (probability times impact). I estimate the probability on a scale from 0.1 (highly unlikely) to 1.0 (certain to happen), and the impact on a relative scale of 1 (no sweat) to 10 (deep tapioca). Multiply these factors together to estimate the exposure from each risk.

Don't try to quantify risks too precisely. Your goal is to differentiate the most threatening risks from those you don't need to tackle immediately. You might find it easier to simply estimate both probability and impact as *high*, *medium*, or *low*. Address those items that have at least one *high* rating first.

Use the Mitigation Plan field to identify the actions you intend to take to control the risk. Some mitigation strategies try to reduce the risk probability, while others reduce the impact. Consider the cost of mitigation when planning; it doesn't make sense to spend $20,000 to control a risk that could only cost you $10,000. Assign every risk that you are going to control to an individual owner and set a date for completing the mitigation actions. Long-term or complex risks might require a multistep mitigation strategy with multiple milestones.

Figure 5-3 illustrates a risk the Chemical Tracking System team leaders discussed at the beginning of this chapter. The team estimated the probability and impact on the basis of their previous experience. Until they evaluate other risk factors, they won't know how serious a risk exposure of 4.2 is. The first two mitigation approaches reduce the probability of this risk becoming a problem by increasing user involvement in the requirements process. Prototyping reduces the potential impact by seeking early feedback on the user interface.

Sample Risk Item from the Chemical Tracking System

ID:
1

Date Opened:
5/4/99

Date Closed:
(open)

Description:
Insufficient user involvement in requirements elicitation leads to extensive user interface rework after beta testing.

Probability:
0.6

Impact:
7

Exposure:
4.2

Mitigation Plan:

1. Gather ease-of-learning and usability requirements early in Phase 1.

2. Hold JAD sessions with product champions to develop the requirements.

3. Develop a throwaway user interface prototype of core functionality interactively with product champions and a human factors consultant. Have product champions and other users evaluate the prototype.

Owner:
Helen

Date Due:
Complete JAD session by 6/16/99

FIGURE 5-3 *Sample risk item from the Chemical Tracking System.*

PLANNING FOR RISK MANAGEMENT

A risk list is not the same thing as a risk management plan. For a small project, you can include your plans for controlling risks in the software project management plan. A large project should write a separate risk management plan that spells out the approaches it will take to identify, evaluate, document, and track risks. This plan should include the roles and responsibilities for the risk management activities. You might wish to appoint a project risk manager to be responsible for staying on top of the things that could go wrong. One company dubbed their risk manager "Eeyore," after the gloomy Winnie-the-Pooh character who constantly bemoaned how bad things could become.

Too often, project teams create plans for their essential activities but fail both to use the plans as a guide throughout the project and to keep them current as realities change. Be sure to follow through on the risk management actions you decide to undertake. The project schedule must allocate enough time for risk management to ensure that the project does not waste its early investment in risk planning. Include risk mitigation activities, status reporting, and updating of the risk list as line items in your project's work breakdown structure.

As with other project management activities, you need to establish a rhythm of periodic monitoring. Keep the ten or so risks that have the highest risk exposure highly visible, and track the effectiveness of your mitigation approaches regularly. When a mitigation action is completed, reevaluate the probability and impact for that risk item, and update the risk list and any other pending mitigation plans accordingly. As the initial top-priority risks are controlled, new items will rise into the top ten. Remember, a risk is not necessarily under control simply because the mitigation actions have been completed. You need to determine whether your mitigation approaches have reduced the exposure to an acceptable level or whether the time window during which a specific risk could have become a problem has passed.

REQUIREMENTS-RELATED RISKS

The risk factors described on the following pages are organized by the requirements engineering subdisciplines of elicitation, analysis, specification, verification, and management. Techniques are suggested that can reduce either the probability of the risk materializing into a problem or the impact on the project if it does. This list is just a starting point; accumulate your own list of risk factors and mitigation strategies, based on the lessons you learn from each project. Use the items here to prompt your thinking when identifying requirements risks, and be sure to write your specific risk statements in the condition–consequence format.

REQUIREMENTS ELICITATION

Product vision and scope   Scope creep is more likely if the team members don't have a clear, shared understanding of what the product is supposed to be and do. Early in the project, write a vision and scope document that contains your business requirements, and use it to guide decisions about new or modified requirements.

Time spent on requirements development   Tight project schedules often pressure managers into glossing over the requirements because they believe that if the programmers don't begin coding right away, they won't finish on time. Projects vary widely depending on their size and application class (such as information systems, systems software, commercial, or military), but a rough guideline is to spend about 15 percent of your project effort on requirements development activities (Rubin 1999). Keep records of how much effort you actually spend on requirements development for each project so you can judge whether it was sufficient and improve your planning for future projects.

Completeness and correctness of requirements specifications   To ensure that the requirements specify what the customer really needs, apply the use-case technique to elicit requirements by focusing on user tasks. Devise specific usage scenarios, write test cases from the requirements, and create prototypes to make the requirements more tangible for users and to elicit specific feedback from them. Enlist customer representatives to formally inspect the requirements specifications and analysis models.

Requirements for highly innovative products   It's easy to misgauge market response to products that are the first of their kind. Emphasize market research, build prototypes, and use customer focus groups to obtain early and frequent feedback about your innovative product visions.

Defining nonfunctional requirements Because of the natural emphasis on product functionality, it is easy to neglect nonfunctional requirements. Query customers about quality characteristics such as performance, usability, integrity, and reliability. Document these nonfunctional requirements and their acceptance criteria as precisely as you can in the SRS.

Customer agreement on product requirements If the diverse customers for your product don't agree on what you should build, someone will be unhappy with the result. Determine who the primary customers are, and use the product champion approach to make sure you have adequate customer representation and involvement. Make sure you are relying on the right people for decision-making authority on the requirements.

Unstated requirements Customers might hold implicit expectations that are not communicated or documented. Try to identify and record any assumptions the customers might be making. Use open-ended questions to encourage customers to share more of their thoughts, ideas, and concerns than you might otherwise hear.

Existing product used as the requirements baseline Requirements development might not be deemed very important on next-generation or reengineering projects. Developers are sometimes told to use the existing product as their source for requirements, "except fix those bugs and add these new features." This forces the developer to glean the new requirements through reverse engineering of the current product. However, reverse engineering is an inefficient and incomplete way to discover requirements, and no one should be surprised if the new system has some of the same shortcomings as the existing system. Document the requirements you discover through reverse engineering and have customers review those requirements to ensure they are correct and still relevant.

Solutions presented as needs User-proposed solutions can mask the users' actual needs, lead to automating ineffective business processes, or pressure developers into making poor design decisions. The analyst must drill down to understand the intent behind the solution the customer has presented.

REQUIREMENTS ANALYSIS

Requirements prioritization   Ensure that every requirement, feature, or use case is prioritized and allocated to a specific product release or implementation stage. Evaluate the priority of every new requirement against the existing body of work remaining to be done so you can make smart trade-off decisions.

Technically difficult features   Evaluate the feasibility of each requirement to identify those that might take longer to implement than planned. Success always seems just around the corner, so use your project status tracking to watch for requirements that are falling behind their implementation schedule. Take corrective action as early as possible.

Unfamiliar technologies, methods, languages, tools, or hardware   Don't underestimate the learning curve of getting up to speed with new techniques that are needed to satisfy certain requirements. Identify those high-risk requirements early on and allow sufficient time for false starts, learning, experimentation, and prototyping.

REQUIREMENTS SPECIFICATION

Requirements understanding   Different understandings of the requirements by developers and customers lead to expectation gaps, where the delivered product does not satisfy customer needs. Formal inspections of requirements documents by teams that include developers, testers, and customers can mitigate this risk. Trained and experienced requirements analysts will ask the right questions of customers and write better specifications. Models and prototypes that represent the requirements from multiple perspectives will also reveal fuzzy and ambiguous requirements.

Time pressure to proceed despite TBDs   It is a good idea to mark areas of the SRS that need further work with TBD (to be determined), but it's risky to proceed with construction if these TBDs have not been resolved. Record the name of the individual responsible for resolving each TBD, how it will be resolved, and the target date for resolution.

Ambiguous terminology   Create a glossary and data dictionary to define all business and technical terms that might be interpreted differently by different readers. In particular, define any terms that have both common and technical or domain-specific meanings. SRS reviews can help participants reach a common understanding of key terms and concepts.

Design included in requirements   Design approaches that are included in the SRS place unnecessary constraints on the options available to developers and can inhibit the creation of optimal designs. Review the requirements to make sure they emphasize what needs to be done to solve the business problem, rather than stating how it will be solved.

REQUIREMENTS VERIFICATION

Unverified requirements   The prospect of inspecting a lengthy SRS is daunting, as is the idea of writing test cases very early in the development process. However, if you verify the quality and correctness of the requirements before construction begins, through inspection, requirements-based test planning, and prototyping, you can greatly reduce expensive rework later in the project. Include time and resources for these quality activities in the project plan. Gain commitment from your customer representatives to participate in requirements inspections. Perform incremental, informal reviews prior to formal inspections to find problems as early and cheaply as possible.

Inspection proficiency   If inspectors do not know how to properly inspect requirements documents and how to contribute to effective inspections, serious defects might be missed. Train all team members who will participate in inspections of requirements documents. Invite an experienced inspector from your organization or an outside consultant to observe, and perhaps moderate, your early inspections to help make them effective.

REQUIREMENTS MANAGEMENT

Changing requirements   Scope creep can be reduced by using a project vision and scope document as the benchmark for approving changes. A collaborative requirements elicitation process with extensive user involvement can reduce requirements creep by almost half (Jones 1996a). Quality control practices that detect requirements errors early can reduce the number of modifications requested later on. To reduce the impact of changing requirements, defer implementation of those requirements that are most likely to change until they are pinned down, and design for modifiability.

Requirements change process   Risks from the way changes to requirements are managed include not having a defined change process, using an ineffective change mechanism, and permitting changes to be made without following the process. You will need to develop a culture and discipline of change management at all levels, which takes time. A requirements change process that includes impact analysis of proposed changes, a change control board to make decisions, and a tool to support the defined procedure is an important starting point.

Unimplemented requirements   The requirements traceability matrix helps to avoid overlooking any requirements during design, construction, or testing. It also helps ensure that a requirement is not implemented by multiple developers because of inadequate communication within the project.

Expanding project scope   If requirements are poorly defined initially, further definition can expand the scope of the project. Vaguely specified areas of the product can consume more effort than anticipated. The project resources that were allocated according to the initial requirements might not be adjustable as the true scope of user needs becomes known. To mitigate this risk, plan on a phased or incremental delivery life cycle. Implement the core functionality in the early releases, and iteratively elaborate the requirements for the later phases.

RISK MANAGEMENT IS YOUR FRIEND

A project manager can use risk management to raise the awareness of conditions that could cause the project to suffer. Consider the manager of a new project who is concerned about getting appropriate users involved in requirements elicitation. The astute manager will realize this condition poses a risk and will document it in the risk list, estimating the probability and impact based on experience with previous projects. If time passes and users are still not involved, the risk exposure for this item will increase, perhaps to the point where the success of the project is compromised. I have been able to convince managers to postpone a project that could not engage sufficient user representatives, by arguing that the company's money should not be invested in a doomed project.

Periodic risk tracking keeps the project manager apprised of the exposure attributable to identified risks. Risks that are not adequately controlled can be brought to the attention of senior managers who can either initiate corrective actions or make a conscious business decision to proceed in spite of the risks. Risk management helps you keep your eyes open and make informed decisions, even if you cannot control every adversity your project might encounter.

 Next Steps

- Identify several requirements-related risks facing your current project. Do not identify current problems as risks, only things that haven't happened yet. Document the risk factors in the condition–consequence format, using the template in Figure 5-2. Suggest at least one possible mitigation approach for each risk.

- Hold a risk brainstorming session with project stakeholders who represent development, marketing, customers, and management. Identify as many requirements-related risk factors as you can. Evaluate each factor for its probability of occurrence and relative impact, and multiply these together to calculate the risk exposure. Sort the risk list in descending order by risk exposure to identify your top five requirements-related risks. Assign each risk to an individual to implement mitigation actions.

SOFTWARE REQUIREMENTS DEVELOPMENT

II

6
Establishing the Project's Vision and Scope

My colleague Karen has successfully introduced formal inspections of software requirements documents in her company. She has observed that many of the issues raised during inspection meetings pertain to project scope. The inspection participants often have different understandings of the intended scope of the project, and they do not always share a common vision of the project's objectives. Consequently, they find it difficult to agree on which functional requirements really belong in the SRS.

As we saw in Chapter 1, the business requirements represent the top level of abstraction in the requirements chain: they define the vision and scope for the software system. The user requirements and software functional requirements must align with the context and objectives established by the business requirements. Requirements that do not support achievement of the project's business objectives should not be included. Your project might include business requirements that do not directly relate to the software, such as hardware purchase, product installation and setup, maintenance, or advertising, but here we are only concerned with those business requirements that have implications for the software product.

A project that lacks a clearly established and well-communicated direction is an invitation for disaster. Project participants can unwittingly work at cross-purposes if they have different objectives and priorities. The requirements will never stabilize if the project stakeholders do not share a common understanding of the business needs the product must satisfy and the benefits it will provide. A clear project vision and scope is especially critical for multisite development projects, where geographical separation inhibits the day-to-day interactions that keep project team members collaborating effectively.

One sign that the business requirements are not sufficiently well defined is that certain features are initially included, then deleted, and then added back in later. Vision and scope issues must be resolved well before the detailed functional requirements are fully specified. An explicit statement of scope and limitations helps greatly with discussions of proposed features and target releases. A well-defined project vision and scope document also provides a point of reference for making decisions about proposed requirement changes.

DEFINING THE VISION THROUGH BUSINESS REQUIREMENTS

The project vision aligns all project participants in a common and clearly expressed direction. The vision describes what the project is about and what the product could ultimately become in a perfect world. In contrast, the scope describes what the product really is and is not going to include. The statement of scope draws the boundary between what's in and what's out, so it also defines the project's limitations.

The project's business requirements are documented in a vision and scope document, which should be drafted prior to funding the project. Organizations that build commercial software often create a marketing requirements document, which serves a similar purpose, but which can go into more detail about the target market segments and issues that pertain to commercial success. The vision and scope document is owned by the project's executive sponsor or someone in a similar role. Business requirements should be gathered from individuals who have a clear sense of why they are undertaking the project and the ultimate value it will provide to the business and to its customers. These individuals might include an executive sponsor, the customer or development organization's senior management, a project visionary such as a product champion, and members of the marketing department.

Business requirements collected from multiple sources might conflict. For example, consider a kiosk product with embedded software that will be sold to retail stores and used by the store's customers. The kiosk developer's business objectives include the following:

- Leasing or selling the kiosk to the retailer

- Selling consumables through the kiosk to the customer

- Attracting customers to the brand

- Modifying the nature of the historical developer-customer relationship

The retailer's business interests could include the following:

- Making money from customer use of the kiosk

- Attracting more customers to the store

- Saving money if the kiosk replaces manual operations

The developer might want to establish a high-tech and exciting new direction for customers, while the retailer wants a simple, turnkey system, and the customer wants convenience and features. The tension among these three parties with their different goals, constraints, and cost factors can lead to conflicting business requirements, which must be resolved before the kiosk's software requirements are detailed.

You can also use the business requirements to set implementation priorities for use cases and their associated functional requirements. For example, a business requirement to generate maximum revenue from the kiosk would imply the early implementation of features directly associated with selling more products or services to the customer, rather than glitzy features that appeal to only a subset of the customers.

The business requirements determine both the set of business tasks (use cases) that the application implements (the application breadth) and the level or depth to which each use case is supported. The depth of support can range from a trivial implementation to full automation with many usability aids. Both breadth and depth need to be determined and documented for each use case. If the business requirements help you determine that a particular use case is outside the application's scope, you are making a breadth decision. The business requirements will also let you determine which use cases demand robust, comprehensive functional implementation and which require merely superficial implementation, at least initially.

VISION AND SCOPE DOCUMENT

The vision and scope document collects the business requirements into a single, concise document that sets the stage for all subsequent development work. The vision and scope document includes a description of the business opportunity, the project's vision and objectives, a statement of product scope and limitations, some characterization of the customers, project priorities, and a description of project success factors. It should be a relatively short document, perhaps three to eight pages long, depending on the nature and size of the project.

Figure 6-1 illustrates a suggested template for a vision and scope document. Document templates standardize the structure of the documents created by your organization's projects. As with any template, you should adapt the one shown in Figure 6-1 to meet the specific needs of your own projects.

1. **Business Requirements**

    1.1   Background
    1.2   Business Opportunity
    1.3   Business Objectives
    1.4   Customer or Market Requirements
    1.5   Value Provided to Customers
    1.6   Business Risks

2. **Vision of the Solution**

    2.1   Vision Statement
    2.2   Major Features
    2.3   Assumptions and Dependencies

3. **Scope and Limitations**

    3.1   Scope of Initial Release
    3.2   Scope of Subsequent Releases
    3.3   Limitations and Exclusions

4. **Business Context**

    4.1   Customer Profiles
    4.2   Project Priorities

5. **Product Success Factors**

FIGURE 6-1   *Template for vision and scope document.*

Let's look at each section in this template.

1. BUSINESS REQUIREMENTS

The business requirements identify the primary benefits that the new system will provide to the customers and to the organization that is developing the product. The emphasis will be different for different kinds of products, such as management information systems, commercial software packages, and systems containing embedded software. However, projects are launched in the belief that the world will be a better place with the new product. In this section, describe why you are undertaking the project and the benefits the product will provide to its builders and buyers.

1.1 Background

In this section, summarize the rationale for the new product. Provide a general description of the history or situation that led to the decision to build this product.

1.2 Business Opportunity

Describe the market opportunity that exists or the business problem that is being solved. Describe the market in which a commercial product will be competing or the environment in which an information system will be used. Include a brief comparative evaluation of existing products and potential solutions, indicating why the proposed product is attractive and what competitive advantages it provides. Identify the problems that cannot currently be solved without the product, and describe how the product aligns with market trends or corporate strategic directions.

1.3 Business Objectives

Summarize the important business benefits the product will provide, preferably in a way that is quantitative and measurable. The value provided to customers is described in Section 1.5 of the vision and scope document, so focus here on the value provided to the business. These objectives could relate to revenue estimates or cost savings, return on investment analysis, and target release dates. If such information appears elsewhere, refer to the other document rather than duplicating it here.

1.4 Customer or Market Requirements

Describe the needs of typical customers, including needs that are not being met by products already in the marketplace or by existing information systems. Present the problems customers are currently encountering that the new product will (or will not) address and provide examples of how customers would use the product. Identify the hardware and software environment in which the product must operate. Define at a high level any known critical interface or performance requirements, but avoid including design or implementation details. Present the requirements in a numbered list so that specific user and functional requirements can be traced back to them.

1.5 Value Provided to Customers

Define the value the customers will receive from this product and indicate how the product will lead to improved customer satisfaction. Express this customer value in terms such as the following:

◆   Improved productivity or reduced rework

◆   Cost savings

◆   Streamlined business processes

◆   Automation of previously manual tasks

◆   Ability to perform entirely new tasks or functions

◆   Compliance with pertinent standards or regulations

◆   Improved usability or reduced frustration level compared to current applications

1.6 Business Risks

Summarize the major business risks associated with developing (or not developing) this product, such as marketplace competition, timing issues, user acceptance, implementation issues, or possible negative impacts on the business. Estimate the severity of the risks, and identify any risk mitigation actions you can take.

2. Vision of the Solution

This section of the document establishes a long-term vision for the system that will address the business objectives. This vision provides the context for making decisions throughout the course of the product development life cycle. It should not include detailed functional requirements or project planning information.

2.1 Vision Statement

Write a concise vision statement that summarizes the long-term purpose and intent of the new product. The vision statement should reflect a balanced view that will satisfy the needs of diverse customers. It can be somewhat idealistic, but should be grounded in the realities of existing or anticipated customer markets, enterprise architectures, organizational strategic directions, and resource limitations.

Here is a sample vision statement for the Chemical Tracking System discussed in earlier chapters:

> *The Chemical Tracking System will allow scientists to request containers of chemicals to be supplied by the chemical stockroom or by vendors. The location of every chemical container within the company, the quantity of material remaining in it, and the complete history of each container's locations and usage will be known by the system at all times. The company will save 25 percent on chemical costs by fully exploiting chemicals already available within the company, by disposing of fewer partially used or expired containers, and by using a standard chemical purchasing process. The Chemical Tracking System will also generate all reports required to comply with federal and state government regulations that require the reporting of chemical usage, storage, and disposal.*

2.2 Major Features

Include a numbered list of the major features or user capabilities the new product will provide, emphasizing those features that distinguish it from previous or competing products. Individual user requirements and functional requirements can be traced back to these features.

2.3 Assumptions and Dependencies

Record any assumptions that were made when conceiving the project and writing this vision and scope document. Often the assumptions that are held by one party are not shared by another. If you write them down and review them, you can reach agreement on the basic assumptions that underlie the project. For example, the management sponsor for the Chemical Tracking System assumed that it would replace the existing chemical stockroom inventory system and that it would interface to the appropriate purchasing department applications. Write such things down to avoid possible confusion and aggravation in the future. Also, note any major project dependencies, such as specific technologies to be used, third-party vendors, development partners, or other business relationships.

3. SCOPE AND LIMITATIONS

When a chemist invents a new reaction that transforms one kind of chemical into another, the published paper includes a "Scope and Limitations" section, which describes what the reaction will and will not do. Similarly, a software project should define its scope and limitations as part of the business requirements.

The project scope defines the concept and range of the proposed solution, and the limitations identify certain capabilities that the product will not include. Clarifying the scope and limitations helps to establish realistic stakeholder expectations. Sometimes customers request features that are too expensive or do not lie within the intended product scope. Proposed requirements that are out of scope must be rejected, unless they are so beneficial that the scope should be enlarged to accommodate them (with accompanying changes in budget, schedule, and staff). Keep a record of such requirements and why they were rejected, as they have a way of reappearing.

3.1 Scope of Initial Release

Summarize the major features that will be included in the initial release of the product. Describe the quality characteristics that will enable the product to provide the intended benefits to its various customer communities. If your goals are to focus the development effort and maintain a reasonable project schedule, avoid the temptation to include in release 1.0 every feature that any potential customer might conceivably want someday. Bloatware and slipped schedules are common outcomes of such insidious scope creep. Focus on those product features that will provide the most value, at the most acceptable development cost, to the broadest community.

For example, my colleague Scott's last project team decided that users had to be able to run their package delivery business with the first software release. Version 1.0 didn't have to be fast, pretty, or easy to use, but it had to be reliable; this focus drove everything the team did. The initial release accomplished the basic objectives of the system, and subsequent releases will include additional features, options, and usability aids.

3.2 Scope of Subsequent Releases

If you envision a staged evolution of the product, indicate which major features will be deferred and the desired timing of subsequent releases.

3.3 Limitations and Exclusions

Defining the boundary between what's in and what's out is a way to manage both scope creep and customer expectations. List any product features or characteristics that a stakeholder might anticipate but that you do not plan to include in the product.

4. BUSINESS CONTEXT

This section summarizes some of the project's business issues, including profiles of major customer categories and management's priorities for the project.

4.1 Customer Profiles

The customer profiles identify some essential characteristics of different categories of customers for this product. Characterize the target market segments and different user classes within those segments. The profile should include the following information for each customer category:

◆ The major benefits that that category of customers will receive from the product

◆ Their likely attitudes toward the product

◆ Key product features of interest

◆ Success drivers for customers in that category

◆ Any known customer constraints that must be accommodated

4.2 Project Priorities

Once the project's priorities are clearly established, the stakeholders and project participants can focus on a common set of objectives. One way to approach this is to consider the five dimensions of a software project: features, quality, schedule, cost, and staff (Wiegers 1996a). In any given project, each of these dimensions can fit in one of three categories:

◆ A *driver* A top-priority objective

◆ A *constraint* A limiting factor within which the project manager must operate

◆ A *degree of freedom* A factor that the project manager can balance against the other dimensions to achieve the drivers within the known constraints

All factors cannot be drivers, and all cannot be constraints. Recording and discussing which factors fit in which categories at the beginning of the project will help align everyone's efforts and expectations with a common set of priorities.

5. PRODUCT SUCCESS FACTORS

Determine how success will be defined and measured for this product, and describe the factors that are likely to have the greatest impact on achieving that success. Include things within the direct control of the organization, as well as external factors. If possible, establish measurable criteria for assessing whether the business objectives have been met. Some examples of these criteria are market share, sales volume or revenue, customer satisfaction measures, and transaction-processing volume and accuracy.

THE CONTEXT DIAGRAM

The scope description establishes the boundary between the system we are developing and everything else in the universe. The context diagram graphically illustrates this boundary by showing the connections between the system being developed, or the problem being addressed, and the outside world. The context diagram identifies the entities outside the system that interface to it in some way (called *terminators* or *external entities*), as well as the flow of data and material between each external entity and the system. The context diagram is used as the top level of abstraction in a data flow diagram developed according to principles of structured analysis (Robertson and Robertson 1994). You can include the context diagram in the vision and scope document, in the SRS, or as part of a data flow model for the system.

Figure 6-2 illustrates a simplified version of the context diagram for the Chemical Tracking System. The entire Chemical Tracking System is depicted as a single circle, so the context diagram provides no visibility into the system's internal processes and data. The flows on the context diagram can represent either information ("chemical request") or physical items ("chemical container"). Terminators, which are shown in rectangles, can represent user classes ("Chemists"), organizations ("Purchasing Department"), or other computer systems ("Training Database").

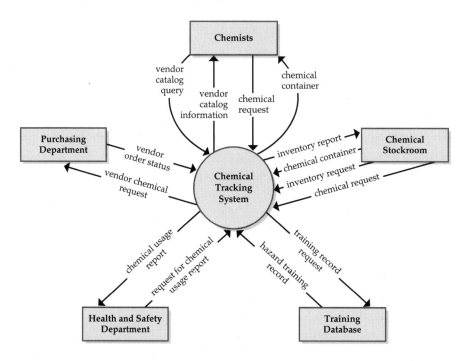

FIGURE 6-2 *Context diagram for the Chemical Tracking System.*

You might expect to see chemical vendors shown as a terminator in this diagram. After all, the company will send orders for chemicals to vendors for fulfillment, chemical containers and invoices will be received from vendors, and checks will be sent to the vendors. However, those processes take place outside the scope of the Chemical Tracking System, as part of the operations of the purchasing and receiving departments. The context diagram makes it clear that this system is not directly involved in placing orders with the vendors, receiving the products, or paying the bills.

Sometimes the context diagram will show connections among terminators that are pertinent to the problem domain, even if they do not communicate directly with the planned system (Jackson 1995). This is fine. Rather than be dogmatic about precisely how to draw a "correct" context diagram, use tools like this to foster clear and accurate communication among the project stakeholders.

KEEPING THE SCOPE IN FOCUS

The business requirements recorded in the vision and scope document provide a valuable weapon in the ongoing battle against scope creep. The vision and scope document enables you to assess whether proposed features and requirements are appropriate for inclusion in the project. The first question you should ask whenever someone proposes a new or changed requirement or feature is, "Is this within scope?"

Some proposed requirements are clearly out of scope. They might be a good idea, but they should be addressed by another project or in a future release. Other proposals obviously lie within the defined project scope. New in-scope requirements could be included in the project, provided they are of appropriately high priority relative to the other requirements that are already planned for a specific release. Including new in-scope requirements might necessitate making trade-off decisions to defer or cancel other requirements or features that are already planned.

The third possibility is that the proposed new requirement is out of scope, but is such a high-value idea that the project's scope should be modified to accommodate it. This will require that you update the vision and scope document, which should be placed under change control at the time it is baselined. When the project's scope is changed, you will usually have to renegotiate the planned budget, resources, schedule, and perhaps staff (especially if new skill sets are needed). Ideally, the original schedule and resources will accommodate reasonable changes. However, unless you originally budgeted for some requirements growth, you will need to replan after requirements changes are approved.

Two major problems inherent in scope creep are that completed activities might have to be redone to accommodate the changes and that quality will suffer if the allocated resources or time are not adjusted when the project scope increases. A defined set of business requirements makes it easier to keep the project going according to plan, to manage legitimate scope growth as the marketplace or business needs change, and to justify saying no when influential people try to stuff more features into an overly constrained project.

Next Steps

◆ Whether you are near the launch of a new project or in the midst of construction, write a vision and scope document using the template in Figure 6-1. This exercise might be difficult if your team doesn't share a common understanding of the project scope. Correct that problem now, rather than letting it slide indefinitely; it will be even more difficult to correct if you wait. This activity will also suggest ways to modify the template to best meet the needs of your organization's projects.

7 Finding the Voice of the Customer

If you share my conviction that customer involvement is a critical factor in delivering excellent software, you'll work hard to engage individuals to provide the voice of the customer for your project from the earliest stages. Success in software requirements, and hence success in software development, depends on getting the voice of the customer as close as possible to the ear of the developer. Chapter 6 discussed how input from one kind of customer—the project's executive sponsor, a project visionary, or the marketing department—provides the project's business requirements. This chapter focuses on the second level of requirements—user requirements. To find the voice of the customer, you must take the following steps:

◆ Identify sources of user requirements on your project

◆ Identify the different classes of users for your product

◆ Gain access to individuals who can represent those various user classes

◆ Agree on who the ultimate decision makers are for your project

Customer involvement is the only way to avoid expectation gaps, those mismatches between the products that customers expect to receive and the products that developers build for them. However, it's not enough to simply ask a customer or two early in the project what they want and then start writing code. If the developers build exactly what customers initially request, they will probably have to build it again because customers often don't know what they really need, and neither do the developers.

The features that users present as their "wants" don't always equate to the functionality they actually need to perform their tasks with the new product. Therefore, once you have collected input from the users, you must analyze and clarify the input until you understand it, document that understanding, and verify that documentation with the customers. This is an iterative process and it takes time. If you don't invest the time to achieve this shared understanding—this common vision of the intended product—the likely outcomes are rework, dissatisfaction, and shelfware.

SOURCES OF REQUIREMENTS

Software requirements can come from many places, depending on the nature of your product and your development environment. The need to gather requirements from multiple perspectives and origins exemplifies the communication-intensive nature of requirements engineering. Following are several typical sources of software requirements.

Interviews and discussions with potential users   The most obvious way to find out what potential users of a new software product want is to ask them. This chapter discusses how to find suitable user representatives, while Chapter 8 addresses techniques for eliciting requirements from those representatives.

Documents that describe current or competing products   Documents can also describe standards that must be followed or government or industry regulations with which the product must comply.

System requirements specifications   A product that contains both hardware and software has a high-level system requirements specification that describes the overall product. A subset of the system requirements is allocated to each software subsystem (Nelsen 1990). Additional detailed software functional requirements will be derived from the system requirements allocated to software.

Problem reports and enhancement requests for a current system   The help desk and field support personnel are valuable sources of requirements. They collect information about the problems users encounter with the current system, as well as ideas users present for improving the system.

Marketing surveys and user questionnaires   Surveys are useful for obtaining a large amount of quantitative or statistical data from a broad spectrum of potential users. Be sure to survey the right people and to ask the right questions in a way that generates useful responses.

Observing users at work   A "Day in the Life" experience in which an analyst observes users of a current system or potential users of the future system can provide much valuable information. Observing a user's workflow in the context of his or her task environment allows the analyst to see problems the user encounters with the current system and to identify ways the new system can effectively support the workflow (McGraw and Harbison 1997; Beyer and Holtzblatt 1998). Watching the users at work provides a more accurate understanding of their activities than simply asking them to write down the steps involved with performing their tasks. The analyst must abstract and generalize beyond the immediate user's activities to ensure that the requirements captured apply to the user class as a whole and not just to that individual. A skillful analyst can often suggest ideas for improving the user's current business processes, also.

Scenario analysis of user tasks   By identifying tasks that users need to accomplish with the system, often through developing specific scenarios or sequences of actions (sometimes called "stories"), the analyst can derive the necessary functional requirements that will let users perform those tasks. This is the essence of the use-case approach. (See Chapter 8.)

USER CLASSES

A product's users differ, among other ways, in the frequency with which they use the product, their application domain and computer systems expertise, the features they use, the business processes they perform, their geographic location, and their access privilege levels. You can group users into a fairly small number of distinct user classes based on these differences. The needs of certain user classes might well be more important to you than those of others (Gause and Lawrence 1999).

Each user class will have its own set of functional and nonfunctional requirements. For example, an inexperienced or occasional user is concerned with how easy the system is to learn (or relearn) to use, so menus, verbose prompts, and wizards are important. However, users who work with the product several hours a day are more concerned about ease of use and efficiency, so they value keyboard shortcuts, macros, and scripting facilities.

Some of the people affected by your application might not be direct users of your product, instead accessing your product's data or services through reports or other applications. These indirect or secondary users can have their own requirements and thus constitute additional user classes. As my colleague Kathy explains it, "Your customer once removed is still your customer."

User classes don't have to be human beings; you can consider other applications or hardware components to which your system interfaces as members of additional user classes. Viewing interapplication interfaces in this way helps ensure that you identify any requirements for your product that relate to those external applications or components.

Identify and characterize the different user classes for your product early in the project, so you can elicit requirements from representatives of each important user class. I know of one company that developed a specialized commercial product for about 65 corporate customers. When they realized they could group their customers into just six distinct user classes, their requirements challenges for future releases were simplified. Document the user classes and their characteristics in the SRS. As an example, the project manager of the Chemical Tracking System discussed in earlier chapters identified the user classes and characteristics shown in Table 7-1.

TABLE 7-1 USER CLASSES FOR THE CHEMICAL TRACKING SYSTEM

Chemists	Chemists will use the system to request chemicals from vendors and from the chemical stockroom. Each chemist will use the system several times per day, mainly for tracking chemical containers in and out of the laboratory. The chemists need to search vendor catalogs for specific chemical structures imported from their current structure drawing tools.
Buyers	Buyers in the purchasing department process chemical requests submitted by other users, and they interface with external vendors to place and track orders. They have little knowledge of chemistry and will need simple query facilities to search vendor catalogs. Buyers will not use the container-tracking features of the system. Each buyer will use the system an average of 10 times per day.
Chemical Stockroom Staff	The chemical stockroom staff consists of three technicians who manage an inventory of more than 500,000 chemical containers. They will process requests from chemists to supply available containers, request new chemicals from vendors, and track the movement of all containers in and out of the stockroom. They are the only users of the inventory and chemical usage reporting features. Because of the high transaction volume, the system functions that are used only by the chemical stockroom staff must be automated and efficient.
Health and Safety Staff	The Health and Safety staff will use the system only to generate quarterly reports that comply with federal and state chemical usage and disposal reporting regulations. The reports must be predefined; no ad hoc query capability is needed. The Health and Safety manager will likely request changes in the reports several times per year as government regulations change. These report changes are of the highest priority.

Finding User Representatives

Every kind of project—including corporate information systems, commercial applications, integrated systems, products that contain embedded software, Web development programs, and contracted software—needs suitable user representatives to serve as the voice of the customer during requirements elicitation. The user representatives should be involved throughout the development life cycle, not just in an isolated requirements phase at the beginning. You need a diversity of user participants to represent different user classes and levels of expertise, although you should emphasize those who represent the most important user communities.

It's easiest to gain access to actual users when you're developing applications for use within your own company. However, if you are developing commercial software, you might engage people from your current beta-testing or early-release sites to provide requirements much earlier in the development process. Build on existing long-term customer relationships or set up focus groups that comprise current users of your products or your competitors' products. If you establish a focus group, be sure that the participants really represent the kinds of users whose needs you wish to have drive your product development. Include a mix of user types, with knowledgeable customers as well as those who are less experienced. If your focus group represents only early adopters or blue-sky thinkers, you might end up with a long list of sophisticated and technically difficult requirements that are not interesting to much of your target market.

Figure 7-1 illustrates some typical communication connections that link the voice of the customer (user) to the ear of the developer. The most direct communication occurs when developers can talk to appropriate users directly; indirect links are often ineffective (Kiel and Carmel 1995). As in the children's game of "Telephone," intervening layers between the user and the developer increase the chance of miscommunications. For example, if developers gather requirements only from the manager of the end users, the requirements are less likely to accurately reflect user needs.

To be sure, some of these intervening layers add value, as when a skilled requirements analyst works with users or other participants to collect, evaluate, and organize their input for the developers. Make certain you understand the risks you assume by using marketing staff or others as surrogates for the actual voice of the customer, and decide whether those risks are worth taking. Despite the obstacles to acquiring optimum customer representation, and despite the costs you might incur, your product and customers will suffer if you don't talk to the people who can provide the best information.

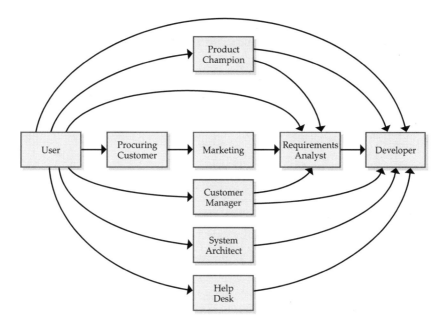

FIGURE 7-1   *Some possible communication pathways between the user and the developer.*

THE PRODUCT CHAMPION

Many years ago, I was a charter member of a small software development group that supported the scientific research activities at a major corporation. When we established the group, we decided that each of our projects would include a small number of key participants from our user community to provide the voice of the customer. We called these people *product champions* (or *project champions*) (Wiegers 1996a). The product champion approach provides an effective way to structure and formalize the customer-developer partnership.

Each product champion represents a specific user class and serves as the primary interface between users in that class and developers. The product champions must be actual users, not surrogate users such as funding sponsors, procuring customers, marketing staff, or software group members pretending to be users. Product champions collect requirements from other members of their user class. Each champion is responsible for reconciling inconsistencies or incompatibilities among the requirements expressed by the people they represent. The goal is for each product champion to work with the analyst to develop a unified set of requirements for that user class. Requirements development is thus a shared responsibility of the analyst and a few key customers, although the analyst will normally write the actual requirements documents.

The best product champions have a clear vision of the new system and are highly enthusiastic because they see how the new product will benefit them and their peers. The champions should be effective communicators who are respected by members of their peer group. They need a thorough understanding of the application domain and enough experience with software to know what is feasible with current technologies and what is realistic in the operations environment. Since the people who make great product champions are usually in demand for other assignments on their principal job, you will have to build a persuasive case for why the participation of particular individuals is so critical to project success.

The product champion approach works best if the champions are fully empowered to make binding decisions on behalf of the customers they represent. If a champion's decisions are routinely overruled by managers or by the software group, the champion's time and goodwill are being wasted. However, the champions must remember that they are not the sole customers. I have seen the product champion approach break down when the individual filling this critical liaison role didn't adequately communicate with his or her peers and presented only his own needs and product concepts.

FINDING PRODUCT CHAMPIONS

If you are developing commercial, rather than internal, software, it's more difficult to find people to serve as product champions from outside your company. If you have a close working relationship with some major corporate customers, they might welcome (or even demand) the opportunity to participate in requirements elicitation. You then face the challenge of how to avoid hearing only the champions' requirements and possibly neglecting the needs of other customers. If you have a diverse customer base, you might identify core requirements that are common to all customers and then define additional requirements that are specific to individual customers or user classes.

Unless they already connect through trade shows or other professional interactions, product champions might not be able to communicate with their counterparts in other companies. There's a risk that discussions could reveal details of internal business processes, potentially hurting each company's competitive edge. What if a champion who knows what you have planned for future products shares this inside information with people who shouldn't be made aware of it? Nondisclosure agreements can help, but they are no guarantee of privacy. Another possibility is that the champion's company might decide not to buy an early release of the product because they know about the better version coming up next. You might want to give your external product champions some economic incentives in exchange for their contributions, such as providing product discounts or even paying for the time they spend working with you on requirements.

Another alternative is to actually hire a suitable product champion who has the right background. One company that developed a retail point-of-sale and back-office system for a particular industry hired three retail store managers to serve as full-time product champions. In another instance, my longtime family physician, Art, left his medical practice and now provides voice-of-the-physician input as a product champion at a medical software company. Art's new employer clearly felt it was worth the expense to hire a doctor to help them build software that would be well accepted by other doctors. Another company hired several former employees from a major customer, who provided valuable subject matter expertise as well as insight into the politics of the customer organization.

Product Champion Expectations

To help the product champion approach succeed, document your expectations of your product champions. While not every champion will perform all of the services you might like, you can use these written expectations to build a case for specific individuals to fill this critical role and as a starting point to negotiate each champion's exact responsibilities. Table 7-2 identifies some activities product champions might perform. Not all of these actions will be necessary or appropriate in every situation, but I've had product champions perform all of them on various projects.

TABLE 7-2   **POSSIBLE PRODUCT CHAMPION ACTIVITIES**

Category	Activities
Planning	• Refine the scope and limitations of the product • Define external interfaces to other systems • Define a transition path from current user applications
Requirements	• Interview other users they represent to gather their requirements • Develop usage scenarios and use cases • Resolve conflicts between proposed requirements • Define implementation priorities • Specify quality attributes and other nonfunctional requirements • Evaluate user interface prototypes
Verification and Validation	• Inspect requirements documents • Define user acceptance criteria • Develop test cases from usage scenarios • Perform beta testing • Provide test data sets
User Aids	• Write portions of user manuals and online help displays • Prepare training materials for tutorials • Present product demonstrations to peers
Change Management	• Evaluate and prioritize defect corrections • Evaluate and prioritize enhancement requests • Evaluate the impact of proposed requirement changes on users • Sit on change control board to participate in change decisions

MULTIPLE PRODUCT CHAMPIONS

The Chemical Tracking System had four user classes, so it needed multiple product champions selected from the internal user community at Contoso Pharmaceuticals. Figure 7-2 illustrates how the project manager set up a group of product champions to collect the right requirements from the right sources. These champions were not assigned full-time, but they spent several hours a week working on the project. Three analysts worked with the four product champions (the Buyer and the Health and Safety user classes were small and had few requirements) to elicit, analyze, and document their requirements. One analyst synthesized all of the input into a single SRS.

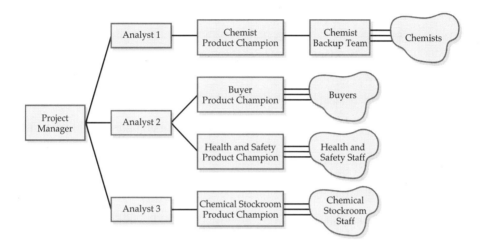

FIGURE 7-2 *Product champion model for the Chemical Tracking System.*

It's not realistic to expect one person to adequately supply all of the diverse needs for a large user class such as the several hundred chemists at Contoso Pharmaceuticals. Therefore, the product champion for the chemist user class assembled a backup team of five other chemists from other parts of the company. These other chemists collected input from their peers in several departments, discussed their issues about the Chemical Tracking System, and provided project status updates to their peers. This hierarchical approach increased the number of users who contributed to requirements elicitation, while avoiding the expense of massive requirements-gathering workshops or a long series of individual interviews that need to be collated and reconciled. The chemist product champion always strove for consensus, but he willingly made the necessary decisions when consensus was not achieved so the project could move ahead rather than become deadlocked.

Who Makes the Decisions?

I once met a project manager at a satellite location for a large development organization. When I asked him who he worked for, he gave me four names: a local development manager, a development manager back at the home office, and two business unit managers from his customer community. This project manager was frustrated by the mixed signals he continually received, by the inability of these four people to make consistent decisions, and by the frequent reversal of decisions.

When requirements fly in from many directions, it can be difficult to resolve conflicts, clarify ambiguities, and reconcile inconsistencies. Someone will also have to arbitrate the questions of scope that inevitably arise. Early in every project, you need to agree on who the decision makers will be for requirements issues. If it is not clear who has the right and responsibility to make these decisions, or if the authorized individuals are unwilling or unable to make the decisions, they will fall to the developers by default. This is usually a poor choice, because the developers usually don't have the necessary information and perspective to make the best business decisions.

There's no globally correct answer to the question of who should make the decisions about requirements on a software project. Analysts sometimes defer to the loudest voice they hear or to the input that comes from the person highest on the food chain. Even with the product champion approach, someone must resolve the conflicting requirements the champions from different user classes present. In general, decisions should be made as low in the organization's hierarchy as possible by people who are close to the issues and well-informed about them. I favor participative decision-making over consensus decision-making. Reaching a consensus is ideal, but you can't hold up progress while waiting for every stakeholder to align on every issue.

Following are some decision-making situations that can arise on projects, with suggested ways to handle them. The leaders on your project need to determine who will decide what to do when such situations arise and who the tiebreaker will be if agreement is not reached.

◆   If individual users disagree on requirements, the product champions decide. The essence of the product champion approach is that the champions are expected to resolve requirements conflicts from those they represent and are authorized to do so.

120

◆   If different user classes have incompatible needs, decide which user classes are more important to satisfy. Knowledge about the kinds of customers that are likely to use the product and how their usage relates to the product's business goals will help you determine which user classes carry the most weight.

◆   Different corporate customers might all demand that the product be designed to satisfy their preferences. Again, use the business objectives for the project to determine which customers you are most concerned about satisfying. One major customer could drive development of the major features, while requirements presented by other customers from whom you expect to receive less revenue might be deferred to a later release.

◆   Requirements expressed by customer managers sometimes conflict with those expressed by the actual users in their departments. While the user requirements must align with the business requirements, managers who will not be using the product hands-on should defer detailed user needs and functionality specification to the product champions who represent their users. Avoid forcing developers to arbitrate among customers who don't agree on the requirements; that's a lose-lose proposition.

◆   When the product the developers think they should build conflicts with what customers say they want, the customer should normally make the decision. However, don't fall into the trap of proclaiming "The customer is always right" and doing whatever any customer demands. In reality, the customer is not always right. The customer always has a point, however, and the developers must understand and respect that point.

◆   A similar situation arises if the marketing department presents requirements that conflict with what developers think they should build. As customer surrogates, marketing's input should carry more weight. Nevertheless, I've seen cases where marketing never said no to a customer request, no matter how infeasible or expensive. I've seen other cases in which marketing provided little input and the developers had to define the product and write the requirements themselves.

There is no single right answer. Decide who will be making decisions on your project's requirements before you confront these issues, lest indecision and the revisiting of previous decisions cause your project to stall.

 Next Steps

◆ Relate Figure 7-1 to the way you hear the voice of the customer in your own environment. Do you encounter any problems with your current communication links? Identify the shortest and most efficient communication paths that you can use to gather user requirements in the future.

◆ Identify the different user classes for your project and decide who would make a good product champion for each. Use Table 7-2 as a starting point to define what functions you would like each of your product champions to perform. Negotiate with the product champion candidates and their managers to increase and structure their contributions to your project.

◆ Determine who the decision makers are for requirements issues and conflict resolution on your project. How well does your current decision-making approach work? Where does it break down? Are the right people making decisions? If not, determine who should be involved in requirements decision making and suggest processes they should use for reaching agreement on the requirements issues before the developers have to resolve these issues themselves.

Hearing the Voice of the Customer

Requirements elicitation lies at the heart of requirements engineering. Elicitation is the process of identifying and understanding the needs and constraints of the different user classes for a proposed software product. Elicitation focuses on gathering the user requirements, the middle level of the software requirements triad. The business requirements from the vision and scope document serve as the anchor point for the user requirements, which address the tasks users need to accomplish with the system. From those tasks, the analyst can derive specific software functional requirements describing the system behaviors that will permit users to perform their tasks. This chapter addresses the principles of requirements elicitation, emphasizing the application of use cases to capture the product's user requirements.

Requirements elicitation is the first step in bridging the gap between the problem domain and the solution that is ultimately constructed. An essential outcome of elicitation is a common understanding among the project stakeholders of the customer needs that are being addressed. Once the needs are understood, the analysts, developers, and customers can explore alternative solutions that will address those needs. Elicitation participants must resist the temptation to begin designing the system until they understand the problem; otherwise, you can expect to do considerable design rework as the requirements become better defined. Focusing elicitation on user tasks—rather than on user interfaces—helps prevent the team from being sidetracked by prematurely exploring design issues.

Elicitation, analysis, specification, and verification don't take place in a tidy linear sequence: these activities are interleaved, incremental, and iterative. As you work with customers, you'll be asking questions and listening to the information they present (elicitation). Concurrently, you'll be processing this information to understand it, classify it into various categories, and relate the customer needs to possible software requirements (analysis). You'll then structure the customer input into written documents and diagrams (specification). Next, you'll ask your customer representatives to review what you've written thus far and correct any errors (verification). This four-step process continues throughout requirements development.

Because of the diversity of software development projects and organizational cultures, there is no single, formulaic approach to requirements development. On the next page are 14 steps you can use to guide your requirements development activities. Once you've completed step 13 for any subset of the requirements, you can proceed with design and construction of that part of the system with confidence that you are building the right product.

REQUIREMENTS ELICITATION GUIDELINES

Requirements elicitation is perhaps the most difficult, most critical, most error-prone, and most communication-intensive aspect of software development. Elicitation can succeed only through an effective customer-developer partnership. The analyst must create an environment conducive to a thorough exploration of issues pertaining to the product being specified. To facilitate

---

SUGGESTED REQUIREMENTS DEVELOPMENT PROCESS

1. Define the project's vision and scope.

2. Identify user classes.

3. Identify appropriate representatives from the user classes.

4. Identify the requirements decision makers and their decision-making process.

5. Select the elicitation techniques that you will use.

6. Apply the elicitation techniques to develop and prioritize the use cases for a portion of the system.

7. Gather information about quality attributes and other nonfunctional requirements from users.

8. Elaborate the use cases into the necessary functional requirements.

9. Review the use-case descriptions and the functional requirements.

10. Develop analysis models, if needed, to clarify the elicitation participants' understanding of portions of the requirements.

11. Develop and evaluate user interface prototypes to help visualize requirements that are not clearly understood.

12. Develop conceptual test cases from the use cases.

13. Use the test cases to verify the use cases, functional requirements, analysis models, and prototypes.

14. Repeat steps 6 through 13 before proceeding with design and construction of each portion of the system.

---

clear communication, capture significant terms in a glossary, rather than assuming that all participants share the same definitions. A thorough examination of requirements issues demands techniques that surface all of the functions that should be considered for the product, as well as discussions about the project's nonfunctional requirements. Make certain your users understand that a discussion about possible functionality is not a commitment to include it in the product. The blue-sky wish list must be focused and prioritized to avoid an infinitely large project that never delivers anything useful.

Elicitation is a highly collaborative activity, not a simple transcription of what customers say they need. As an analyst, you must probe beneath the surface of the requirements the customers present to understand their true needs. Ask open-ended questions to help you better understand the user's current business processes and to see how the new system could enable or improve their performance. Inquire about variations in the user tasks that might be encountered or ways that other possible users might need to use the system. Imagine yourself learning the user's job. What tasks would you need to perform? What questions would you have? Use this perspective to guide your requirements explorations.

Also, probe around the exceptions: What could prevent the user from successfully completing a task? How does the user think the system should respond to error conditions? Ask questions that begin with, "What else could...," "What happens when...," "Would you ever need to...," and "Does anyone ever..." Note the source of each requirement so that you can trace downstream development back to specific customer origins.

Try to bring to light any assumptions the customers might hold, particularly those that conflict. Read between the lines to identify features or characteristics the customers expect to be included without their having explicitly said so. Gause and Weinberg (1989) suggest the use of "context-free questions"—high-level questions that elicit information about global characteristics of both the business problem and the potential solutions. The customer's response to questions such as "What kind of precision is required in the product?" or "Can you help me understand why you don't agree with Person X's reply?" can lead to insights that more direct, closed-end questions do not.

Elicitation draws on all available sources of input that describe the problem domain or the characteristics desired in the software solution. Chapter 7 identified several sources of software requirements. One study indicated that highly successful projects used more kinds of communication links between developers and customers than did less successful projects (Kiel and Carmel 1995). Interviews with individual customers or groups of potential users are a traditional source of input on requirements for both commercial package software and MIS applications. (For guidance on how to conduct user interviews, see Beyer and Holtzblatt [1998], Wood and Silver [1995], and McGraw and Harbison [1997].) Engaging users directly in the elicitation process is a way to gain support and buy-in for the project.

After each interview, list the items you discussed and ask the people you interviewed to review the list and make corrections. Early and frequent review is a key element of successful requirements elicitation, because only those individuals who supplied the requirements can determine whether they were captured accurately. Use further elicitation and analysis to resolve any conflicts and inconsistencies.

Try to understand the thought processes that led the users to present the requirements they state. Walk through the processes that users follow to make decisions when performing their tasks, and extract the underlying logic. Flowcharts and decision trees are useful ways to depict these logical decision paths.

When eliciting requirements, avoid becoming distracted by prematurely excessive detail. It's easy for users to begin itemizing the precise layout of items in a report or a dialog box before you've reached a common understanding of the pertinent user task. If such details are recorded as requirements, they can place unnecessary constraints on the subsequent design process. You might have to reel in the elicitation participants periodically to keep them focused on the appropriate level of abstraction for today's conversation. Assure them that you'll address all of their details as requirements development continues, and then make sure that you do.

Plan to elaborate the requirements iteratively in successive layers of detail. Begin by identifying user goals and tasks, represented as use cases. Then elaborate those tasks into functional requirements that will enable the users to perform the tasks, as well as into a set of nonfunctional requirements that describe the system constraints and the users' quality expectations. Detailed user interface design comes later, although preliminary screen sketches can be helpful at any point to illustrate your understanding of the requirements.

THE USE-CASE APPROACH

For many years, analysts have used scenarios or stories that describe ways a user will interact with a software system to help elicit requirements (McGraw and Harbison 1997). More recently, Ivar Jacobson (1992) and others formalized this into the use-case approach to requirements elicitation and modeling. Although use cases emerged from the object-oriented development world, they can be applied to projects that follow any development approach because the user doesn't care how you build the software. Some design methods include notations for modeling use cases (Regnell, Kimbler, and Wesslén 1995; Booch, Rumbaugh, and Jacobson 1999). However, the shift in perspective and thought process that use cases bring to requirements development is more important than whether you draw formal use-case diagrams. The focus on what the *users* need to do with the system is much more powerful than the traditional elicitation approach of asking users what they want the *system* to do.

A *use case* describes a sequence of interactions between a system and an external "actor" that results in the actor accomplishing a task that provides benefit to someone. An actor is a person, another software application, a piece of hardware, or some other entity that interacts with the system to achieve some goal (Cockburn 1997a,b). Actors map to roles that the members of one or more user classes can perform. For example, the Chemical Tracking System's "Request a Chemical" use case involves an actor called "Requester." There is no Chemical Tracking System user class called Requester, but chemists and members of the chemical stockroom staff both can assume that role.

Use cases provide a way to represent the user requirements, which must align with the system's business requirements. The analyst and customers should examine every proposed use case to determine whether it lies within the defined project scope before accepting it into the requirements baseline. The objective of the use-case approach to requirements elicitation is to describe all the tasks the users will need to perform with the system. In theory, the resulting set of use cases will encompass all the desired functionality of the system. In practice, you are unlikely to reach complete closure, but the use-case approach will bring you closer than any other elicitation approach I know of.

USE CASES AND USAGE SCENARIOS

A single use case might include a number of logically related tasks and several interaction sequences that lead to completing the tasks. A use case is therefore a collection of related usage scenarios, and a scenario is a specific instance of a use case. One scenario is identified as the *normal course* of events for the use case, also called the main course, the basic course, the normal flow, and the "happy path." The normal course is described by listing a sequence of dialogue elements or interactions between the actor and the system. When this dialogue is completed, the actor has accomplished the intended goal. The normal course for the "Request a Chemical" use case results in a user requesting that a chemical be ordered from an outside vendor.

Figure 8-1 shows a use-case diagram for "Request a Chemical," using Unified Modeling Language (UML) notation (Booch, Rumbaugh, and Jacobson 1999).[1] The actor (Requester) is shown as a simple stick figure, with a line drawn from the actor to each use case (shown in the ovals) that he needs. The major use case of interest in this diagram is "Request a Chemical." The other use cases, "See Available Stockroom Containers" and "Enter Charge Number," illustrate the two other possible use-case relationships of <<extend>> and <<include>>, which are described later in this section. Use-case diagrams provide a high-level visual representation of the user requirements.

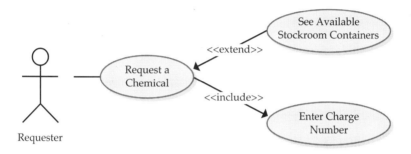

FIGURE 8-1   *The "Request a Chemical" use case from the Chemical Tracking System.*

Other scenarios within the use case are described as *alternative courses.* Alternative courses also result in successful task completion, but they represent variations in the specifics of the task or in the path used to accomplish the task. The normal course can branch off into an alternative course at some decision point in the dialogue sequence, then rejoin the normal course later. An alternative course for the "Request a Chemical" use case is "Request a Chemical from the Chemical Stockroom." Although the user is requesting a chemical in both the normal and the alternative courses, the specific interactions between the user and the system will differ in several respects. In the alternative course, the user must still specify the desired chemical, but she might be able to choose from among several existing containers in the chemical stockroom.

---

1. The conventions and terminology of evolving software design languages such as UML change from time to time, so the representation described here might become obsolete some day. The use-case concepts described in this chapter are more important than the formalisms used to represent them.

Some of the steps in an alternative course will be the same as those in the normal course, but certain unique actions are needed to accomplish the alternative path. (See Figure 8-2.) It is sometimes convenient to *extend* the normal course by inserting into the flow a separate use case that defines the alternative course. The use case that is being extended must be a complete use case that can be performed on its own. Figure 8-1 shows that the use case "See Available Stockroom Containers" extends the "Request a Chemical" use case. That extension leads to the alternative course of "Request a Chemical from the Chemical Stockroom."

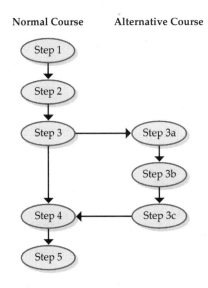

FIGURE 8-2   *Dialogue flow in the normal and alternative courses of a use case.*

Several use cases might share some common functionality. To avoid duplication, you can define a separate use case that contains the common functionality and indicate that other use cases should *include* that common use case. This is logically equivalent to calling a common subroutine in a programming language. The included use case is essential to the completion of the task, whereas a use case that extends another one is optional because the normal course can take place on its own (Rumbaugh 1994). As an example, the "Request a Chemical" use case is one of several that includes a separate use case called "Enter Charge Number," as was shown in Figure 8-1.

Conditions that result in the task not being successfully accomplished are documented as *exceptions*, which are sometimes regarded as a type of alternative course. It is important to describe the exception paths when defining use cases, because they represent the user's vision of how the system should behave under specific conditions. One exception for the "Request a Chemical" use case is "Chemical Is Not Commercially Available". If you don't document exceptions, the developer might overlook those possibilities during design and construction, which could cause the system to fail when it encounters an exception condition.

IDENTIFYING AND DOCUMENTING USE CASES

You can identify use cases by using several approaches (Ham 1998; Larman 1998):

- Identify actors and their roles first, then identify the business processes in which each participates to reveal use cases.

- Identify the external events to which the system must respond, then relate these events to participating actors and specific use cases.

- Express business processes or daily activities in terms of specific scenarios, derive use cases from the scenarios, and identify the actors involved in each use case.

- Derive likely use cases from existing functional requirement statements. If any requirements don't align with a use case, consider whether you really need them.

Because use cases represent the user requirements, you should gather them directly from representatives of the various user classes for your system or, less desirably, from their surrogates. The analysts on the Chemical Tracking System project facilitated a series of two- to three-hour use-case elicitation workshops, held every other day. Facilitated, structured group workshops are one of the most effective techniques for linking customers and developers (Kiel and Carmel 1995). Each workshop's participants included the product champion who represented a particular user class, other selected user representatives, and one or more developers. Developers serve as the voice of reality when infeasible requirements are suggested, and participating in the elicitation workshops gives them early insight into the product they will be expected to build. Members of the various Chemical Tracking System user classes participated in separate workshops, which worked well because only a few use cases were common to multiple user classes.

Prior to holding the workshops, each analyst asked the users to think of tasks or business processes they would need to execute with the new system. Each of these tasks became a candidate use case, which the analyst numbered and named with a succinct statement of the task, such as "Request a Chemical" or "Print the Safety Datasheet for a Chemical." As the group explored the use cases in the workshops, they found that some of them really represented related scenarios that could be consolidated into a single abstract use case. A few proposed use cases were discarded because they were judged to be out of scope for the project. The group also discovered additional use cases beyond those in the initial set they identified.

Users tend to identify the most important use cases first, so the discovery sequence gives some clues to priority. Another prioritization approach is to write just a two- or three-sentence description of each candidate use case as it is proposed. Prioritize these candidate use cases, fill in the details for those with the highest priority first, and then reevaluate the priorities for your remaining candidate use cases.

Each elicitation workshop explored several use cases, documenting each one according to a standard template. Figure 8-3 illustrates the template for a simplified version of the "Request a Chemical" use case. The participants began by identifying the actor who would benefit from the first use case. Next, they defined any preconditions that had to be satisfied to perform the use case, and postconditions that would describe the state of the system after the use case was completed. The estimated frequency of use provided an early indicator of concurrent usage and capacity requirements. Next, the analyst asked the participants how they envisioned interacting with the system to perform the task. The resulting dialogue sequence of actor actions and system responses became the flow that was identified as the normal course of events. Although each participant had a different mental image of the actual user interface and interaction mechanisms, the group was able to reach a common vision of the steps in the actor-system dialogue.

The analyst captured the individual actor actions and system responses on sticky notes, which were placed on a flipchart sheet for each use case. Another way to conduct such a workshop is to project a use case template onto a large screen from a computer and complete the template during the discussion. For dialogue sequences that involve complex logic or multiple decisions, a graphical representation such as a flowchart is more illuminating than a numbered series of steps.

Use Case ID	UC-5		
Use Case Name	**Request a Chemical**		
Created By	Tim	Last Updated By	Janice
Date Created	10/4	Date Last Updated	10/27
Actor	Requester		
Description	The Requester specifies the chemical to request, either by entering its chemical ID number or by importing its structure from a chemical drawing tool. The system can satisfy the request either by offering the Requester a new or used container of the chemical from the chemical stockroom or by letting the Requester place an order to an outside vendor.		
Preconditions	1. User's identity has been authenticated. 2. Chemical inventory database is online.		
Postconditions	1. Completed request is stored in the Chemical Tracking System. 2. Request was e-mailed to Chemical Stockroom or Purchasing for fulfillment.		
Priority	High		
Frequency of Use	Approximately 5 times per week by each chemist, 100 times per week by each member of chemical stockroom staff.		

Normal Course	**5.0 Request a Chemical from a Vendor**		
	Actor Actions	*System Responses*	
	1. Enter the chemical ID number or the name of the file that contains the chemical structure. 4. Specify vendor (continue) or chemical stockroom (Alternative Course 5.1).	2. Verify the chemical ID is valid. 3. Ask Requester if he wants a new vendor order or a container from the chemical stockroom. 5. <continue dialogue until request is completed>	

Alternative Course	**5.1 Request a Chemical from the Chemical Stockroom** (branch after 5.0.4)		
	Actor Actions	*System Responses*	
	2. Optionally, ask to view the history of any container. 3. Select a specific container or ask to place a vendor order.	1. Display a list of containers of the desired chemical that are in the chemical stockroom.	
		(continued)	

FIGURE 8-3   *Partial description of the "Request a Chemical" use case for the Chemical Tracking System.*

FIGURE 8-3 *continued*

Exceptions	**5.E.1 Chemical Is Not Commercially Available**	
	Actor Actions	*System Responses*
	3. Ask to request another chemical.	1. Display message: No vendors.
		2. Ask Requester if he wishes to request another chemical or exit.
		4. Start Normal Course over.
Includes	**UC-12 Enter Charge Number**	
Special Requirements	The system must be able to import a chemical structure in the standard encoded form from any of the supported chemical drawing packages.	
Assumptions	Imported chemical structures are assumed to be valid.	
Notes and Issues	Tim will find out if management approval is needed to request a chemical on the Level 1 hazard list. Due date 11/4.	

The elicitation team developed similar dialogues for the alternative courses and exceptions they identified. Many exception conditions were revealed when the analyst asked questions like "What should happen if the database isn't online at that moment?" or "What if that chemical is not commercially available?" After each use case was fully explored and no additional variations, exceptions, or details were proposed, the workshop participants moved on to another use case. They did not try to cover all the use cases in one marathon session. Instead, they planned to explore the use cases in increments, and then review and refine them iteratively, elaborating details of the functional requirements and possible user interface approaches.

Figure 8-4 shows the sequence of events associated with the use-case elicitation workshops and subsequent activities. After each workshop, the analyst took the use-case descriptions and began to derive functional requirements from them. Some of these were obvious, such as "Each submitted request shall be identified by a unique, system-assigned sequence number." Others were subtler, representing the functionality the developer would have to build to permit users to carry out the steps in their interaction with the system. The analyst documented these functional requirements in a hierarchical structured form, suitable for inclusion in a software requirements specification.

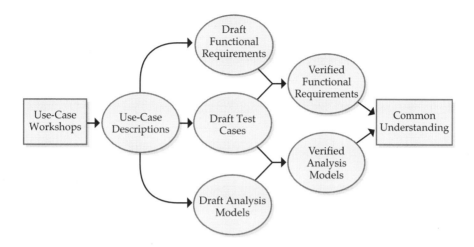

FIGURE 8-4   *Use-case elicitation approach.*

The analyst found it helpful to draw graphical analysis models for some of the complex use cases. Such models include data flow diagrams, entity-relationship diagrams, state-transition diagrams, object class and interaction diagrams, and dialog maps of possible user interface architectures. These models depict different views of the requirements, which can often reveal omissions, ambiguities, and inconsistencies that aren't easy to spot in text. Chapter 10 illustrates several of these analysis models for the Chemical Tracking System.

Within a day after the workshop, the analyst gave the use-case descriptions and their associated functional requirements to the workshop participants, who reviewed them prior to the next workshop. These frequent informal reviews revealed many errors, such as previously undiscovered alternative courses and exceptions, incorrect functional requirements, and missing steps in the actor-system dialogues. The use-case approach provides a powerful way to improve requirements quality through such incremental reviews.

There is a limit to how frequently you can hold effective use-case elicitation workshops. One analyst who held workshops every day learned that the participants had difficulty finding errors in the documents they reviewed because the information was too fresh in their minds. The mental relaxation that comes after a day or two away from an intellectually intensive activity allows you to view your earlier work from a fresh perspective. Two or three workshops per week is the maximum if you want to reap the benefits of interim reviews.

Early in the requirements development process, the test lead for the Chemical Tracking System developed conceptual test cases from the use cases. These test cases helped the team document a clear, shared understanding of how the system should behave in specific usage scenarios. The test cases let the analyst verify whether she had captured all of the functional requirements needed to generate the system behaviors documented in the test cases. She also used the test cases to determine whether the analysis models were complete, accurate, and consistent with the functional requirements. Chapter 14 discusses generating test cases from requirements in more detail.

Large systems can have hundreds of use cases, and considerable time will be needed to identify, elaborate, document, and verify them. Nonetheless, defining the system's intended functionality through use-case workshops is an excellent investment in building a high-quality software system that will meet the needs of diverse users.

Use Cases and Functional Requirements

The use-case descriptions in themselves don't provide developers with enough detail about the functionality they must build. If you stop requirements development at the user requirements stage, you'll find that at construction time the developers have to ask many questions to fill their information gaps. To reduce this uncertainty, you need to elaborate each use case into its detailed functional requirements (Arlow 1998).

Each use case leads to a number of functional requirements that will enable an actor to perform the pertinent task, and several use cases might need the same functional requirement. For example, if five use cases require that the user's identity be authenticated, you don't want to write five different blocks of code for that purpose. You can document the functional requirements associated with a use case in several ways. The approach you take depends on whether you expect your team to perform the design, construction, and testing from the use-case documents, from the SRS, or from a combination of both. None of these methods is perfect, so select the approach that best fits with how you wish to document and manage your project's software requirements. Avoid duplicating information in multiple locations, as redundancy makes requirements management more difficult.

Use Cases Only

One possibility is to include the functional requirements right in each use-case description, although you'll probably still need a separate SRS to contain those requirements that are not associated with specific use cases. You should cross-reference functional requirements that are duplicated in multiple use cases. One way to address this is through the "include" relationship discussed earlier, in which common functionality (such as user authentication) is split out into a separate, reusable use case.

Use Cases and SRS

Another alternative is to restrict the use-case descriptions to the user requirements level of abstraction and to document the functional requirements you derive from each use case in the SRS. In this approach, you'll need to establish traceability between the use cases and their associated functional requirements. The best way to do this is to store all use cases and functional requirements in a database or a commercial requirements management tool that will let you define these traceability links. (See Chapter 19.)

SRS Only

A third approach is to organize the SRS by use case and include both the use case and the functional requirements descriptions. With this approach, you won't have to write separate detailed use-case documents; however, you'll need to identify duplicated functional requirements or to state every functional requirement only once and refer to its initial statement whenever the requirement reappears in another use case.

BENEFITS OF USE CASES

The power of the use-case approach to requirements elicitation comes from its task-centric and user-centric perspective. The users will have clearer expectations of what the new system will let them do than if you take a function-centric approach. The customer representatives on several Web development projects found that the use-case approach really helped them clarify their ideas of what visitors to the Web site should be able to do. Use cases help analysts and developers understand both the user's business and the application domain. Carefully thinking through the actor-system dialogue sequences can reveal ambiguity and vagueness early in the development process, as does generating test cases from the use cases.

It's frustrating for developers to write code that never gets used. With use cases, the functional requirements are derived specifically to allow the user to perform certain tasks. The use-case technique prevents "orphan" functionality—those functions that seem like a good idea during elicitation, but that no one ever uses because they don't really relate to user tasks.

There are technical benefits too. The use-case perspective reveals domain objects and their responsibilities to each other. Developers using object-oriented design methods can turn use cases into object models. Furthermore, as the business processes change over time, the tasks that are embodied in specific use cases will change. If you've traced functional requirements, designs, code, and tests back to their parent use cases—the voice of the customer—it will be easy to see how those business-process changes cascade throughout the entire system.

USE-CASE TRAPS TO AVOID

Watch out for the following traps when applying the use-case approach:

- *Too many use cases.* If you find yourself caught in a use-case explosion, you might not be writing them at the appropriate level of abstraction. Don't create a separate use case for every possible scenario. Instead, include the normal course, alternative courses, and exceptions as scenarios within a single use case. Don't treat every step in the interaction sequence as a separate use case, either. Each use case should describe an independent task. You'll typically have many more use cases than business requirements, but many more functional requirements than use cases. Every use case should tell a story about a way the user would interact with the system to attain a particular goal.

- *Duplication across use cases.* If identical functionality appears in multiple use cases, there's a risk of implementing that functionality multiple times. To avoid the repetition, use the "include" relationship, in which common functionality is split out into a separate use case that is invoked by all use cases that need it.

◆ *User interface design included in the use cases.* Use cases should focus on what the users need to do with the system, not how the screens will look. Emphasize understanding the conceptual dialogues between the actors and the system, and defer the user interface details to the design stage. Any screen sketches or user interface architecture maps should be used only to help visualize the actor-system interactions, not as firm design specifications.

◆ *Including data definitions in use cases.* I've seen use cases that included definitions of the data items and structures that are manipulated in the use case, including data type, length, format, and valid values. This approach makes it difficult for project participants to find the definitions they need, as it is not obvious which use-case description includes each data definition. It can also lead to redundant definitions, which easily get out of synch when one instance is changed and others are not. Collect data definitions in a project-wide data dictionary (discussed in Chapter 9), which will reduce the chance of using them inconsistently.

◆ *Attempting to associate every requirement with a use case.* While use cases can effectively capture the majority of desired system behaviors, you'll probably have some requirements that do not relate specifically to user tasks or to interactions with other actors. You still need a separate requirements specification in which to document nonfunctional requirements, external interface requirements, and functional requirements that weren't derived from a use case.

CLASSIFYING CUSTOMER INPUT

Don't expect your customers to present the requirements analyst with a succinct, complete, and well-organized list of needs. Analysts must classify into various categories the myriad bits of information that make up the voice of the customer, so they can document the information appropriately and use it in the most sensible way. Figure 8-5 illustrates several such classification categories. Information that doesn't fit into one of these "buckets" might represent a non-software project requirement, such as a requirement to deliver user training for the new system, or it could simply be extraneous information. The following discussion suggests some phrases to listen for that will help you in this classification process.

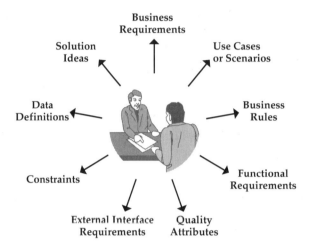

FIGURE 8-5   *Classifying the voice of the customer.*

Business requirements. Anything that describes the financial, marketplace, or other business benefit that either customers or the developing organization can gain from the product is most likely a business requirement. Listen for statements about the value that direct or indirect users of the software will receive, such as "Increase market share by X%," "Save $Y per year," or "Replace Z high-maintenance legacy systems."

Use cases or scenarios. General statements of user goals or business tasks they need to perform with the system are probably use cases, while specific task descriptions represent usage scenarios. Work with the customers to generalize specific tasks into broader use cases. You can often glean use cases by asking customers to describe their business workflow activities.

Business rules. When a customer says that some activity can be performed only by certain individuals or roles, under certain conditions, he might be describing a business rule, for example, "A chemist can order a chemical on the Level 1 hazard list only if his hazardous-chemical training is current." Business rules are operating principles about a business process. You might derive some software functional requirements to enforce the rules, such as making the training record database accessible to the Chemical Tracking System. As stated, though, business rules are not functional requirements.

Functional requirements. A customer statement that begins with "The user must be able to <perform some function>" or "The system should <demonstrate some behavior>" is most likely a functional requirement. Functional requirements describe the observable behaviors the system will exhibit, often in the context of an actor action–system response sequence. Functional requirements define what the system will do; they make up the bulk of the SRS. The analyst should make certain that everyone understands why the system "must" perform certain functions. Proposed functional requirements sometimes reflect obsolete or ineffective business processes that should not be incorporated into a new system.

Quality attributes. Statements that indicate how well the system performs some behavior or lets the user take some action are quality attributes, one kind of nonfunctional requirement. Listen for words that describe desirable characteristics: fast, easy, intuitive, user-friendly, robust, reliable, secure, and efficient. You'll have to work with the users to define precisely what they mean by these ambiguous and subjective terms, as described in Chapter 11.

External interface requirements. This class of requirement describes the connections between your system and the rest of the universe. The SRS should include sections for these requirements, including interfaces and communication mechanisms for users, hardware, and other software systems. Phrases that indicate the customer is describing an external interface requirement include:

- "Must read signals from <some device>"
- "Must send messages to <some other system>"
- "Must be able to read files in <some format>"
- "Must control <some piece of hardware>"

Constraints. Constraints are conditions that legitimately limit the choices available to the designer or programmer. They represent another type of nonfunctional requirement that you should document in the SRS. Try to prevent the customer from imposing unnecessary constraints, as they can inhibit creating the best solution. Unnecessary constraints will also reduce your ability to use commercially available software components as part of the solution. Certain constraints can help satisfy quality attributes. An example is to improve portability by using only the standard commands of a programming language, not permitting vendor-specific extensions. Following are some phrases that indicate the customer is describing a constraint:

- "Must use <a specific database product or language>"
- "Can't require more than <some amount of memory>"
- "Must operate identically to <some other system>"
- "Must be consistent with <another application>"

Data definitions. Whenever customers describe the format, allowed values, or default value for a data item or the composition of a complex business data structure, they are presenting a data definition. For example, "The ZIP code consists of five digits, followed by an optional hyphen and an optional four digits, defaulted to 0000" is a data definition. Collect these in a data dictionary to provide a master reference that project participants can use throughout the product's development and maintenance. (See Chapter 9.)

Solution ideas. If a customer describes a specific way to interact with the system to carry out some action (for example, "The user selects the item he wants from a dropdown list"), you are hearing a suggested solution, not a requirement. Proposed solutions can distract the elicitation team from surfacing the actual underlying requirements. When eliciting requirements, focus on what needs to be done rather than how the new system will be designed or built. Explore why the customer suggested a specific implementation method, as that will help you understand both the real need and the customer's implicit expectations about how the system will work.

SOME CAUTIONS ABOUT ELICITATION

During requirements elicitation you might find that the product scope is ill defined, either too large or too small (Christel and Kang 1992). If the scope is too large, you'll collect more requirements than you really need to deliver adequate business and customer value, and the elicitation process will drag on. If the project is scoped too small, customers will present needs that are clearly important yet just as clearly lie beyond the limited scope currently established for the product. The present scope could be too small to provide a satisfactory product. Requirements elicitation can result in modifying the project's scope and vision, but make such far-reaching changes cautiously.

It is often stated that requirements are about *what* the system has to do, while *how* the solution will be implemented is the realm of design. Though attractively concise, this is an oversimplification. Requirements elicitation should indeed focus on the *what*, but there is a gray area between analysis and design. You can use hypothetical *how*s to clarify and refine your understanding of what the users need. Analysis models, screen sketches, and prototypes help make the concepts expressed during requirements elicitation more tangible and thus provide a way to find errors and omissions. View the models and screens you generate during requirements development as conceptual suggestions that facilitate effective communication, not as constraints on the options available to the designer.

Requirements elicitation workshops that involve too many participants can slow to a contentious crawl. My colleague Debbie once was frustrated at the sluggish progress of the use-case workshops she was facilitating for a Web development project. The twelve participants engaged in extended discussions of unnecessary details and had a hard time agreeing on how each use case should work. The team's progress accelerated nicely when she reduced the number of participants to six who represented the key project roles of customer, system architect, developer, and visual designer.

Conversely, collecting input from too few representatives, or hearing only the voice of the loudest, most opinionated customer, can also be a problem. It can lead to overlooking requirements that are important to certain user classes, or to specifying requirements that don't represent the needs of a majority of the users. The best balance will involve a few product champions who have authority to speak for their user classes, with each champion backed up by a small group of other representatives from that same class.

HOW DO YOU KNOW WHEN YOU'RE DONE?

No simple, clear signal will indicate when you're done gathering requirements. As customers and developers talk with their colleagues, read industry and business literature, and muse in the shower each morning, they will generate ideas for potential inclusion in the product. You'll never be completely done, but the following cues suggest that you're reaching the point of diminishing returns on requirements elicitation:

- If the users can't think of any more use cases, perhaps you're done. Users tend to identify use cases in sequence of decreasing importance.

- If users propose new use cases, but you've already derived the associated functional requirements from other use cases, perhaps you're done. These new use cases might really be alternative courses for other use cases you've already captured.

- If users begin to repeat issues they already covered in previous discussions, perhaps you're done.

- If suggested new use cases or functional requirements are all deemed to be out of scope, perhaps you're done.

- If proposed new requirements are all of low priority relative to the ones you've already specified, perhaps you're done.

- If the users are proposing capabilities that might be included "sometime in the lifetime of the product," rather than "in the specific product we're talking about right now," perhaps you're done.

Early in the project, make a list of the functional areas that the system is likely to include. You might create a checklist of common functions to consider for many projects, such as writing error logs, backup and restore, reporting, printing, preview capabilities, formatting, and user preferences. Late in requirements development, compare your original list with the functions you've specified. If you don't find gaps, perhaps you're done.

Next Steps

♦ Select a section of any documented voice-of-the-customer input on your project or from the SRS. Classify every item contained in that section into the categories shown in Figure 8-5. If you discover items that are incorrectly documented as functional requirements, move them to the correct location in the SRS or to another appropriate document.

♦ Write a use case for your current project, using the use-case template in Figure 8-3. Include any pertinent alternative courses and exceptions. Define the functional requirements that will allow the user to successfully complete this use case. Check whether your current SRS already includes all of these functional requirements.

♦ List the requirements elicitation methods used on your current project. Which ones worked well? Why? Which ones did not work very well? Why not? Identify elicitation techniques that you think would work better and decide how you'd apply them next time. Identify any barriers you might encounter to making those techniques work, and brainstorm ways to overcome those barriers.

9
Documenting the Requirements

Requirements development has a final product: a documented agreement between the customers and the development group about the product to be built. This agreement spans the triad of business requirements, user requirements, and software functional requirements. As we saw earlier, the vision and scope document contains the business requirements, while the user requirements are captured in use-case documents. You must also document both the functional requirements derived from use cases and the product's nonfunctional requirements, including quality attributes and external interface requirements. Unless you write these requirements in an organized and readable fashion, and have key project stakeholders review and approve them, people will not be sure what they are agreeing to.

You can document software requirements in three ways:

◆ Textual documents that use well-structured and carefully written natural language

◆ Graphical models that illustrate transformational processes, system states and changes between them, data relationships, logic flows, or object classes and their relationships

◆ Formal specifications that define requirements by using mathematically precise formal logic languages

While formal specifications provide the greatest rigor and precision, few software developers, and virtually no customers, are familiar with formal notation. Despite its many shortcomings, structured natural language remains the most practical way of documenting requirements for most software projects. A text-based software requirements specification that contains the functional and nonfunctional requirements will meet the needs of most projects. Graphical analysis models augment the SRS by providing alternative views of the requirements.

This chapter addresses the purpose and structure of the SRS, including a suggested document template. Guidelines for writing functional requirements are also presented, along with several examples of imperfect requirement statements and suggestions for improving them. Graphical modeling techniques for representing the requirements are the topic of Chapter 10. Formal specification methods are not addressed further in this book; see Alan Davis's *Software Requirements: Objects, Functions, and States* (1993) for references to further discussions of formal specification methods.

The Software Requirements Specification

The software requirements specification is also known as the functional specification, requirements agreement, and system specification. The SRS precisely states the functions and capabilities that a software system must provide and the constraints that it must respect. The SRS is the basis for all subsequent project planning, design, and coding, as well as the foundation for system testing and user documentation. The SRS should describe as completely as possible the intended external, user-visible behaviors of the system. It should not contain design, construction, testing, or project management details other than known design and implementation constraints. Several audiences use the SRS for various purposes:

- ◆   Customers and the marketing department rely on the SRS to know what product they can expect to be delivered.

- ◆   Project managers base their plans and estimates of schedule, effort, and resources on the product description contained in the SRS.

- ◆   The software development team relies on the SRS to understand what it is to build.

- ◆   The testing group uses the product behavior descriptions contained in the SRS to derive test plans, cases, and procedures.

- ◆   Software maintenance and support staff refer to the SRS to understand what each part of the product is supposed to do.

- ◆   The publications group writes user documentation, such as manuals and help screens, based on both the SRS and the user interface design.

- ◆   Training personnel can use both the SRS and the user documentation to help them develop educational materials.

As the ultimate repository for the product requirements, the SRS must be comprehensive: *all* requirements should be included. Developers and customers should make no assumptions. If any desired functional or nonfunctional requirement is not identified in the SRS, it isn't part of the agreement and no one should expect it to appear in the product.

Nothing says you have to write the product's entire SRS before you begin design and construction. You can also approach requirements specification iteratively or incrementally, depending on a number of factors: whether you can identify all of the requirements at the outset, whether the same people who write the SRS will build the product, the number of planned releases, and so forth. However, every project must have a baselined agreement for each set of requirements that will be implemented. *Baselining* is the process of transitioning an SRS under development into one that has been reviewed and approved. Changes in a baselined SRS should be made through the project's defined change control process.

All participants must work from the same set of approved requirements to avoid unnecessary rework and miscommunication. I know of one project that suddenly experienced a flood of bug reports from the testers. It turned out they had been testing against an older version of the SRS, and what they thought were bugs really were features. Much of their testing effort was wasted, because the testers were looking for the wrong system behaviors.

Chapter 1 presented several characteristics of high-quality requirements documents: they must be complete, consistent, modifiable, and traceable. Structure and write the SRS so that users and other readers can understand it (Sommerville and Sawyer 1997). Keep the following readability suggestions in mind:

- Number sections, subsections, and individual requirements consistently.

- Leave text ragged on the right margin, rather than being fully justified.

- Make liberal use of white space.

- Use visual emphasis (such as **bold**, <u>underline</u>, *italics*, and `different fonts`) consistently and judiciously.

- Create a table of contents and an index to help readers find the information they need.

- Number and label all figures and tables and refer to them by number.

- Use your word processor's cross-reference facility, rather than hard-coded page or section numbers, to refer to other items or locations within the document.

LABELING REQUIREMENTS

To satisfy the SRS quality criteria of traceability and modifiability, every software requirement must be uniquely identified. This allows you to refer to specific requirements in a change request, modification history, cross-reference, or requirements traceability matrix. Because simple and bulleted lists are not adequate for this purpose, I will describe several different requirements-labeling methods with their advantages and shortcomings. Select whichever technique makes the most sense for your situation.

Sequence number. The simplest approach is to give every requirement a unique sequence number, such as UR-2 or SRS13. Commercial requirements management tools assign such a number when a new requirement is added to the tool's database (most such tools also support hierarchical numbering). The prefix indicates the requirement type, such as UR for "user requirement." The numbers are not reused, so a deleted requirement is simply flagged as deleted in the database, and a new requirement gets the next available number. This simple numbering approach does not provide any logical or hierarchical grouping of related requirements, and the labels give you no clue as to what each requirement is about.

Hierarchical numbering. This is perhaps the most commonly used convention. If the functional requirements appear in section 3.2 of your SRS, they will all have labels such as 3.2.4.3. More digits in the label indicate a more detailed, lower-level requirement. This method is simple and compact, and your word processor can probably assign the numbers automatically. However, the labels can expand to many digits in even a medium-sized SRS, and they tell you nothing about the purpose of each requirement. If you have to insert a new requirement, the numbers of all following requirements in that section will be incremented. Delete or move a requirement, and the numbers below it in that section will be decremented. These changes can create havoc for any references to the requirements elsewhere in the system.

An improvement on the simple hierarchical numbering approach is to number the major sections of the requirements hierarchically and then identify individual functional requirements in each section with a short text code followed by a sequence number. For example, the SRS might contain "Section 3.2.5 – Editor Functions," and the requirements in that section could be labeled ED-1, ED-2, and so forth. This approach provides some hierarchy and organization while keeping the labels short, somewhat meaningful, and positionally independent. Inserting new requirement ED-9 between ED-1 and ED-2 does not force you to renumber the rest of the section.

Hierarchical textual tags. Consultant Tom Gilb suggests a text-based hierarchical tagging scheme for labeling individual requirements (Gilb 1988). Consider this requirement: "The system shall ask the user to confirm any request for printing more than ten copies." This requirement might be tagged PRINT.COPIES.CONFIRM, which indicates that it is part of the print function and is related to the issue of setting the number of copies to be printed. Hierarchical textual tags are structured, semantically meaningful, and unaffected by adding, deleting, or moving other requirements. Their primary drawback is that they are bulkier than the hierarchical numeric labels.

DEALING WITH INCOMPLETENESS

Sometimes you know that you lack a piece of information about a specific requirement. You might need to consult with a customer, check an interface description for another system, or define another requirement before you can resolve this uncertainty. Use the notation *TBD* ("to be determined") as a standard indicator to highlight these knowledge gaps in the SRS. This way, you can search the SRS for TBDs to identify the spots where you know clarification is needed. Document who will resolve each issue, how, and by when. Number each TBD and create a list of all TBDs to help you track each item to closure.

Resolve all TBDs before you proceed with construction of a set of requirements, because any uncertainties that remain increase the risk of making errors and having to rework the requirements. When the developer encounters a TBD or other ambiguity, he might not go back to the requirement's originator to clarify or resolve it. More likely, the developer will make his best guess, which won't always be correct. If you must proceed with construction while TBDs remain, defer those requirements' implementation if you can, or design those portions of the product to be easily modifiable when the open issues are resolved.

USER INTERFACES AND THE SRS

Incorporating user interface designs in the SRS has both drawbacks and benefits. On the minus side, screen images and user interface architectures are descriptions of solutions (designs), not of requirements. If you cannot baseline the SRS until the user interface design is completed, the requirements development process will take longer than it would otherwise. This can try the patience of managers, customers, or developers who are already concerned about the time being spent on requirements development. User interface layouts are not a substitute for defining the functional requirements. Don't expect developers to deduce the underlying functionality and data relationships from screen shots. Including user interface designs in the SRS also implies that developers must follow the requirements change process every time they want to alter a user interface element.

On the plus side, exploring potential user interfaces can help you refine the requirements and makes the user–system interactions more tangible to both the users and the developers. User interface displays can also assist with project planning and estimation. You can count graphical user interface

(GUI) elements or calculate the number of function points[1] associated with each screen and then estimate the effort it will take to implement the screens, based on your previous experience with similar development activities.

A sensible balance is to include conceptual images—sketches—of selected user interface components in the SRS, without creating an expectation that the implementations must precisely follow those models. This enhances communication by representing the requirements in another fashion, but without overconstraining the developers and overloading your change management process. For example, a preliminary sketch of a complex dialog box will illustrate the intent behind a portion of the requirements, but a skilled designer might turn it into a tabbed dialog or employ another approach that enhances usability.

A SOFTWARE REQUIREMENTS SPECIFICATION TEMPLATE

Every software development organization should adopt a standard SRS template for its projects. Several recommended SRS templates are available (Davis 1993; Robertson and Robertson 1999). Dorfman and Thayer (1990) collected some 20 requirements standards and several examples from the National Bureau of Standards, the U.S. Department of Defense, NASA, and several British and Canadian sources. Many people use templates derived from IEEE Standard 830-1998, "IEEE Recommended Practice for Software Requirements Specifications" (IEEE 1998). This is a well-structured, flexible template that is suitable for many kinds of software projects.

Figure 9-1 illustrates an SRS template that was adapted and extended from the IEEE 830 standard. Modify this template to fit the needs and nature of your projects. If a particular section of the template doesn't apply to your project, leave the section heading in place but specify that it does not apply. This will prevent the reader from wondering whether something important was omitted inadvertently. Use this template to guide your thinking, and add any sections that are pertinent to your project. As with any software project document, include a table of contents and a revision history that lists

---

1. Function points are a measure of the quantity of user-visible functionality of an application, independent of how it is constructed. You can estimate the function points from an understanding of the user requirements, based on the counts of internal logical files, external interface files, and external inputs, outputs, and queries (IFPUG 1999).

the changes that were made to the SRS, including the date of the change, who made the change, and the reason.

---

1. Introduction

   1.1 Purpose
   1.2 Document Conventions
   1.3 Intended Audience and Reading Suggestions
   1.4 Product Scope
   1.5 References

2. Overall Description

   2.1 Product Perspective
   2.2 Product Functions
   2.3 User Classes and Characteristics
   2.4 Operating Environment
   2.5 Design and Implementation Constraints
   2.6 Assumptions and Dependencies

3. External Interface Requirements

   3.1 User Interfaces
   3.2 Hardware Interfaces
   3.3 Software Interfaces
   3.4 Communications Interfaces

4. System Features

   4.x System Feature X
       4.x.1 Description and Priority
       4.x.2 Stimulus/Response Sequences
       4.x.3 Functional Requirements

5. Other Nonfunctional Requirements

   5.1 Performance Requirements
   5.2 Safety Requirements
   5.3 Security Requirements
   5.4 Software Quality Attributes
   5.5 Business Rules
   5.6 User Documentation

6. Other Requirements

Appendix A: Glossary

Appendix B: Analysis Models

Appendix C: To-Be-Determined List

FIGURE 9-1   *Template for software requirements specification.*

The rest of this section describes the information you would include in each section of the template in Figure 9-1. You can incorporate sections by reference to other existing project documents (such as a vision and scope document or an interface specification), rather than duplicating information in the SRS or bundling everything together into a single document. Don't follow the template dogmatically; do what makes sense for you.

1. INTRODUCTION

The introduction presents an overview of the SRS to help the reader understand how the document is organized and how to read and interpret it.

1.1 Purpose

Identify the product whose software requirements are specified in this document, including the revision or release number. If this SRS pertains to only part of the entire system, identify the portion or subsystem that it addresses.

1.2 Document Conventions

Describe any standards or typographical conventions that were followed when writing this SRS, including text styles, highlighting, or significant notations. For instance, state whether the priority shown for a high-level requirement is inherited by all of its detailed requirements, or whether every requirement statement has its own priority.

1.3 Intended Audience and Reading Suggestions

List the different readers to whom the SRS is directed, such as developers, project managers, marketing staff, users, testers, and documentation writers. Describe what the rest of the SRS contains and how it is organized. Suggest a sequence for reading the document that is most appropriate for each type of reader.

1.4 Product Scope

Provide a short description of the software being specified and its purpose, including benefits and goals. Relate the software to corporate goals or business strategies. If a separate vision and scope document is available, refer to it rather than duplicating its contents here.

1.5 References

List any documents or other resources to which this SRS refers. These might include user interface style guides, contracts, standards, system requirements specifications, use-case documents, or the SRS for a related product. Provide enough information so that the reader can access each reference, including its title, author, version number, date, and source or location.

2. OVERALL DESCRIPTION

This section presents a high-level overview of the product being specified and the environment in which it will be used, the anticipated users of the product, and the known constraints, assumptions, and dependencies.

2.1 Product Perspective

Describe the context and origin of the product being specified in this SRS. State whether this product is the next member of a product family, the next release of a mature product, a replacement for existing applications, or a new, self-contained product. If this SRS defines a component of a larger system, state how this software relates to the overall system and identify interfaces between the two.

2.2 Product Functions

Summarize the major functions the product must perform. Details will be provided in Section 4, so you only need a high-level summary here, such as a bulleted list. Organize the functions to make them understandable to any reader. A picture of the major groups of requirements and how they are related, such as a top-level data flow diagram or a class diagram, can be helpful.

2.3 User Classes and Characteristics

Identify the various user classes that you anticipate will use this product and describe their pertinent characteristics. (See Chapter 7.) Some requirements might pertain only to certain user classes. Distinguish the most important user classes for this product from those whom it is less critical to satisfy.

2.4 Operating Environment

Describe the environment in which the software will operate, including the hardware platform, operating system and versions, and other software components or applications with which it must peacefully coexist.

2.5 Design and Implementation Constraints

Identify any issues that will restrict the options available to the developers and describe why they are constraints. Constraints might include the following:

◆ Specific technologies, tools, programming languages, and databases that must be used or avoided

◆ Required development conventions or standards (for instance, if the customer's organization will be maintaining the software, it might specify design notations and coding standards that a subcontractor must use)

◆ Corporate policies, government regulations, or industry standards

◆ Hardware limitations, such as timing requirements or memory restrictions

◆ Standard data interchange formats

2.6 Assumptions and Dependencies

List any assumed factors (as opposed to known facts) that could affect the requirements stated in the SRS. These could include commercial components that you plan to use, or issues around the development or operating environment. You might assume that the product will conform to a particular user interface design convention, whereas another SRS reader might assume something different. The project could be affected if these assumptions are incorrect, are not shared, or change.

Also, identify any dependencies the project has on external factors. For example, if you expect to integrate into the system some components that are being developed by another project, you are dependent upon that project to supply the correctly operating components on schedule. If these dependencies are already documented elsewhere, such as in the project plan, refer to those other documents here.

3. EXTERNAL INTERFACE REQUIREMENTS

Use this section to specify any requirements that ensure the new product will connect properly to external components. The context diagram shows the external interfaces at a high level of abstraction. Place detailed descriptions of the data and control components of the interfaces in the data dictionary.

If different portions of the product have different external interfaces, incorporate an instance of this section within the detailed requirements for each such portion.

3.1 User Interfaces

State the software components for which a user interface is needed. Describe the logical characteristics of each user interface. The following are some characteristics you might include:

- GUI standards or product family style guides that are to be followed

- Screen layout or resolution constraints

- Standard buttons, functions, or navigation links that will appear on every screen (such as a help button)

- Shortcut keys

- Error message display standards

Document the user interface design details, such as specific dialog box layouts, in a separate user interface specification, not in the SRS.

3.2 Hardware Interfaces

Describe the characteristics of each interface between the software and hardware components of the system. This description might include the supported device types, the nature of the data and control interactions between the software and the hardware, and communication protocols to be used.

3.3 Software Interfaces

Describe the connections between this product and other external software components (identified by name and version), including databases, operating systems, tools, libraries, and integrated commercial components. Identify and describe the purpose of the data items or messages exchanged among the software components. Describe the services needed and the nature of the intercomponent communications. Identify data that will be shared across software components. If the data-sharing mechanism must be implemented in a specific way, such as a global data area in a multitasking operating system, specify this as an implementation constraint.

3.4 Communications Interfaces

Describe the requirements associated with any communication functions the product will use, including e-mail, Web browser, network communications standards or protocols, electronic forms, and so on. Define any pertinent message formatting. Specify communication security or encryption issues, data transfer rates, and synchronization mechanisms.

4. SYSTEM FEATURES

The template in Figure 9-1 shows the functional requirements organized by system features, the major services provided by the product. You might prefer to organize this section by use case, mode of operation, user class, object class, or functional hierarchy (IEEE 1998). You can also use hierarchical combinations of these elements. Select an organizational approach that makes it easy for readers to understand the intended product.

4.x System Feature X

State the name of the feature in just a few words, such as "4.1 Spell Check and Spelling Dictionary Management." You will repeat subsections 4.x.1 through 4.x.3 for each system feature.

4.x.1 Description and Priority

Provide a short description of the feature and indicate whether it is of high, medium, or low priority. Alternatively, you could include specific priority component ratings, such as benefit, penalty, cost, and risk, each rated on a relative scale of 1 (low) to 9 (high). (See Chapter 13.)

4.x.2 Stimulus/Response Sequences

List the sequences of input stimuli (user actions, signals from external devices, or other triggers) and system responses that define the behaviors for this feature. These sequences will correspond to the dialogue elements associated with use cases, as was discussed in Chapter 8.

4.x.3 Functional Requirements

Itemize the detailed functional requirements associated with this feature. These are the software capabilities that must be present for the user to carry out the services provided by the feature or to perform the task specified by a use case. Describe how the product should respond to anticipated error conditions or invalid input or actions. Uniquely identify each requirement, as described earlier in this chapter.

5. OTHER NONFUNCTIONAL REQUIREMENTS

Use this section to list any nonfunctional requirements other than external interface requirements and constraints.

5.1 Performance Requirements

State any product performance requirements for various usage scenarios, and explain their rationale to help the developers make suitable design choices. Specify the number of concurrent users or operations to be supported, response times, and the timing relationships for real-time systems. You could also specify capacity requirements here, such as memory and disk space requirements or the maximum number of rows stored in database tables. Quantify the performance requirements as specifically as possible. You might need to state performance requirements for individual functional requirements or features, rather than collecting them all in one section. For example, "95% of catalog database queries shall be completed within 2 seconds on a 450-MHz Pentium II PC running Microsoft Windows 2000 with at least 50% of the system resources free."

5.2 Safety Requirements

Specify those requirements that are concerned with possible loss, damage, or harm that could result from the use of the product. Define any safeguards or actions that must be taken, as well as potentially dangerous actions that must be prevented. Identify any safety certifications, policies, or regulations to which the product must conform. An example of a safety requirement is: "An operation shall be terminated within 1 second if the measured tank pressure exceeds 95 percent of the specified maximum pressure."

5.3 Security Requirements

Specify any requirements regarding security, integrity, or privacy issues that affect the use of the product and protection of the data used or created by the product. Define any user authentication or authorization requirements. Identify any security or privacy policies or certifications the product must satisfy. You might prefer to address these requirements through the quality attribute called integrity, which is described in Chapter 11. An example of a security requirement is: "Every user must change his initially assigned login password immediately after his first login. The initial password cannot be reused."

5.4 Software Quality Attributes

Specify any additional product quality characteristics that will be important to either customers or developers. (See Chapter 11.) These characteristics should be specific, quantitative, and verifiable when possible. At the least, indicate the relative preferences for various attributes, such as ease of use over ease of learning, or portability over efficiency.

5.5 Business Rules

List any operating principles about the product, such as which individuals or roles can perform which functions under specific circumstances. These are not functional requirements in themselves, but they might imply certain functional requirements to enforce the rules. An example of a business rule is: "Only users having supervisory job codes can issue cash refunds of $100.00 or more."

5.6 User Documentation

List the user documentation components that will be delivered along with the software, such as user manuals, online help, and tutorials. Identify any known user documentation delivery formats or standards.

6. OTHER REQUIREMENTS

Define any other requirements that are not covered elsewhere in the SRS, such as internationalization requirements or legal requirements. You could also add sections on operations, administration, and maintenance to cover requirements for product installation, configuration, startup and shutdown, recovery and fault tolerance, and logging and monitoring operations. Add any new sections to the template that are pertinent to your project. If you don't have to add any other requirements, omit this section.

APPENDIX A: GLOSSARY

Define all the terms necessary for a reader to properly interpret the SRS, including acronyms and abbreviations. You might wish to build a separate glossary that spans multiple projects for the entire organization and include only terms that are specific to a single project in each SRS.

APPENDIX B: ANALYSIS MODELS

This optional section includes, or refers to the existence and locations of, pertinent analysis models such as data flow diagrams, class diagrams, state-transition diagrams, or entity-relationship diagrams. (See Chapter 10.)

APPENDIX C: TO-BE-DETERMINED LIST

Compile a numbered list of the TBD (to be determined) references that remain in the SRS so that they can be tracked to closure.

GUIDELINES FOR WRITING REQUIREMENTS

There is no formulaic way to write excellent requirements; the best teacher is experience. Learning from the problems you have encountered in the past will teach you much. Many requirements documents can be improved by following effective technical-writing style guidelines and by employing user terminology rather than computer jargon (Kovitz 1999). Keep the following recommendations in mind as you document software requirements:

◆ Keep sentences and paragraphs short.

◆ Use the active voice.

◆ Write complete sentences that have proper grammar, spelling, and punctuation.

◆ Use terms consistently and as defined in the glossary.

◆ State requirements in a consistent fashion, such as "The system shall" or "The user shall," followed by an action verb, followed by the observable result. For example, "The stockroom manager subsystem shall display a list of all containers of the requested chemical that are currently in the chemical stockroom."

◆   To reduce ambiguity, avoid vague, subjective terms such as user-friendly, easy, simple, rapid, efficient, support, several, state-of-the-art, superior, acceptable, and robust. Find out what the customers really mean when they say "user-friendly" or "fast" or "robust" and state those expectations in the requirements.

◆   Avoid comparative words such as improve, maximize, minimize, and optimize. Quantify the degree of improvement that is needed, or state the maximum and minimum acceptable values of some parameter. Make sure you know what the customers mean when they say the new system should "process," "support," or "manage" something. Ambiguous language leads to unverifiable requirements.

Because requirements are written hierarchically, decompose an ambiguous top-level requirement into sufficient lower levels to clarify it and remove the ambiguity. Write requirements in enough detail so that if the requirement is satisfied, the customer's need will be met, but not with so much detail as to unnecessarily constrain the design. If you could satisfy a requirement in several ways and all are acceptable, the level of detail is probably adequate. However, if a designer who is reviewing the SRS is not clear on the customer's intent, you need to include additional detail to reduce the risk of reworking the product if a misunderstanding is subsequently revealed.

Requirements authors often struggle to find the right level of granularity. A helpful guideline is to write individually testable requirements. If you can think of a small number of related test cases to verify that a requirement was correctly implemented, it is probably at the right level of detail. If the tests you envision are numerous and diverse, perhaps several requirements were lumped together that need to be separated. Testable requirements have been suggested as a metric for software product size (Wilson 1995).

Write requirements at a consistent level of detail. I have seen requirement statements in the same SRS that varied widely in their scope. For example, "The keystroke combination Control-S shall be interpreted as File Save" and "The keystroke combination Control-P shall be interpreted as File Print" were split out as separate requirements. However, "The product shall respond to editing directives entered by voice" describes an entire subsystem, not a single functional requirement.

Avoid long narrative paragraphs that contain multiple requirements. Conjunctions such as "and" and "or" in a requirement suggest that several requirements have been combined. Never use "and/or" or "et cetera" in a requirement statement.

Avoid stating requirements redundantly in the SRS. Although including the same requirement in multiple places might make the document easier to read, it also makes it harder to maintain. The multiple instances of the requirement all have to be updated at the same time, lest an inconsistency creep in. Cross-reference related items in the SRS to help keep them synchronized when making changes. Storing individual requirements just once in a requirements management tool or database alleviates the redundancy problem.

Think about the most effective way to represent each requirement. Consider a set of requirements that fit the following pattern: "The Text Editor shall be able to parse <*format*> documents that define <*jurisdiction*> laws." There are three possible values for <*format*> and four possible values for <*jurisdiction*>, for a total of 12 similar requirements. When you review a list of requirements that are this similar, it is hard to spot one that is missing, such as "The Text Editor shall be able to parse untagged documents that define international laws." Represent requirements that follow a pattern like this in a table, as illustrated in Table 9-1, to make sure you haven't missed any. The higher-level requirement could be stated as "ED-13. The Text Editor shall be able to parse documents in several formats that define laws in various jurisdictions, as shown in Table <xx>."

TABLE 9-1   SAMPLE TABULAR FORMAT FOR LISTING
                 REQUIREMENT NUMBERS THAT FIT A PATTERN

Jurisdiction	Tagged Format	Untagged Format	ASCII Format
Federal	ED-13.1	ED-13.2	ED-13.3
State	ED-13.4	ED-13.5	ED-13.6
Territorial	ED-13.7	ED-13.8	ED-13.9
International	ED-13.10	ED-13.11	ED-13.12

SAMPLE REQUIREMENTS, BEFORE AND AFTER

Chapter 1 identified several characteristics of high-quality requirement statements: complete, correct, feasible, necessary, prioritized, unambiguous, and verifiable. Because requirements that don't exhibit these characteristics will cause confusion and rework down the road, you need to find and correct any problems as early as possible. Below are several requirements, adapted from real projects, that have some problems. Examine each statement in the context of these quality characteristics to see if you can spot the problems. I've presented my thoughts about what is wrong with each one and a suggested improvement. I have no doubt that another pass through my suggestions would make them even better, but your goal is not to write perfect requirements. It is to write requirements that are good enough to let your team proceed with design and construction at an acceptable level of risk.

Example 1

"The product shall provide status messages at regular intervals not less than every 60 seconds."

This requirement seems to be incomplete: What are the status messages and under what conditions are they "provided" to the user? How long do they remain visible? What part of "the product" are we talking about? The timing interval is confusing, too. Is the interval between status messages supposed to be at least 60 seconds, so showing a new message every year is okay? If the intent is to have no more than 60 seconds elapse between messages, would one millisecond be too short? How consistent does the message display interval have to be? The word "every" just muddles the issue. Because of these problems, the requirement is not verifiable.

Here is one way we could rewrite the requirement to address those shortcomings (making some guesses about what was intended, which we must confirm with the customer):

1. The Background Task Manager (BTM) shall display status messages in a designated area of the user interface.

1.1 The messages shall be updated every 60 (plus or minus 10) seconds after background task processing begins and shall remain visible continuously.

1.2   If background task processing is progressing normally, the BTM shall display the percentage of the background task processing that has been completed.

1.3   The BTM shall display a "Done" message when the background task is completed.

1.4   The BTM shall display an error message if the background task has stalled.

I split this into multiple requirements because each will require separate test cases and to make each one individually traceable. If several requirements are strung together in a paragraph, it is easy to overlook one during construction or testing. Notice that the revised requirement does not specify precisely how the status messages will be displayed. That's a design issue, and if you specify it here, it becomes a design constraint placed on the developer. Prematurely constrained design options frustrate the programmers and can result in a suboptimal product design.

Example 2

"The product shall switch between displaying and hiding nonprinting characters instantaneously."

Computers cannot do anything instantaneously, so this requirement isn't feasible. It is also incomplete because it does not state the cause of the state switch. Is the software making the change on its own under certain conditions, or does the user take some action to initiate the change? Also, what is the scope of the display change within the document: selected text, the entire document, or what? There is an ambiguity problem too. Are "nonprinting" characters hidden text, or are they attribute tags or control characters of some kind? Because of these problems, this requirement cannot be verified.

This might be a better way to write the requirement: "The user shall be able to toggle between displaying and hiding all HTML markup tags in the document being edited with the activation of a specific triggering mechanism." Now it's clear that the nonprinting characters are HTML markup tags. The modified requirement indicates that the user triggers the display change, but it doesn't constrain the design because it doesn't define the precise mechanism used. When the designer selects an appropriate triggering mechanism (such as a hot key, a menu command, or voice input), you can write specific tests to verify whether the toggle operates correctly.

Example 3

"The parser shall produce an HTML markup error report that allows quick resolution of errors when used by HTML novices."

The word "quick" is ambiguous. The lack of definition of what goes into the error report indicates incompleteness. I'm not sure how you would verify this requirement. Find someone who calls herself an HTML novice and see if she can resolve errors quickly enough using the report? It is also not clear whether the HTML novice's usage refers to the parser or the error report. And when is the report generated?

Let's try this instead:

1.   After the HTML Parser has completely parsed a file, it shall produce an error report that contains the line number and text of any HTML errors found in the parsed file and a description of each error found.

2.   If no parsing errors are found, the error report shall not be produced.

Now we know when the error report is generated and what goes in it, but we've left it up to the designer to decide what the report should look like. We've also specified an exception condition: if there aren't any errors, don't generate a report.

Example 4

"Charge numbers should be validated online against the master corporate charge number list, if possible."

I give up: What does "if possible" mean? If it's technically feasible? If the master charge number list can be accessed online? If you aren't sure whether a requested capability can be delivered, use TBD to indicate that the issue is unresolved. The requirement is incomplete because it doesn't specify what happens if the validation passes or fails. Avoid imprecise words such as "should." The customer either needs this functionality or he doesn't. Some requirements specifications use subtle distinctions among keywords such as *shall, should,* and *may* as a way to indicate importance. I prefer to stick with *shall* or *will* as a clear statement of the requirement's intent and to specify the priorities explicitly.

Here is an improved version of this requirement:

"The system shall validate the charge number entered against the on-line master corporate charge number list. If the charge number is not found on the list, the system shall display an error message and the order shall not be accepted."

A second related requirement might document the exception condition of the master corporate charge number list not being available at the time the validation was attempted.

Example 5

"The product shall not offer search and replace options that could have disastrous results."

The notion of "disastrous results" is certainly subject to interpretation. Making an unintended global change while editing a document could be disastrous if the user does not detect the error or has no way to correct it. You should also be judicious in the use of inverse requirements, which describe things the system will not do. The underlying concern seems to pertain to protecting the file contents from inadvertent damage. Perhaps the real requirements are for a multilevel undo capability and confirmation of global changes or other actions that might result in data loss.

THE DATA DICTIONARY

Long ago, I worked on a project in which, on several occasions, the three programmers inadvertently used different variable names, lengths, and validations for the same data item. This caused confusion about what the real data definition was, truncation of data when it was stored in a variable that was too small, and maintenance headaches. We suffered from the lack of a data dictionary—a shared repository that defines the meaning, type, data size and format, units of measurement, precision, and allowed range or list of values for all data elements and structures used in the application.

The data dictionary is the glue that holds the various requirements documents and analysis models together. Integration problems are reduced if all developers comply with the contents of a data dictionary. To avoid redundancy and inconsistencies, establish a separate data dictionary for your project, rather than defining each data item in every requirement in which it appears. Maintain the data dictionary separately from the SRS, in a location that any stakeholder can access at any stage of the product's development or maintenance.

Items in the data dictionary are represented using a simple notation (Robertson and Robertson 1994). The item is shown on the left side of an equal sign, with its definition on the right. This notation defines primitive data elements, the composition of multiple data elements into structures, iteration (repeats) of a data item, enumerated values for a data item, and optional data items. The examples shown below are from (of course!) the Chemical Tracking System.

Primitive data elements   A primitive data element is one for which no decomposition or subdivision is possible or sensible. It can be assigned a scalar value. The primitive's definition should identify its data type, size, range of allowed values, and so on. Primitives typically are defined with a comment, which is any text delimited by asterisks:

> *Request ID = * 6-digit system-generated sequential integer, beginning with 1, that uniquely identifies each request **

Composition   A data structure or record contains multiple data items. If an element in the data structure is optional, enclose it in parentheses:

> *Requested Chemical   = Chemical ID*
> *+ Quantity*
> *+ Quantity Units*
> *+ (Vendor Name)*

This structure identifies all the information associated with a request for a specific chemical. The Vendor Name is optional because the person placing the request might not care from which vendor the chemical is ordered. Each data item that appears in a structure must itself appear in the data dictionary. Structures can incorporate other structures.

Iteration   If multiple instances of an item can appear in a data structure, enclose that item in curly braces. If you know the allowed number of possible repeats, show that number in the form *minimum:maximum* in front of the opening brace:

> *Request   = Request ID*
> *+ Charge Number*
> *+ 1:10{Requested Chemical}*

This example shows that a chemical request must contain at least one chemical, but not more than ten chemicals. Each request also has a single request ID and one charge number whose format would be defined elsewhere in the data dictionary.

Selection   If a primitive data element can take on a limited number of discrete values, enumerate those values in a list:

> *Quantity Units = ["grams" | "kilograms" | "each"]*
> ** 9-character text string indicating the units associated*
> *with the quantity of chemical requested **

This entry shows that there are just three allowed values for the text string Quantity Units. The comment provides the informal definition of the data element.

The time you invest in creating a data dictionary and a glossary will be more than repaid by the time gained in avoiding the mistakes that happen when project participants do not share the same understanding of critical pieces of information. If you keep the glossary and data dictionary current, they will remain valuable tools throughout the system's maintenance life and during the development of related or follow-on systems.

 Next Steps

- ◆ Take a page of functional requirements from your project's SRS. Examine each statement to see how well it complies with the characteristics of excellent requirements. Rewrite any requirements that don't measure up.

- ◆ If your organization doesn't already have a standard format for documenting requirements, convene a small working group to adopt a standard SRS template. Begin with the template in Figure 9-1 and adapt it to best meet the needs of your organization's projects and products. Agree on a convention for labeling individual requirements.

◆   Convene a group of three to seven project stakeholders to formally review the SRS for your project. Make sure each requirement statement is clear, feasible, verifiable, unambiguous, and so forth. Look for any conflicts between different requirements in the specification, for missing requirements, and for missing sections of the SRS. Follow through to make sure the defects you find are corrected in the SRS and in any downstream work products based on those requirements.

10

A Picture Is Worth 1024 Words

The Chemical Tracking System project team was holding its first SRS review. The participants were Dave (project manager), Lori (requirements analyst), Helen (lead programmer), Ramesh (test lead), Tim (product champion for the chemists), and Roxanne (product champion for the chemical stockroom). Tim began by saying, "I read the whole SRS. Most of the requirements seemed okay to me, but I had a hard time following some parts of it. I wasn't sure if we identified all of the steps in the chemical request process."

Ramesh added, "It was hard for me to think of all the test cases I'll need to cover the status changes for a request as it goes through the system. I found a bunch of requirements sprinkled throughout the SRS about the status changes, but I couldn't tell if any are missing or inconsistent."

Roxanne had a similar problem. "I got confused when I read about the way I would actually request a chemical," she said. "The individual requirements made sense, but I had trouble visualizing the sequence of steps I would go through."

After the reviewers raised several other concerns, Lori concluded, "It looks like this SRS doesn't tell us everything we need to know to understand the system and make sure we haven't missed a requirement or made any mistakes. I'll draw some pictures to help us visualize the requirements and see if that clarifies these problem areas. Thanks for the feedback."

According to requirements authority Alan Davis, no single view of the requirements provides a complete understanding of them (Davis 1995). You need a combination of textual and graphical requirements representations to paint a full picture of the intended system and to help you detect inconsistencies, ambiguities, errors, and omissions. These graphical representations, or analysis models, improve your understanding of the requirements. Diagrams communicate certain types of information among the project participants more efficiently than text can, and they help bridge language and vocabulary barriers among different team members. This chapter provides a brief overview of several requirements modeling techniques, all of which I have found helpful in understanding the user's business problems and software needs.

MODELING THE REQUIREMENTS

When I began drawing analysis models many years ago, I hoped to find one technique that could pull everything together into a holistic depiction of the requirements. Eventually I concluded that there is no such all-encompassing diagram. An early goal of structured systems analysis was to replace entirely the classical functional specification with graphical diagrams and representations more formal than narrative text (DeMarco 1979). However, experience has shown that analysis models should augment, rather than replace, a natural language requirements specification (Davis 1995).

Models that present graphical views of the requirements include data flow diagrams (DFD), entity-relationship diagrams (ERD), state-transition diagrams (STD), dialog maps, and class diagrams. Less conventional modeling approaches can also be valuable. One project team successfully used a project-scheduling tool to diagram the timing requirements for an embedded software product, working at the millisecond time scale, rather than in days and weeks. These models are useful for elaborating and exploring the requirements, as well as for designing software solutions. Used as requirements analysis tools, these diagrams let you model the problem domain or create conceptual representations of the new system. The diagrams help analysts and customers arrive at a shared, comprehensive understanding of the requirements, and they reveal requirement errors.

Whether you are using the models for requirements analysis or for design depends on both the timing and the intent of the modeling. During requirements development, you create models to make sure you understand the requirements. The models depict the logical aspects of the problem domain's data components, transactions and transformations, real-world objects, and allowed states. You can either draw the models from the textual requirements to represent them from different perspectives, or you can derive the functional requirements from models you drew based on user input. During design, you draw physical, not logical, models to represent specifically how you intend to implement the system: the actual database you plan to create, the object classes you will instantiate, and the code modules you will develop.

The analysis modeling techniques described in this chapter are supported by a variety of commercial computer-aided software engineering, or CASE, tools. CASE tools provide several benefits over ordinary drawing tools. First, they make it easy for you to improve the diagrams you draw through iteration. You will never get a model right the first time you draw it, so iteration is a key to success in system modeling (Wiegers 1996a). Second, CASE tools "know" the rules for each modeling method they support. They can validate the models and identify syntax or logic errors that people who review the diagrams might not see. The tools also link multiple system diagrams together and to their shared data definitions in a data dictionary. CASE tools can help you keep the models consistent with each other and with the functional requirements in the SRS.

Analysis models facilitate communication among the project participants about certain aspects of the system. You probably won't need a complete set of models for the entire system. Focus your modeling on the most complex and most critical portions of the system, and on those portions most subject to ambiguity or uncertainty. The notations presented here provide a common language for project participants to use, but you can also use less formal diagrams to augment your verbal and written project communications.

FROM VOICE OF THE CUSTOMER TO ANALYSIS MODELS

By listening carefully to how customers present their requirements, the analyst can pick out keywords that translate into specific analysis model elements. Table 10-1 suggests possible mappings of significant nouns and verbs from the customer's input into specific model components, which are described later in this chapter. As you craft customer input into written requirements and models, you should be able to trace every model component back to a requirement.

TABLE 10-1 **RELATING THE CUSTOMER'S VOICE TO ANALYSIS MODEL COMPONENTS**

Type of Word	Examples	Analysis Model Components
Noun	• People, organizations, software systems, data items, or objects that exist	• Terminators or data stores (DFD) • Entities or their attributes (ERD) • Classes or their attributes (class diagram)
Verb	• Actions, things a user can do, or events that can take place	• Processes (DFD) • Relationships (ERD) • Transitions (STD) • Class operations (class diagram)

Throughout this book, I've used the Chemical Tracking System as a case study. Building on this example, consider the following paragraph of user needs supplied by the product champion who represented the Chemist user class. Significant unique nouns are highlighted in **bold** and verbs are in *italics*; look for these keywords in the analysis models shown in this chapter. For the sake of illustration, some of the models show information that goes beyond that contained in this one paragraph, while other models depict just part of the information presented here.

"A **chemist** or a member of the **chemical stockroom staff** can *place* a **request** for one or more **chemicals**. The request can be *fulfilled* either by *delivering* a **container** of the chemical that is already in the **chemical stockroom's inventory** or by *placing* an **order** for a new container of the chemical with an outside **vendor**. The **person** placing the request must be able to *search* **vendor catalogs** online for specific chemicals while *preparing* his or her request. The system needs to *track* the **status** of every chemical request from the time it is prepared until it is either *fulfilled* or *canceled*. It also needs to *keep track* of the **history** of every chemical container from the time it *arrives* at the **company** until it is fully consumed or disposed of."

Data Flow Diagram

The *data flow diagram* is the basic tool of structured systems analysis (DeMarco 1979; Robertson and Robertson 1994). A DFD identifies the transformational processes of a system, the collections (stores) of data or material the system manipulates, and the flows of data or material between processes, stores, and the outside world. Data flow modeling takes a hierarchical decomposition approach to systems analysis, which works well for transaction-processing systems and other function-intensive applications. By adding control flow elements, the DFD technique has been extended to permit modeling of real-time systems.

The DFD is a way to represent the steps involved in a current business process or the operations of a proposed new system. Data flow diagrams can represent systems over a wide range of abstraction. High-level DFDs provide a holistic, bird's-eye view of the data and processing components in a multistep activity, which complements the precise, detailed view embodied in the SRS. A DFD illustrates how the functional requirements in the SRS combine to let the user perform specific tasks, such as requesting a chemical. I have often sketched DFDs when discussing business processes with users. The immediate feedback I received on my diagrams helped me to refine my understanding of the task flow we were exploring.

The context diagram that was illustrated in Figure 6-2 is the highest level of abstraction of the DFD. The context diagram represents the entire system as a single, black-box process, depicted as a circle (a *bubble*). It also shows the external entities or *terminators* that connect to the system and the data or material *flows* between the system and the terminators. Flows between elements in the context diagram often represent complex data structures, which are defined in the data dictionary.

You can elaborate the context diagram into the level 0 DFD, which partitions the system into its major components or processes. Figure 10-1 shows the level 0 DFD for the Chemical Tracking System (somewhat simplified). The single process bubble that represented the entire Chemical Tracking System on the context diagram has been subdivided into seven major processes (the bubbles). As with the context diagram, the terminators are shown in rectangles. All data flows from the context diagram also appear on the level 0 DFD. In addition, the level 0 diagram contains several *data stores*, depicted as a pair of parallel horizontal lines, which are internal to the system and therefore do not appear on the context diagram. A flow from a bubble to a store indicates that data is being placed into the store, a flow out of the store indicates a read operation, and a bidirectional arrow between a store and a bubble indicates an update operation.

Each process that appears as a separate bubble on the level 0 diagram can be further expanded into a separate DFD to reveal progressively more detail about the system. This progressive refinement is continued until the lowest-level diagrams depict only primitive process operations that can be clearly represented in narrative text, pseudocode, a flowchart, or program code. The functional requirements in the SRS will define precisely what happens within each primitive process. Every level of the DFD must be balanced and consistent with the level above it so that all of the input and output flows on the child diagram match up with flows on its parent. Complex data flows on the higher-level diagrams can be split into their constituent elements, as defined in the data dictionary, on the lower-level DFDs.

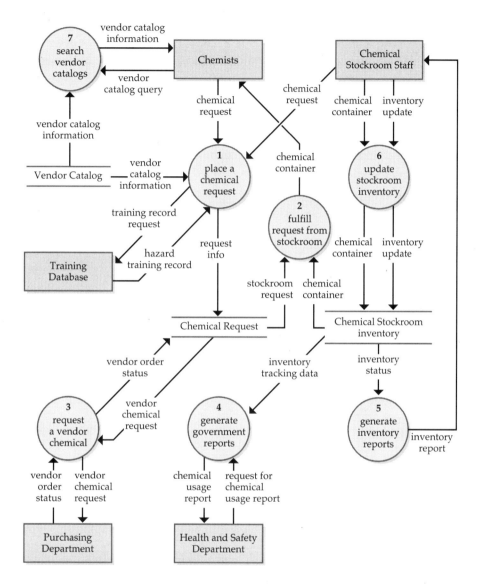

FIGURE 10-1   *Level 0 data flow diagram for the Chemical Tracking System.*

At first glance, Figure 10-1 might seem confusing. However, if you examine the immediate environment of any one process, you will see the data items that it consumes and produces and their sources and destinations. The flows connected to a store lead to the processes that either create or consume the store's contents. To see exactly how a process uses the data items, you will need to either draw a more detailed child DFD or refer to the functional requirements for that part of the system.

Following are several conventions for drawing data flow diagrams. Not everyone adheres to these conventions, but I find them helpful. Using the models to enhance communication among the project participants is more important than dogmatic conformance to these principles.

- Place the data stores only on the level 0 DFD and lower levels, not on the context diagram.

- Processes communicate through data stores, not by direct flows from one process to another. Similarly, data cannot flow directly from one store to another; it must pass through a process bubble.

- Do not attempt to imply anything about the processing sequence using the DFD.

- Name the processes as a concise action: verb plus object. Use names throughout the DFD that are meaningful to the customers and pertinent to the business or problem domain.

- Number the processes uniquely and hierarchically. On the level 0 diagram, number each process with an integer. If you create a child DFD for process 3, number the processes in that child diagram 3.1, 3.2, and so on.

- Do not show more than seven to ten processes on a single diagram or it becomes difficult to draw, change, and understand.

- Do not have bubbles with flows that are only coming in or only going out. The processing that a DFD bubble represents normally requires both input and output.

Entity-Relationship Diagram

Just as the data flow diagram illustrates the processes that take place in a system, the *entity-relationship diagram* depicts the system's data relationships (Wieringa 1996). If your ERD represents logical groups of information from the problem domain and their connections, you're using the ERD as a requirements analysis tool. An analysis ERD helps you understand and communicate the data components of the business or system, without implying that the product will necessarily include a database. In contrast, when you create an ERD during system design, you're generally defining the physical structure of the system's database.

Entities are physical items (including people) or aggregations of data items that are important to the business you're analyzing or to the system you intend to build (Robertson and Robertson 1994). Entities are named as singular nouns and are shown in rectangles. Figure 10-2 illustrates a portion of the entity-relationship diagram for the Chemical Tracking System. Notice that the entities named Chemical Request, Vendor Catalog, and Chemical Stockroom Inventory appeared as data stores in the data flow diagram in Figure 10-1. Other entities represent actors who interact with the system (Requester), physical items that are part of the business operations (Chemical Container), and blocks of data that were not shown on the level 0 data flow diagram but would appear on a lower level DFD (Container History, Chemical).

Each entity is described by several *attributes*; individual instances of an entity will have different attribute values. For example, the attributes for each chemical include a unique chemical identifier, its formal chemical name, and a graphical representation of its chemical structure. The data dictionary contains the detailed definitions of those attributes, which guarantees that entities in the ERD and their corresponding data stores from the DFD are defined identically.

The diamonds in the ERD represent *relationships*, which identify the logical and numeric linkages between pairs of entities. Relationships are named in a way that describes the nature of the connections. For example, the relationship between the Requester and the Chemical Request is called "placing," because a Requester places a Chemical Request, or, alternatively, a Chemical Request is placed by a Requester.

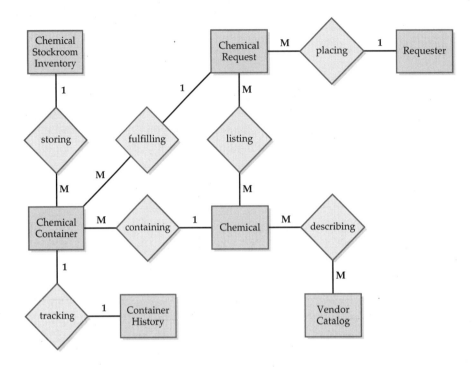

FIGURE 10-2 *Entity-relationship diagram for the Chemical Tracking System.*

The cardinality, or multiplicity, of each relationship is shown with a number or letter on the lines that connect entities and relationships. Different ERD notations use different conventions to represent cardinality; this example illustrates one common approach. Because each Requester can place multiple requests, there is a one-to-many relationship between Requester and Chemical Request. This cardinality is shown with a "1" on the line connecting Requester and the "placing" relationship, and an "M" (for many) on the line connecting Chemical Request and the "placing" relationship. Other possible cardinalities are as follows:

◆ One-to-one (every Chemical Container is tracked by a single Container History)

◆ Many-to-many (every Vendor Catalog describes many Chemicals, and some Chemicals are described in multiple Vendor Catalogs)

If you know that a more precise cardinality exists than simply "many," you can show the specific number or range of numbers instead of the generic "M."

Drawing an ERD during requirements analysis is an excellent way to organize what you've learned about the significant data elements of the business or the new system. I used this technique when I was the information technology representative on a business process reengineering team. After the team had proposed a new process flow, I asked the team member who represented the role responsible for each new process step what data items were needed to perform the step. I also asked which data items created by the step should be stored for subsequent use.

After interviewing all of the process step owners, we aligned the data needed and the data produced for all steps. This correlation identified required data items that weren't generated anywhere in the system, and it also revealed data that was being stored but not used. Finally, I documented these data relationships with an ERD and a data dictionary, which provided a conceptual picture of the data components for the new business process. These analysis tools improved our understanding of the problem, which was valuable even if we never built a software system to support the new business process.

STATE-TRANSITION DIAGRAM

Real-time systems and process control applications can exist in one of a limited number of states at any given time. A change in state can take place only when well-defined criteria are satisfied, such as receiving a specific input stimulus under certain conditions. Such systems are examples of finite-state machines. In addition, many information systems deal with business objects (such as sales orders, invoices, or inventory items) that pass through complex life cycles; these life cycles also can be treated as finite-state machines. Most software systems require some kind of state modeling or analysis, just as most involve transformational processes, data entities, and business objects.

Describing a complex finite-state machine in natural language creates a high probability of overlooking a permitted state change or including a disallowed change. Depending on how the SRS is organized, requirements that pertain to the state machine's behavior might appear in multiple locations throughout the SRS. This makes it difficult to reach an overall understanding of the system's behavior.

The *state-transition diagram* provides a concise, complete, and unambiguous representation of a finite-state machine (Davis 1993). The STD contains three types of elements:

◆   Possible system *states*, shown as rectangles.

◆   Allowed state changes or *transitions*, shown as arrows connecting pairs of rectangles.

◆   Conditions that cause each transition to take place, shown as text labels on each transition arrow. The labels often indicate both the conditions and the corresponding system output.

The STD does not show the processing that the system performs, only the possible state changes that are the outcome of that processing. You can use an STD to model a portion of a software system that can only exist in specific states, the behavior of a real-world entity such as an automobile cruise control system, or the status of individual items that the system manipulates.

An STD helps developers understand the intended behavior of the system. It is a good way to check whether all the required states and transitions have been correctly and completely described in the written functional requirements. Testers can derive test cases from the STD that cover all allowed transition paths. Customers can read an STD with just a little coaching about the notation.

Recall that a primary function of the Chemical Tracking System was to permit actors called Requesters to place requests for chemicals, which can be fulfilled either from the inventory in the chemical stockroom or by placing orders to outside vendors. Each request will pass through a series of possible states between the time it is created and the time it is either fulfilled or canceled. Thus, we can treat the life cycle of a chemical request as a finite-state machine and model it as shown in Figure 10-3. This STD shows that an individual request can take on one of seven possible states:

◆   *In Preparation*—the Requester is creating a new request, having entered that function from some other part of the system.

◆   *Postponed*—the Requester saved his or her work for future completion without submitting the request to the system or canceling the request operation.

◆   *Accepted*—the user submitted a completed chemical request, and the system determined it was in good order and accepted it for processing.

◆ *Placed*—the request must be satisfied by an outside vendor and a buyer has placed an order with the vendor.

◆ *Fulfilled*—the request has been satisfied, either by delivering a chemical container from the chemical stockroom to the Requester or by receipt of a chemical from a vendor.

◆ *Back-ordered*—the vendor did not have the chemical available and he notified the buyer that it is back-ordered for future delivery.

◆ *Canceled*—the Requester canceled an accepted request before it was fulfilled, or the buyer canceled a vendor order before it was fulfilled or while it was back-ordered.

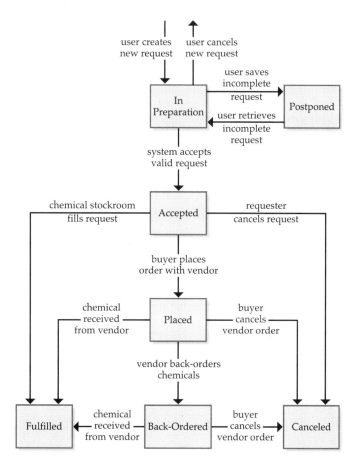

FIGURE 10-3   *State-transition diagram for a chemical request in the Chemical Tracking System.*

When the Chemical Tracking System user representatives reviewed the initial chemical request STD, they identified one state that was not needed, another essential state that the analyst hadn't documented, and two incorrect transitions. No one had found those errors when they reviewed the functional requirements that addressed the request states.

The STD does not provide enough detail for a developer to know what software to build. Therefore, the SRS must include the functional requirements associated with processing a chemical request and its possible state changes. However, the STD provides a compact visual representation of the possible request states and how they are permitted to change.

The STD for a real-time system is similar to that shown in Figure 10-3, except that a special state called Idle is included, to which the system returns whenever it is not doing other processing. In contrast, the STD for an object that passes through a defined life cycle, such as a chemical request, will have one or more termination states; these are the Fulfilled and Canceled states in Figure 10-3.

DIALOG MAP

The user interface in many applications can be regarded as a finite-state machine. Only one dialog element (such as a menu, workspace, line prompt or dialog box) is available at any given time for user input. The user can navigate to a limited number of other dialog elements based on the action he takes at the active input location. The number of possible navigation pathways can be very large in a complex graphical user interface, but the number is finite and the options usually are known. Therefore, many user interfaces can be modeled with a form of state-transition diagram called a *dialog map* (Wiegers 1996a).

The dialog map represents a user interface architecture at a high level of abstraction. It shows the dialog elements in the system and the navigation links among them, but it does not reveal the detailed screen designs. A dialog map allows you to explore hypothetical user interface concepts based on your understanding of the requirements. Users and developers can study a dialog map to reach a common vision of how the user might interact with the system to perform a task. Dialog maps are also useful for modeling the visual architecture of a Web site, where they are sometimes called "site maps."

Any navigation links that you build into the Web site appear as transitions on the dialog map. Dialog maps are related to system storyboards, which also include a short description of each screen's purpose.

Dialog maps capture the essence of the user–system interactions and task flow without getting you bogged down too soon in specifying the details of screen layouts and data elements. Users can trace through a dialog map to find missing, incorrect, or superfluous transitions, and hence missing, incorrect, or superfluous requirements. You can use the dialog map developed during requirements analysis as a guide during detailed user interface design, ultimately developing an implementation dialog map that documents the actual user interface architecture of the product.

Just as in ordinary state-transition diagrams, the dialog map shows each dialog element as a state (rectangle) and each allowed navigation option as a transition (arrow). The condition that triggers a user interface navigation is shown as a text label on the transition arrow. There are several types of trigger conditions:

- A user action, such as pressing a function key or clicking on a hyperlink or dialog box button

- A data value, such as an invalid user input that triggers an error message display

- A system condition, such as detecting that a printer is out of paper

- Some combination of these, such as typing a menu option number and pressing the Enter key

To simplify the dialog map, you can omit global functions such as pressing the F1 key to bring up a help display. The SRS section on user interfaces should specify that this functionality will be available, but showing it on the dialog map adds little value to the model as a communication tool. Similarly, when modeling a web site, you need not include standard navigation links that will appear on every page in the site. You can also omit the transitions that reverse the flow of a Web page navigation sequence because the web browser's Back button handles that navigation.

A dialog map is an excellent way to represent the interactions between an actor and the system that are described in a use case. The dialog map can depict alternative courses as branches off the normal course flow. I found that sketching dialog map fragments on a whiteboard was helpful during use-case elicitation workshops in which a team explored the sequence of actor actions and system responses that would lead to task completion.

Chapter 8 presented a use case for the Chemical Tracking System called Request a Chemical. The normal course for this use case involved requesting a chemical to be supplied by placing an order to an outside vendor. An alternative course was to supply a container of the chemical from the chemical stockroom's inventory. The user placing the request wanted the option to view the history of the available stockroom containers of that chemical before selecting one. Figure 10-4 shows a dialog map for this use case.

This diagram might look complicated at first, but if you trace through it one line and box at a time, it's not difficult to understand. Remember, during requirements analysis, the dialog map represents possible interactions between the user and the system at a conceptual level; the actual implementation might be different. The user initiates this use case by selecting an option to "request a chemical" from a menu in the Chemical Tracking System. The main workspace for this use case is a list of the chemicals in this request, on a display called the Current Request List. The arrows leaving that box on the dialog map show all the navigation options—and hence functionality—available to the user in that context:

- Cancel the entire request.

- Submit the request if it contains at least one chemical.

- Add a new chemical to the request list.

- Delete a chemical from the list.

Note that the last operation, deleting a chemical, doesn't involve another dialog element; it simply refreshes the current request list display after the user makes the change.

As you trace through this dialog map, you will see elements that reflect the rest of the Request a Chemical use case:

- One flow path for requesting a chemical from a vendor

- Another path for fulfillment from the chemical stockroom

- An optional path to view the history of a specific chemical stockroom container

- An error message display to handle entry of an invalid chemical identifier

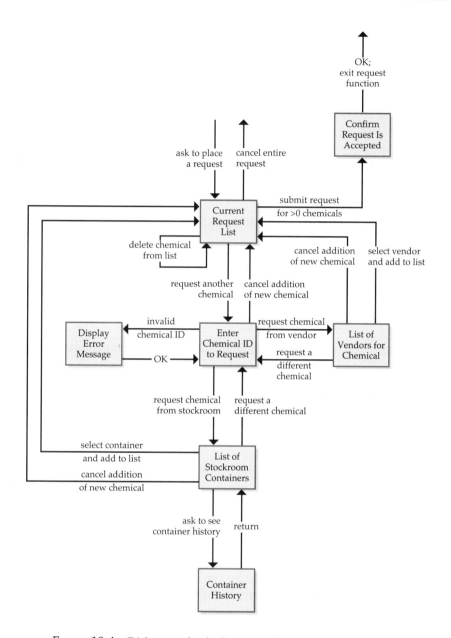

FIGURE 10-4   *Dialog map for the Request a Chemical use case from the Chemical Tracking System.*

Some of the transitions on the dialog map allow the user to back out of operations. The dialog map is a good way to see whether any such usability requirements have been overlooked, as when a Back button is missing from a wizard and the user is forced to complete an unwanted action.

When a user reviews this dialog map, she might spot a missing requirement. For example, a cautious user might think it's a good idea to confirm the operation that leads to canceling an entire request, to prevent inadvertently losing data. Adding this new function costs very little at the analysis stage but can be expensive to add in a delivered product. Because the dialog map represents just the conceptual view of the possible elements involved in the interaction between the user and the system, don't try to pin down all of the user interface design details at the requirements stage. Instead, use these models to make sure the project stakeholders share a common understanding of the system's intended functionality.

CLASS DIAGRAMS

Object-oriented software development has superceded structured analysis and design on many projects, spawning the domains of object-oriented analysis, design, and programming. *Objects* typically correspond to real-world items in the business or problem domain. Objects represent individual instances derived from a generic template called a *class*. Class descriptions encompass attributes (data) and the operations that can be performed on the attributes. A *class diagram* is a graphical way to depict the classes that you identify during object-oriented analysis and the relationships among them.

Products developed using object-oriented methods do not demand unique requirements development approaches. This is because requirements development focuses on what the users need to do with the system and the functionality it must contain, not with how it will be constructed. Users don't care how you build the system and they don't care about objects or classes. However, if you know that you're going to build the system using object-oriented techniques, it can be helpful to begin identifying classes and their attributes and behaviors during requirements analysis. This facilitates the transition from requirements development to design, as you decide how the problem-domain objects will map into the system's objects and further detail each class's attributes and operations.

Many different object-oriented methods and notations have been advanced over the years. Recently, several of them have been subsumed into the Unified Modeling Language (UML) (Booch, Rumbaugh, and Jacobson 1999). At the level of abstraction that is appropriate for requirements analysis, you can use the UML notation to draw class diagrams, as illustrated in Figure 10-5, for a portion of (you guessed it) the Chemical Tracking System. You can easily elaborate these conceptual class diagrams, which are free from implementation specifics, into more detailed class diagrams for object-oriented design and implementation. Interactions among the classes and the messages they exchange can be shown using *sequence diagrams* and *collaboration diagrams*, which are not addressed further in this book. (See Booch, Rumbaugh, and Jacobson 1999.)

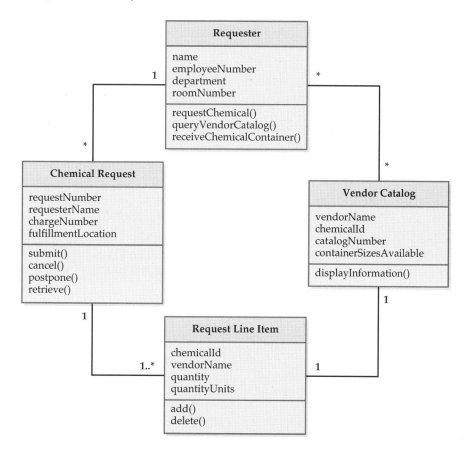

FIGURE 10-5   *Class diagram for part of the Chemical Tracking System.*

Figure 10-5 shows four classes, each in a large box: Requester, Vendor Catalog, Chemical Request, and Request Line Item. There are some similarities between the information in this class diagram and that shown in the other analysis models. The Requester appeared in the entity-relationship diagram in Figure 10-2, where it represented an actor role that could be played by a member of either the Chemist or Chemical Stockroom Staff user classes. The data flow diagram in Figure 10-1 also showed that both of these user classes can place requests for chemicals. Do not confuse a user class with an object class; despite the similarity in names, there is no intentional connection.

The attributes associated with the Requester class are shown in the middle portion of its class box: name, employeeNumber, department, and roomNumber (the capitalization is a UML convention). Those are the data items associated with each object that is a member of the Requester class. Similar attributes will appear in the definitions of the stores on a data flow diagram.

The operations that an object in the Requester class can perform are shown in the bottom portion of the class box and are followed by empty parentheses. In a class diagram that represents a design, these operations will correspond to the class's functions or methods, and the function arguments can be shown in the parentheses. The analysis class model simply has to show that a Requester can request chemicals, query vendor catalogs, and receive chemical containers. The operations shown in the class diagram correspond to the processes that appear in bubbles on low-level data flow diagrams.

The lines that connect the class boxes in Figure 10-5 represent associations between the classes. The numbers on the lines show the multiplicity of the association, much as the numbers on lines in the entity-relationship diagram show the multiplicity relationships between entities. In Figure 10-5, an asterisk indicates a one-to-many association between a Requester and a Chemical Request: one requester can place many requests, but each request belongs to just one requester.

A FINAL REMINDER

Each of the modeling techniques described in this chapter has its advantages and its limitations. Keep in mind that you create analysis models to provide a level of requirements understanding and communication that goes beyond what a textual SRS or any other single representation can provide. Avoid getting caught up in the dogmatic mindsets and religious wars that sometimes take place in the world of software development methods and models.

 Next Steps

◆   Practice using the modeling techniques described in this chapter by documenting the design of some completed software.

◆   Identify a portion of your SRS that has proven difficult for readers to understand or in which defects have been found. Choose an analysis model described in this chapter that is appropriate for representing that portion of the requirements. Draw the model and assess whether it would have been helpful had you created it earlier during requirements development.

◆   The next time you need to document some requirements, select a modeling technique that complements the textual description. Sketch the model on paper once or twice to make sure you're on the right track, and then use a commercial CASE tool that supports the model notation you are using. Gradually integrate iterative modeling of portions of the requirements into your standard requirements development process.

11

Software
Quality Attributes

Many years ago, I was involved with a project that replaced several existing mainframe applications with a new one. Based on user requests, the development team designed a window-based user interface and defined new data files that contained twice as much data as the old files held. Although the new system satisfied its technical specifications, it did not achieve the desired level of customer acceptance. Users complained about the sluggish performance of the user interface and the disk space the new data files consumed.

The users had some unstated expectations about the new product's characteristics that were not realistic given the functional requirements they had stated. Unfortunately, the developers and users hadn't explicitly discussed the possible performance implications of the new technical approaches, resulting in an expectation gap. There is more to software success than just delivering the functionality the customers request.

Nonfunctional Requirements

Users focus on specifying their functional, or behavioral, requirements—the things the software will let them do. In addition, though, users often have implicit expectations about *how well* the product will work. These characteristics include how easy the product is to use, how quickly it executes, how reliable it is, and how well it behaves when unexpected situations arise. Such characteristics, known as software quality attributes, or quality factors, are part of the system's nonfunctional (also called nonbehavioral) requirements.

Quality attributes are difficult to define, yet often they make the difference between a product that merely does what it is supposed to and one that delights its customers. As Robert Charette (1990) pointed out, "In real systems, meeting the nonfunctional requirements often is more important than meeting the functional requirements in the determination of a system's perceived success or failure." Excellent software products reflect an optimum balance of these competing quality characteristics. If you don't explore the customers' quality expectations during requirements elicitation, you're simply lucky if the product satisfies them. Disappointed users and frustrated developers are the more likely outcome.

Customers don't generally volunteer their nonfunctional expectations, although the information they provide during elicitation can supply some clues about important quality characteristics. The trick is to pin down just what the users have in mind when they say the software must be "robust," "reliable," or "efficient." Quality, in its many dimensions, must be defined both by the customers and by those who will build, test, and maintain the software. Questions that explore the user's implicit expectations can lead to quality goal statements and design criteria that help the developers create a fully satisfactory product.

Quality Attributes

Several dozen product characteristics can be called quality attributes, although most projects need to carefully consider only a handful of them. If developers know which of these characteristics are most crucial to project success, they can select software engineering approaches to achieve the specified quality goals (Glass 1992; DeGrace and Stahl 1993). Quality attributes have been classified according to various schemes (Boehm 1976; DeGrace and Stahl 1993). One way to classify attributes distinguishes those characteristics that are discernible at run time from those that are not (Bass, Clements, and Kazman 1998). Another approach is to distinguish the visible characteristics that are primarily important to the users from under-the-hood characteristics that are primarily significant to developers and maintainers. The attributes that are of most significance to developers indirectly contribute to customer satisfaction by making the product easier to change, correct, verify, and move to new platforms.

Table 11-1 identifies several quality attributes in both categories that every project should consider; there are many others (Charette 1990). Some attributes are critical to embedded systems (efficiency and reliability), while others might be more pertinent to mainframe applications (availability and maintainability) or to desktop systems (interoperability and usability). In an ideal universe, every system would exhibit the maximum possible value for all of its attributes. The system would be available at all times, would never fail, would supply instantaneous results, and would be intuitively obvious to use. Because nirvana is unattainable, you have to learn which subset of the attributes from Table 11-1 is most important to your project's success. Then define the user and developer goals in terms of these essential attributes so that the product designers can make appropriate choices.

TABLE 11-1   **SOFTWARE QUALITY ATTRIBUTES**

Important Primarily to Users	Important Primarily to Developers
Availability	Maintainability
Efficiency	Portability
Flexibility	Reusability
Integrity	Testability
Interoperability	
Reliability	
Robustness	
Usability	

Different parts of the product can have different combinations of desired quality characteristics. Efficiency might be critical for certain components, while usability is paramount for others. Differentiate quality characteristics that apply to the entire product from those that are specific to certain components, certain user classes, or particular usage situations. Document any global attribute requirements in section 5.4 of the SRS template presented in Chapter 9, and associate specific goals with the features, use cases, or functional requirements listed in section 4 of the SRS.

Defining Quality Attributes

You must specify quality attributes in terms of how users expect the system to behave. Quantitatively specifying the important attributes provides a clear understanding of user expectations, which will help designers devise the most appropriate solutions (Gilb 1988). However, most users won't know how to answer questions such as "How important is interoperability to you?" or "How reliable does the software have to be?" On one project, the analysts developed several prompting questions based on each attribute that they thought might be significant to various user classes. They asked several representatives of each user class to rank each attribute on a scale of 1 (don't give it another thought) to 5 (critically important). The responses helped the analysts determine which quality characteristics were most important to use as design criteria.

The analysts then worked with users to craft specific, measurable, and verifiable requirements for each attribute (Robertson and Robertson 1997). If the quality goals are not verifiable, you cannot tell whether you have achieved them. Where appropriate, indicate the scale or units of measure for each attribute and the target, minimum, and maximum values. If you cannot quantify some of the quality attributes that are important for your project, at least define the priorities and preferences. The *IEEE Standard for a Software Quality Metrics Methodology* presents an approach for defining software quality requirements in the context of an overall quality metrics framework (IEEE 1992).

Another way to define an attribute is to specify any system behaviors that would violate your quality expectations (Voas 1999). By defining unacceptable behaviors—a kind of inverse requirement—you can devise tests that attempt to force the system to demonstrate those behaviors. If you can't force them, you've probably achieved your attribute goals. This approach is particularly valuable for safety-critical applications, where a system that violates reliability or performance tolerances poses a risk to life or limb.

The remainder of this section briefly describes each of the quality attributes listed in Table 11-1 and suggests some questions that might help users state their expectations with respect to the attribute. Sample goal statements are provided, drawn from the Chemical Tracking System or other projects, although these examples are a bit simplified. You'll need to choose the best way to state each quality attribute requirement for your project to guide the developers in making design choices.

ATTRIBUTES IMPORTANT TO USERS

Availability   Availability refers to the percentage of the planned "up time" during which the system is actually available for use and fully operational. More formally, availability equals the mean time to failure (MTTF) for the system divided by the sum of the MTTF and the mean time to repair the system after a failure is encountered. Some tasks are more time-critical than others, and users become frustrated when they need to perform a task and the system isn't available at that moment. Ask users what percentage of up time is really needed and whether there are any times for which availability is imperative to meet business or safety objectives. An availability requirement might read: "The system shall be at least 99.5 percent available on weekdays between 6:00 A.M. and midnight local time, and at least 99.95 percent available between 4:00 P.M. and 6:00 P.M. local time."

Efficiency   Efficiency is a measure of how well the system utilizes processor capacity, disk space, memory, or communication bandwidth (Davis 1993). If a system is consuming all available resources, users will encounter degraded performance, a visible indication of inefficiency. Poor performance can simply be an irritant to the user who is waiting for a database query to display results, or it can represent serious risks to safety, as when a real-time process control system is overloaded. To allow safety buffers for unanticipated conditions, you might specify something like the following: "Ten percent of the available processor capacity and 15 percent of the available system memory shall be unused at the planned peak load conditions." It's important to consider minimum hardware configurations when defining performance, capacity, and efficiency goals.

Flexibility   Also known as extensibility, augmentability, extendability, and expandability, flexibility indicates how much effort is needed to add new capabilities to the product. If developers anticipate system enhancements, they can choose design approaches that maximize the software's flexibility. This attribute is essential for products that are developed in an incremental, iterative fashion through a series of successive releases. A graphics project I once worked on set the following flexibility goal: "A maintenance programmer who has at least six months of experience supporting the product shall be able to add a new supported hardcopy output device with no more than one hour of labor."

Integrity   Integrity (or security) deals with precluding unauthorized access to system functions, preventing information loss, ensuring that the software is protected from virus infection, and protecting the privacy of data entered into the system. Integrity has become a major issue with software executed through the World Wide Web. Users of e-commerce systems are concerned about protecting credit card information, and Web surfers don't want personal information or a record of the sites they visit to be used inappropriately. Integrity requirements do not have any tolerance for error: data and access must be completely protected in the specified ways. State integrity requirements in unambiguous terms: user identity verification, user privilege levels, access restrictions, or the precise data that must be protected. A sample integrity requirement is: "Only users who have Auditor access privileges shall be able to view customer transaction histories."

Interoperability   Interoperability indicates how easily the product can exchange data or services with other systems. To assess the required degree of interoperability, you need to know which other applications the users will employ in conjunction with your product and what data they expect to exchange. Users of the Chemical Tracking System were accustomed to drawing chemical structures with several commercial tools, so they presented the following interoperability requirement: "The Chemical Tracking System shall be able to import any valid chemical structure from the ChemiDraw and Chem-Struct tools."

Reliability   Reliability is the probability of the software executing without failure for a specific period of time (Musa, Iannino, and Okumoto 1987). Robustness and availability are sometimes considered aspects of reliability. Ways to measure software reliability include the percentage of correctly performed operations, the length of time the system runs before revealing a new defect, and defect densities. Establish quantitative reliability requirements based on how severe the impact would be if a failure occurs and whether the cost of maximizing reliability is justifiable. If the software satisfies its reliability requirements, it can be considered shippable with respect to the reliability goals even if it still contains defects. Systems that require high reliability should also be designed for high testability.

My team once wrote some software to control laboratory equipment that performed daylong experiments using scarce, expensive chemicals. The users required the software component that actually ran the experiments to be highly reliable, while other system functions, such as logging temperature data periodically, were less critical. A reliability requirement for this system could be stated as "No more than five experimental runs out of 1000 can be lost because of software failures."

Robustness Robustness is the degree to which a system or component continues to function correctly when confronted with invalid input data, defects in connected software or hardware components, or unexpected operating conditions. Robust software recovers gracefully from problem situations and is forgiving of user errors. When eliciting robustness goals from users, ask about known error conditions the system might encounter and how users would like the system to react.

I once led a project to develop a reusable software component called the Graphics Engine, which processed data files describing graphical plots and rendered the plots on a designated output device (Wiegers 1996b). Many applications that needed to generate plots invoked the Graphics Engine. Since we would have no control over the data these applications fed into the Graphics Engine, robustness was an essential quality. One of our robustness requirements was "All plot description parameters shall have default values specified, which shall be used if the input data is missing or invalid." This example reflects a design approach to achieving robustness for a product whose "users" are other software applications.

Usability Also referred to as "ease of use" and "human engineering," usability addresses the myriad factors that constitute "user-friendliness." Usability measures the effort required to prepare input for, operate, and interpret the output of the product. You need to balance ease of use against the ease of learning how to operate the product. The Chemical Tracking System analysts asked their users questions such as "How important is it that you be able to request chemicals quickly and simply and view other information?" and "On average, how long do you think it should take you to request a chemical?" These are simple starting points toward defining the many characteristics that will make the software easy to use. Discussions about usability can lead to measurable goals such as "A trained user shall be able to request a chemical selected from a vendor catalog in an average of three and a maximum of five minutes."

Also, inquire whether the new system must conform to any user interface standards or conventions, or whether its user interface should be consistent with that of other frequently used systems. Here is a sample usability requirement: "All functions on the File menu shall have shortcut keys defined that use the Control key pressed simultaneously with one other key. Menu commands that also appear on the Microsoft Word 2000 File menu shall use the same shortcut keys used in Word."

Usability also encompasses how easy it is for new or infrequent users to learn to use the product. Ease-of-learning goals can often be quantified and measured, for example, "A new user shall be able to place a request for a chemical with no more than 30 minutes of orientation" or "New operators shall perform 95 percent of their required tasks correctly after a one-day training class." When you define usability or learnability requirements, consider how expensive it will be to test the product to determine whether it satisfies the requirements.

ATTRIBUTES IMPORTANT TO DEVELOPERS

Maintainability   Maintainability indicates how easy it is to correct a defect or make a change in the software. Maintainability depends on how easily the software can be understood, changed, and tested, and is closely related to flexibility. High maintainability is critical for products that will undergo periodic revision and for products that are being built quickly (and perhaps cutting corners on quality). You can measure maintainability in terms of the average time required to fix a problem and the percentage of fixes that are made correctly.

The Chemical Tracking System included the following maintainability requirement: "Modifications made in existing reports shall be operational within one calendar week of receiving revised chemical-reporting regulations from the federal government." On the Graphics Engine project, we knew we would be doing frequent software surgery to satisfy evolving user needs, so we specified design criteria to enhance its overall maintainability: "Function calls shall not be nested more than two levels deep" and "Each software module shall have a ratio of nonblank comments to source code statements of at least 0.5." State such design goals carefully and precisely to discourage developers from taking silly actions that conform to the letter, but not the intent, of the goal.

Portability   The effort required to migrate a piece of software from one operating environment to another is a measure of portability. The design approaches that make software portable are similar to those that make it reusable (Glass 1992). Portability is typically either immaterial to project success or critical to the project's outcome. Portability goals should state the portions of the product that must be able to migrate to other environments and identify those target environments. Developers can then select design and coding approaches that will enhance the product's portability appropriately.

Reusability   A long-sought goal of software development, reusability indicates the extent to which a software component can be used in applications other than the one for which it was initially developed. Developing reusable software costs considerably more than creating a component that you intend to use in just one application. Reusable software has to be modular, well-documented, independent of a specific application and operating environment, and somewhat generic (DeGrace and Stahl 1993). Specify which elements of the new system need to be constructed in a manner that facilitates their reuse, or stipulate the libraries of reusable components that should be created as a spin-off from the project.

Testability   Testability refers to the ease with which the software components or integrated product can be tested to find defects. Designing for testability is critical if the product has complex algorithms and logic, or if it contains subtle functionality interrelationships. Testability is also important if the product will be modified often, because it will undergo frequent regression testing to determine whether the changes damaged any existing functionality.

Because we knew we would have to test the Graphics Engine many times as it was repeatedly enhanced, we included this design goal: "The maximum cyclomatic complexity of a module shall not exceed 20." Cyclomatic complexity is a measure of the number of logic branches in a source code module (McCabe 1982). Adding more branches and loops to a module makes it harder to test, understand, and maintain. The project was not going to be a failure if some module had a cyclomatic complexity higher than 20, but documenting such design criteria helps the developers achieve a desired quality objective.

ATTRIBUTE TRADE-OFFS

Certain attribute pairs have inescapable trade-offs. Users and developers must decide which attributes are more important than others, and they must respect those priorities consistently as they make decisions. Figure 11-1 illustrates some typical interrelationships among the quality attributes from Table 11-1, although you might encounter exceptions to these (Charette 1990; IEEE 1992; Glass 1993). A plus sign in a cell indicates that increasing the attribute in the corresponding row has a positive effect on the attribute in the column. For example, design approaches that increase a software component's reusability can also make the software more flexible, easier to connect to other software components, easier to maintain, more portable, and easier to test.

A minus sign in a cell means that increasing the attribute in that row adversely affects the attribute in the column. Efficiency has a negative impact on many other attributes. If you're writing the tightest, fastest code you can, using a specific compiler and operating system, it's likely to be hard to maintain and enhance, as well as not very portable to another environment. Similarly, systems that optimize the operator's ease of use or that are intended to be flexible, reusable, and interoperable with other software or hardware components often pay a performance penalty. For example, using the external, general-purpose Graphics Engine tool to generate plots resulted in a significant performance degradation compared to the old applications that had integral custom graphics code. You have to balance the threat of performance reductions against the anticipated benefits of your proposed solution to ensure you're making sensible trade-offs.

To reach the optimum balance of product characteristics, you must identify, specify, and prioritize the pertinent quality attributes during requirements elicitation. As you define the important quality attributes for your project, use Figure 11-1 to avoid making commitments to conflicting goals. Following are some examples:

◆   Don't expect to optimize the usability if the software has to run
    on multiple platforms (portability).

◆ Reusable software might be so generalized for use in multiple environments that it cannot achieve specific error tolerance (reliability) or integrity objectives.

◆ It's hard to completely test the integrity requirements of highly secure systems; reused generic components or interconnections with other applications might compromise security mechanisms.

	Availability	Efficiency	Flexibility	Integrity	Interoperability	Maintainability	Portability	Reliability	Reusability	Robustness	Testability	Usability
Availability								+		+		
Efficiency			−		−	−	−	−		−	−	−
Flexibility		−		−	+	+	+			+		
Integrity		−			−			−		−		−
Interoperability		−	+	−			+					
Maintainability	+	−	+					+		+		
Portability		−	+		+	−			+	+		−
Reliability	+	−	+			+			+		+	+
Reusability		−	+	−	+	+	+	−			+	
Robustness	+	−						+				+
Testability	+	−	+			+		+				+
Usability		−								+	−	

FIGURE 11-1   *Positive and negative relationships between selected quality attributes.*

Achieving the right balance of quality characteristics in the software won't happen by itself. Include discussions of quality attribute expectations in requirements elicitation, and document what you learn in the SRS. As a result, you're more likely to deliver a product that satisfies all the project stakeholders.

Next Steps

◆   Identify several quality attributes from Table 11-1 that might be important to users on your current project. Formulate one or two questions about each attribute that will help your users articulate their expectations. Based on the user responses, write one or two specific goals for each important attribute.

12 *Risk Reduction Through Prototyping*

I recently met with a software team that had the unpleasant experience of having users reject a completed product as unsuitable. The users hadn't seen the user interface prior to product delivery, and they found problems both with the interface and with the underlying requirements. Software prototyping is a technique you can employ to reduce the risk of customer dissatisfaction. Early feedback from users ensures that the development team properly understands the requirements and knows how best to implement them.

Even if you apply the requirements elicitation, analysis, and specification practices described in earlier chapters, portions of your requirements might still be uncertain or unclear to either the customers or the developers. If you don't correct these problems, an expectation gap between the user's vision of the product and the developer's understanding of what to build is a certain outcome. It's hard to visualize exactly how a software product will behave under specific circumstances by reading textual requirements or studying analysis models. Prototyping makes the new product tangible, brings use cases to life, and closes gaps in your understanding of the requirements. Users are generally more willing to try out a prototype (which is fun) than to read the entire SRS (which is tedious).

Prototype has multiple meanings, and participants in a prototyping activity can have very different expectations. For example, a prototype airplane actually flies—it is the first version of the real airplane. In contrast, a software prototype is generally only a portion or a model of an actual system, and it might not do anything useful at all. This chapter examines different kinds of software prototypes, their application to requirements development, and ways to make prototyping an effective part of your software engineering process (Wood and Kang 1992).

PROTOTYPING: WHAT AND WHY

A software prototype is a partial implementation of a proposed new product. You can use prototypes for three major purposes:

- *Clarify and complete the requirements.* Used as a requirements tool, the prototype is a preliminary implementation of a part of the system that is not well understood. User evaluation of the prototype points out problems with the requirements, which you can correct at low cost before you construct the actual product.

- *Explore design alternatives.* Used as a design tool, a prototype lets you explore different user interface techniques, optimize system usability, and evaluate possible technical approaches.

- *Grow into the ultimate product.* Used as a construction tool, a prototype is a fully functional implementation of an initial subset of the product, which you can elaborate into the complete product through a sequence of small-scale development cycles.

The primary reason for creating a prototype is to resolve uncertainties early in the development cycle. Use these uncertainties to decide which parts of the system you need to prototype and what you hope to learn from user evaluations of the prototypes. A prototype is also an excellent way to reveal and resolve ambiguity in the requirements. Ambiguity and incompleteness leave the developer unsure of what to build, and creating a prototype helps illuminate and rectify that uncertainty. Users, managers, and other nontechnical project stakeholders find that prototypes give them something concrete to visualize as the product is being specified and designed. Prototypes are easier to understand than the technical jargon developers sometimes use.

HORIZONTAL AND VERTICAL PROTOTYPES

When people say "software prototype," they are usually thinking about a *horizontal prototype* of a possible user interface. A horizontal prototype is also called a *behavioral prototype* or a *mock-up*. It lets you explore some specific behaviors of the intended system, with the goal of refining the requirements. The prototype gives users something tangible to work with as they contemplate whether the functionality implied by the prototype will let them perform their business tasks. Note that this type of prototype often implies functionality without actually implementing it.

A horizontal prototype is like a movie set. It displays the facades of user interface screens, possibly allowing some navigation between them, but it contains little or no real functionality. Think of your typical Western: the cowboy walks into the saloon and then walks out of the livery stable, yet he doesn't have a drink and he doesn't see a horse because there really isn't anything behind the false fronts of the buildings.

A mock-up shows users the functional and navigational options that are available in the prototyped screens. Some of the navigations will work, but the user might only see a message that describes what would really be displayed at that point. The information that appears in response to a database query is faked or constant, and report contents are hard-coded. The prototype doesn't actually perform any useful work, although it looks like it does. The simulation is often enough to let the users judge whether any functionality is missing, wrong, or unnecessary. The prototype represents the developer's concept of how a specific use case might be implemented. The user's evaluation of the prototype can point out alternative courses for the use case, missing process steps, or previously undetected exception conditions.

When you construct such prototypes at a fairly abstract level, the user can focus on broad requirement and workflow issues without becoming distracted by the precise appearance or positioning of screen elements (Constantine 1998). After you have clarified the requirements and determined the general structure of the interface, you can create more detailed prototypes to explore the specifics of user interface design. You can create horizontal prototypes using a variety of screen design tools, or even with paper and pencil, as discussed later.

The *vertical prototype*, also known as a *structural prototype* or *proof of concept*, implements a slice of application functionality. Develop a vertical prototype when you're uncertain whether a proposed architectural approach is sound or when you want to optimize algorithms, evaluate a proposed database schema, or test critical timing requirements. Vertical prototypes are generally constructed with production tools in the production operating environment, to make the results meaningful. The vertical prototype is used more to reduce risk during software design than for requirements development.

I once worked on a project where we wanted to implement an unusual client/server architecture as part of a transitional strategy from a mainframe-centric world to an application environment based on networked Unix servers and workstations (Thompson and Wiegers 1995). A vertical prototype that implemented just a bit of the user interface client and the corresponding server functionality allowed us to evaluate the communication components, performance, and reliability of our proposed architecture. The experiment was a success, as was the implementation we based on that architecture.

THROWAWAY AND EVOLUTIONARY PROTOTYPES

Before you construct a prototype, make an explicit and well-communicated decision whether the prototype will be discarded after evaluation or will evolve into a portion of the delivered product. You build a *throwaway prototype* (or *exploratory prototype*) to answer questions, resolve uncertainties, and improve requirements quality (Davis 1993). Because you intend to discard the prototype after it has served its purpose, build it as quickly and cheaply as you can. The more work you invest in the prototype, the more reluctant the project participants become to discard it.

When you build a throwaway prototype, you ignore much of what you know about solid software construction techniques. Emphasize quick implementation and modification over robustness, reliability, performance, and long-term maintainability. For this reason, you must not allow code from a throwaway prototype to migrate into a production system unless it meets your production-quality code standards. Otherwise, you and the users will suffer the consequences for the life of the product.

The throwaway prototype is most appropriate when you face uncertainty, ambiguity, incompleteness, or vagueness in the requirements. You need to resolve these issues to reduce the risk of proceeding with construction. A prototype that helps users and developers visualize how the requirements might be implemented can reveal gaps in the requirements. It also allows the users to judge whether the requirements will enable the necessary business processes.

Figure 12-1 shows a sequence of development activities that move from user tasks to detailed user interface design with the help of a throwaway prototype. Each use-case description includes a sequence of actor actions and system responses, which you can model in the form of a dialog map to depict a possible user interface architecture. (See Chapter 10.) A throwaway prototype elaborates the dialog elements into specific screens, menus, and dialog boxes. When users evaluate the prototype, their feedback might lead to changes in the use-case descriptions (for example, if a new alternative course is discovered) and to corresponding changes in the dialog map. Once the requirements are refined and the screens are sketched out, you can design the details of each user interface element for optimum usability. This progressive refinement approach is cheaper than leaping directly from use-case descriptions to a complete user interface implementation and then discovering major errors in the requirements.

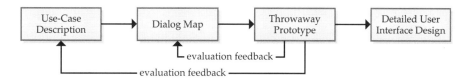

FIGURE 12-1   *Activity sequence from user tasks to user interface design using a throwaway prototype.*

In contrast to a throwaway prototype, an *evolutionary prototype* provides a solid architectural foundation for building the product incrementally as the requirements become clearly defined over time. Evolutionary prototyping is a component of the spiral software development life cycle model (Boehm 1988) and of some object-oriented software development processes (Kruchten 1996). In contrast to the quick-and-dirty nature of throwaway prototyping, an evolutionary prototype must be built with robust, production-quality code from the outset. Therefore, an evolutionary prototype takes longer to create than a throwaway prototype that addresses the same functionality. An evolutionary prototype must be designed for easy growth and frequent enhancement, so you need to emphasize software architecture and solid design principles. There's no room for shortcuts in the quality of an evolutionary prototype.

Think of the first increment of an evolutionary prototype as a pilot release that implements a well-understood and stable portion of the requirements. Lessons learned from testing and initial usage can lead to modifications in the next iteration, on the way to eventual implementation of the full product through a series of evolutionary prototypes. Such prototypes provide a way to quickly get useful functionality into the hands of the users.

Evolutionary prototyping is well suited for Web development projects. On one Web project I managed, we created a series of four prototypes, based on the requirements we developed from a use-case analysis. Several users evaluated each prototype, and based on their responses to specific questions we posed, we revised the prototype. The revisions following the fourth prototype evaluation resulted in our production Web site.

Figure 12-2 illustrates several ways you can combine the various types of prototyping into your software development process. For example, you can use the knowledge gained from a series of throwaway prototypes to refine the requirements, which you might then implement incrementally through an evolutionary prototyping sequence. An alternative path through Figure 12-2 would use a throwaway horizontal prototype to clarify the requirements prior to finalizing the user interface design, while a parallel vertical prototyping effort would validate the core application algorithms. What you *cannot* do successfully is turn the intentional low quality of a throwaway prototype into the maintainable robustness demanded of a production system. Table 12-1 summarizes some typical applications of throwaway, evolutionary, horizontal, and vertical prototypes.

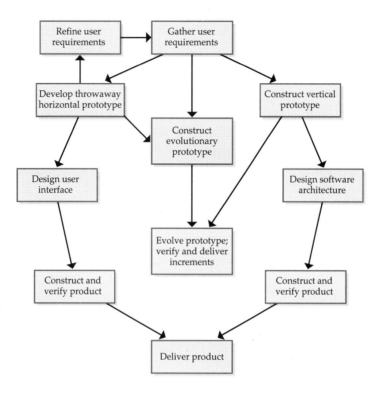

FIGURE 12-2   *Several possible ways to incorporate prototyping into the software development process.*

TABLE 12-1   **TYPICAL APPLICATIONS OF SOFTWARE PROTOTYPES**

	Throwaway	**Evolutionary**
Horizontal	• Clarify and refine use cases and functional requirements. • Identify missing functionality. • Explore user interface approaches.	• Implement core use cases. • Implement additional use cases based on priority. • Develop and refine Web sites.
Vertical	• Demonstrate technical feasibility.	• Implement and grow core client/server functionality and communication layers. • Implement and optimize core algorithms.

PAPER AND ELECTRONIC PROTOTYPES

In many cases, an executable prototype isn't necessary to elicit the information you need to resolve uncertainties about the requirements. Paper prototypes (sometimes called lo-fi prototypes) are a cheap, fast, and low-tech way to explore what a portion of an implemented system might look like (Rettig 1994; Hohmann 1997). Paper prototypes help you test whether the users and developers have reached a shared understanding of the requirements. They let you take a tentative and low-risk step into a possible solution space prior to developing production code.

Paper prototypes involve tools no more sophisticated than paper, index cards, sticky notes, clear plastic sheets, whiteboard, and markers. You sketch your idea of what the screens might look like without worrying about exactly how and where the buttons and widgets will appear. Users willingly provide feedback that can lead to profound changes on a few pieces of paper. Sometimes they are less eager to critique a lovely computer-based prototype in which it appears the developer has invested a lot of work. Developers, too, will often resist making substantial changes in a carefully crafted electronic prototype.

With lo-fi prototyping, a person plays the role of the computer while a user walks through an evaluation scenario. The user initiates actions by saying aloud what she would like to do at a specific screen: "I'm going to select Print Preview from the File menu." The person simulating the computer then displays the page or index card that represents the display that would appear when the user takes that action. The user can judge whether that is indeed the expected response and whether the item displayed contains the correct elements. If it's wrong, you simply take a fresh piece of paper or index card and draw it again.

No matter how efficient your prototyping tools are, sketching displays on paper is faster. Paper prototyping facilitates rapid iteration of the prototypes, and iteration is a key success factor in requirements development. Paper prototyping is an excellent technique for refining the requirements prior to prototyping detailed user interfaces with automated tools, constructing an evolutionary prototype, or undertaking traditional design and construction activities. It also provides a useful tool for managing customer expectations.

If you decide to build an electronic throwaway prototype, several appropriate tools are available (Andriole 1996). These include:

- Programming languages such as Microsoft Visual Basic, IBM VisualAge Smalltalk, and Inprise Delphi

- Scripting languages such as Perl, Python, and Rexx

- Commercial prototyping toolkits, screen painters, and graphical user interface builders

Web-based approaches using HTML (hypertext markup language) pages, which can be modified quickly, are useful for creating prototypes that are intended to clarify requirements, not to explore specific user interface designs. Suitable tools will let you quickly implement and modify user interface components, regardless of how inefficient the code behind the interface is. Of course, if you're building an evolutionary prototype, you must use the production development tools from the outset.

PROTOTYPE EVALUATION

You can improve the effectiveness of prototype evaluation by creating scripts that guide the users through a series of steps and ask specific questions to elicit the information you need. This activity is a valuable supplement to the more general invitation to "tell me how you like this prototype." Derive the evaluation scripts from the use cases or functions addressed in the prototype. The script should ask the user to perform specific tasks and steer them through the parts of the prototype about which you have the most uncertainty. At the end of each task, the script should present the evaluator with specific task-related questions. In addition, you might ask the following general questions:

- Does this prototype implement the functionality in the way you expected?

- Is any functionality missing?

- Can you think of any error conditions that the prototype does not address?

- Are any unnecessary functions present?

◆ How logical and complete does the navigation seem to you?

◆ Can you think of easier ways to perform this task?

Make sure the right people evaluate the prototype from the appropriate perspective. The prototype evaluators should be representative of the expected user population. Include in the evaluation group experienced and inexperienced users drawn from the user classes who would be using the functionality incorporated in the prototype. Before you present the prototype to the evaluators, stress that it does not contain all of the actual business logic, which will be implemented during development of the actual product.

You will learn more by watching users work with the prototype than if you simply ask them to evaluate it on their own and tell you what they think. Formal usability tests of user interface prototypes are powerful, but you can also learn a lot through low-tech observation. Watch where the user's fingers try to go instinctively. Spot places where the prototype's approach conflicts with operating paradigms from other applications to which the users are accustomed. Look for the furrowed brow that indicates a puzzled user who isn't sure how to do something or how to navigate to a desired destination. Ask users to share their thoughts out loud as they evaluate the prototype so that you can understand what they're thinking and detect any requirements that the prototype improperly addresses. Strive to create a nonjudgmental environment in which the evaluators feel free to express their thoughts, ideas, and concerns. Avoid the temptation to coach users on the "right" way to perform some function as they work with the prototype.

Document what you learn from the prototype evaluation. For a horizontal prototype, use the information you gather to refine the requirements in the SRS. If the prototype evaluation led to some user interface design decisions or the selection of specific interaction techniques, record those conclusions and how you arrived at them. Decisions that are not accompanied by the attendant thought processes tend to be revisited over and over, a needless waste of time. For a vertical prototype, document the evaluations you performed and their results, culminating in the decisions you made about the viability of the technical approaches you explored.

THE BIG RISK OF PROTOTYPING

Prototyping is a technique for reducing the risk of software project failure. However, prototyping introduces its own risks. The biggest risk is that a user or manager will see a running prototype and conclude that the product is nearly completed. "Wow, it looks like you're almost done!" says the enthusiastic prototype evaluator. "It looks really good. Can you just finish this up and give it to me?"

In a word: NO! If you're demonstrating or evaluating a throwaway prototype, it was never intended for production use, no matter how much it looks like the real thing. It is merely a model, a simulation, or an experiment. Managing stakeholder expectations is a key element of successful prototyping, so make certain that all who see the prototype understand why and how it is being built. Resist the often considerable pressure to deliver a throwaway prototype. Delivering the prototype will actually cause the project to be completed later than planned, because the design and code were intentionally created without regard to quality or durability.

Don't let the fear of encountering premature delivery pressure dissuade you from creating prototypes, but make it absolutely clear to those who see the prototype that you will not release the prototype and call it production software. One way to control this risk is to use paper, rather than electronic, prototypes. No one who evaluates a paper prototype will think the product is nearly ready for delivery. Another possibility is to use prototyping tools that are different from those used for actual development; this will help you resist pressure to "just finish up" the prototype and deliver it as a product.

Continue to manage expectations during prototype evaluations. If evaluators see the prototype respond instantaneously to a simulated database query, they might expect the same fabulous performance in the production software. Consider building in time delays to more realistically simulate the expected behavior of the final product (and perhaps make the prototype look even less ready for immediate delivery).

PROTOTYPING SUCCESS FACTORS

Software prototyping provides a powerful set of techniques that can shorten development schedules, increase customer satisfaction, produce higher quality products, and reduce requirement errors and user interface shortcomings.

To help make prototyping an effective part of your requirements development process, follow these guidelines:

♦ Include prototyping tasks in your project plan. Schedule time to develop, evaluate, and possibly modify the prototypes.

♦ Plan to develop multiple prototypes, because you will rarely get them right on the first try.

♦ Create throwaway prototypes as quickly and cheaply as possible. Invest the minimum amount of work in developing prototypes that will answer questions or resolve uncertainties about the requirements. Don't try to perfect a throwaway prototype's user interface.

♦ Don't include code comments, input data validations, defensive coding techniques, or error-handling code in a throwaway prototype.

♦ Don't prototype requirements you already understand.

♦ Resist the temptation—or the pressure from users—to keep adding more functionality. Don't allow a simple throwaway prototype to become more elaborate than is necessary to meet the prototyping objectives.

♦ Don't infer anything about production performance from the performance of a horizontal prototype. The prototype might not run in the intended production environment, and you might have built it with tools that differ in efficiency from the production development tools.

♦ Use plausible dummy data in prototype screen displays and reports. The users who evaluate the prototype can be distracted by unrealistic data and fail to focus on the prototype as a model of how the real system might look and behave.

♦ Don't expect a prototype to replace written requirements. A lot of behind-the-scenes functionality is only implied by the prototype and should be documented in an SRS to make it complete, specific, and traceable.

Next Steps

◆ Identify a portion of your project, such as a use case, that suffers from confusion about requirements. Sketch out a portion of a possible user interface that represents your understanding of the requirements and how they might be implemented—a paper prototype. Have some users walk through your prototype to simulate performing a task or use case. Identify any places where the initial understanding of the requirements was incomplete or incorrect. Modify the prototype accordingly and walk through it again.

◆ Present a summary of the information in this chapter to your prototype evaluators. This will help them understand the rationale behind your prototyping and have realistic expectations for the prototyping effort's outcome.

13

Setting Requirement Priorities

After most of the user requirements for the Chemical Tracking System were documented, the project manager, Dave, and the requirements analyst, Lori, met with two of the product champions. Tim represented the chemist community and Roxanne represented the chemical stockroom staff.

"As you know," Dave began, "the product champions collected a lot of requirements for the Chemical Tracking System. It doesn't look as if we can include all of the functionality you want in the first release. Since most of the requirements came from the chemists and the chemical stockroom, I'd like to talk with you about prioritizing your requirements."

Tim was puzzled. "Why do you need the requirements prioritized? They're all important, or we wouldn't have given them to you."

Dave explained, "I know they're all important, but we can't fit everything in and still deliver a high-quality product on schedule. No more resources are available, so we want to make sure we address the most important requirements in the first release, which is due at the end of next quarter. We're asking you to help us distinguish the requirements that absolutely must be included initially from those that can wait for a later release."

"I know the chemical usage and disposal reports that the Health and Safety office needs to generate for the government have to be available by the end of the quarter," Roxanne pointed out. "We can use the chemical stockroom's current inventory system for a few more months if we have to. But the barcode labeling and scanning features are essential, more important than searchable vendor catalogs for the chemists."

Tim raised a protest. "I promised the online catalog search function to the chemists as a way for this system to save them a lot of time. The catalog search has to be included from the beginning," he insisted.

Lori, the analyst, said, "While I was exploring use cases with the chemists, it seemed that some would be performed very often and others just once in a while or only by a few people. Could we look at the complete set of use cases from all the product champions and figure out which ones you don't need immediately? I'd also like to defer some of the bells and whistles from the top-priority use cases, if we can."

Tim and Roxanne weren't thrilled that they'd have to wait for some of their system's functionality to be delivered. However, they realized that if the development team couldn't implement every requirement by the time release 1.0 had to ship, it would be better if everyone could agree on the subset to implement first.

Every software project with resource limitations has to understand the relative priorities of the requested features, use cases, and functional requirements. Prioritization helps the project manager resolve conflicts, plan for staged deliveries, and make the necessary trade-offs. This chapter discusses the importance of prioritizing requirements and suggests a prioritization scheme based on value, cost, and risk.

WHY PRIORITIZE REQUIREMENTS?

When customer expectations are high, timelines short, and resources limited, you need to make sure the product delivers the most essential functionality as early as possible. Establishing the relative importance of each function lets you plan construction to provide the greatest product value at the lowest cost. Prioritization is particularly critical if you are doing time-boxed or incremental development in which the release schedules are tight and immovable and you need to eliminate or defer the less critical functions.

A project manager has to balance the desired project scope against the constraints of schedule, budget, staff resources, and quality goals. One way to accomplish this is to drop, or defer to a later release, low-priority requirements when new, higher priority requirements are accepted or other project conditions change. If the customers do not differentiate their requirements by importance and urgency, project managers must make these decisions on their own. Because customers might not agree with a project manager's priorities, customers must indicate which requirements are needed initially and which can wait. Establish priorities early in the project, while you have more options available for achieving a successful project outcome.

It's difficult enough to get any one customer to decide which of his requirements are most important; achieving consensus among multiple customers with diverse expectations is even more challenging. People naturally have their own interests at heart, and they aren't always eager to compromise their needs for some other group's benefit. However, prioritizing requirements is one of the customer's responsibilities in the customer-developer partnership, as discussed in Chapter 2.

Customers and developers must both provide input to requirements prioritization. Customers place a high priority on those functions that provide the greatest benefit to users. However, once a developer points out the cost, difficulty, technical risk, or other trade-offs associated with a specific requirement, the customers might decide it isn't as essential as they initially thought. The developer might also determine that certain lower priority functions should be implemented early on because of their impact on the system's architecture. Prioritization means balancing the business benefit of each requirement against its cost and any implications it has for the architectural foundation and future evolution of the product.

GAMES PEOPLE PLAY WITH PRIORITIES

The knee-jerk response to a request for customers to set priorities is, "I need all of these features. Just make it happen somehow." It can be difficult to persuade customers to set priorities if they know that low-priority requirements might never be implemented. A developer told me once that priorities aren't necessary, because if he wrote something in the SRS, he intends to build it. However, that doesn't consider the issue of *when* each piece of functionality gets built. Developers might prefer to avoid prioritization, thinking that establishing priorities conflicts with the "we can do it all" attitude they want to convey to their customers and managers.

In reality, some features are more essential than others. This becomes apparent during the all-too-common "rapid descoping phase" late in the project, when nonessential features are jettisoned to make sure something is shipped on schedule. Setting priorities early in the project helps you make those trade-off decisions along the way, rather than in emergency mode at the end. Implementing half of a feature before you determine it is of low priority is wasteful and frustrating.

If left to their own devices, customers will establish perhaps 85 percent of the requirements as high priority, 10 percent as medium, and 5 percent as low. This doesn't give the project manager much flexibility. Scrubbing the requirements by eliminating any that aren't essential and simplifying those that are unnecessarily complicated has been identified as a best practice for rapid software development (McConnell 1996).

On one large project, the management steering team exhibited impatience over the analyst's insistence on prioritizing the requirements. The managers pointed out that often they can do without a particular feature, but another feature might need to be beefed up to make up for the omitted requirements. If they defer too many requirements, the resulting system won't achieve the revenue that was projected in the business plan. When you evaluate priorities, look at the connections and interrelationships among different requirements and their alignment with the project's business requirements.

PRIORITIZATION SCALES

A common approach to prioritization is to group requirements into three categories. Table 13-1 shows several such three-level scales. They are all subjective and imprecise, so everyone involved must agree on what each level means in the scale they use. If relative terms such as *high, medium,* and *low* confuse people, use more definitive labels like *committed, time permitting,* and *future release.*

TABLE 13-1   SEVERAL REQUIREMENTS PRIORITIZATION SCALES

Name	Meaning	Reference
High	A mission-critical requirement; required for next release	--
Medium	Supports necessary system operations; required eventually but could wait until a later release if necessary	
Low	A functional or quality enhancement; would be nice to have someday if resources permit	
Essential	Software not acceptable unless these requirements are provided in an agreed manner	(IEEE 1998)
Conditional	Would enhance the product, but would not make it unacceptable if absent	
Optional	A class of functions that might or might not be worthwhile	
3	Must be implemented perfectly	(Kovitz 1999)
2	Needs to work, but not spectacularly well	
1	Can contain bugs	

The priority of each requirement should be included in the SRS or use case descriptions. Establish a convention for your SRS so the reader knows whether the priority assigned to a high-level requirement is inherited by all of its subordinate requirements, or whether every individual requirement should have its own priority attribute.

Even a medium-sized project can have hundreds or thousands of functional requirements, too many to classify analytically and consistently. To keep it manageable, you need to choose an appropriate level of abstraction for the prioritization—use cases, features, or detailed functional requirements. Within a single use case, certain alternative courses might have a higher priority than others. You might decide to do an initial prioritization at the feature level and then to prioritize the functional requirements within certain features separately. This will help you distinguish the core functionality from refinements that could be added in later releases. Document even the low-priority requirements, because their priority might change later and knowing about them now will help the developers plan ahead for future enhancements.

Prioritization Based on Value, Cost, and Risk

On a small project, the stakeholders can probably agree on requirement priorities informally. Larger or more contentious projects demand a more structured approach, which removes some of the emotion, politics, and guesswork from the process. Several analytical and mathematical techniques have been proposed to assist with requirements prioritization. These methods involve estimating the relative value and relative cost of each requirement. The highest priority requirements are those that provide the largest fraction of the total product value at the smallest fraction of the total cost (Karlsson and Ryan 1997; Jung 1998). Subjectively estimating the cost and value by pairwise comparisons of all the requirements is impractical for more than a couple of dozen requirements.

Another alternative is Quality Function Deployment (QFD), which provides a comprehensive method for relating customer value to the features for a proposed product (Cohen 1995). A third approach, borrowed from

Total Quality Management (TQM), rates each requirement against several weighted project success criteria and computes a score to rank the priority of the requirements. However, few software organizations seem to be willing to undertake the rigor of QFD or TQM.

Table 13-2 illustrates a simple spreadsheet model to help you estimate the relative priorities for a set of use cases, product features, or individual functional requirements. This example depicts several features from the Chemical Tracking System. This scheme borrows from the QFD concept of customer value depending on both the benefit provided to the customer if a specific product feature is present and the penalty paid if that feature is absent (Pardee 1996). A feature's attractiveness is directly proportional to the value it provides and inversely proportional to its cost and the technical risk associated with implementing it. All other things being equal, those features that have the highest risk-adjusted value/cost ratio should have the highest priority. This approach distributes a set of estimated priorities across a continuum, rather than grouping them into just a few priority levels.

You should apply this prioritization scheme only to negotiable features, those that are not top priority. For example, you wouldn't include in this priority analysis items that implement the core business functions of the product, that you view as key product differentiators, or that are required for compliance with government regulations. You are going to build those features into the next release, no matter what. Once you've identified those features that absolutely must be included for the product to be shippable, use the model to scale the relative priorities of the remaining features.

The typical participants in the prioritization process include:

◆ The project manager, who leads the process, arbitrates conflicts, and adjusts input from the other participants if necessary

◆ Key customer representatives, such as product champions, who supply the benefit and penalty ratings

◆ Development representatives, such as team tech leads, who provide the cost and risk ratings

TABLE 13-2   SAMPLE PRIORITIZATION MATRIX FOR THE CHEMICAL TRACKING SYSTEM

Relative Weights:	2	1			1		0.5		
Feature	Relative Benefit	Relative Penalty	Total Value	Value %	Relative Cost	Cost %	Relative Risk	Risk %	Priority
1. Query status of a vendor order.	5	3	13	8.4	2	4.8	1	3.0	1.345
2. Generate a chemical stockroom inventory report.	9	7	25	16.2	5	11.9	3	9.1	0.987
3. See history of a specific chemical container.	5	5	15	9.7	3	7.1	2	6.1	0.957
4. Print a chemical safety datasheet.	2	1	5	3.2	1	2.4	1	3.0	0.833
5. Maintain a list of hazardous chemicals.	4	9	17	11.0	4	9.5	4	12.1	0.708
6. Modify a pending chemical request.	4	3	11	7.1	3	7.1	2	6.1	0.702
7. Generate an individual laboratory inventory report.	6	2	14	9.1	4	9.5	3	9.1	0.646
8. Search vendor catalogs for a specific chemical.	9	8	26	16.9	7	16.7	8	24.2	0.586
9. Query training database for a hazardous-chemical training record.	3	4	10	6.5	4	9.5	2	6.1	0.517
10. Import chemical structures from structure drawing tools.	7	4	18	11.7	9	21.4	7	21.2	0.365
Totals	54	46	154	100	42	100	33	100	--

Follow the steps below to use this prioritization model.

1. List in a spreadsheet all the requirements, features, or use cases that you wish to prioritize; in this example, we'll use features. All the items must be at the same level of abstraction; don't mix individual requirements with product features. If certain features are logically linked—for example, you would implement feature B only if feature A were included—list only the driving feature in the analysis. This model will work with up to several dozen features before it becomes unwieldy. If you have more items than that, group related features together to create a manageable initial list. You can do a second round of analysis at a finer level of detail if you need to.

2. Estimate the relative benefit that each feature provides to the customer or to the business on a scale of 1 to 9, where 1 indicates negligible benefit and 9 means enormously valuable. These benefit ratings indicate alignment with the product's business requirements. Your customer representatives are the best people to judge these benefits.

3. Estimate the relative penalty the customer or business would suffer if the feature were not included. Again, use a scale of 1 to 9, where 1 means essentially no penalty and 9 indicates a very serious downside. Failing to conform to an industry standard could incur a high penalty even if the customer benefit is low, as would omitting a feature that customers would reasonably expect to be present, whether or not they explicitly requested it. Requirements that have both a low benefit and a low penalty add cost but little value; they might be instances of gold-plating.

4. The Total Value column is the sum of the relative benefit and relative penalty. By default, benefit and penalty are weighted equally. As a refinement, you can change the relative weights for these two factors. In the example in Table 13-2, all benefit ratings are weighted twice as heavily as the penalty ratings. The spreadsheet totals the feature values and calculates the percentage of the total value from these features that is attributable to each feature (Value % column).

5. Estimate the relative cost of implementing each feature, again on a scale of 1 (low) to 9 (high). The spreadsheet will calculate the percentage of the total cost that is contributed by each feature. Developers can estimate the cost ratings based on the requirement's complexity, the extent of user interface work required, the potential ability to reuse existing code, the amount of testing and documentation that will be needed, and so on.

6. Similarly, have developers estimate the relative degree of technical or other risks associated with each feature on a scale of 1 to 9. A rating of 1 means you can program it in your sleep, while 9 indicates serious concerns about feasibility, the lack of staff with the needed expertise, or the use of unproven or unfamiliar tools and technologies. The spreadsheet will calculate the percentage of the total risk that comes from each feature. By default, benefit, penalty, cost and risk are weighted equally, but you can adjust the weightings in the spreadsheet. In Table 13-2, risk has half the weight of the cost factor, which has the same weight as the penalty term. If you don't want to consider risk at all in the model, set the risk weighting value to zero.

7. Once you have entered all of the estimates into the spreadsheet, it will calculate a priority value for each feature, using the following formula:

$$\text{priority} = \frac{\text{value \%}}{(\text{cost \%} * \text{cost weight}) + (\text{risk \%} * \text{risk weight})}$$

8. Sort the list of features in descending order by calculated priority. The features at the top of the list have the most favorable balance of value, cost, and risk, and thus should have highest priority.

This semiquantitative method is not mathematically rigorous, and its accuracy is limited by your ability to estimate the benefit, penalty, cost, and risk for each item. Therefore, use the calculated priority sequence only as a guideline. Customer and development representatives should review the completed spreadsheet to reach agreement on the ratings and the resulting sorted priority sequence. Calibrate this model for your own use with a set of completed requirements from a previous project. Adjust the weighting factors until the calculated priority sequence correlates well with your after-the-fact evaluation of how important the requirements in your test set really were.

This model can also help you make trade-off decisions when you are evaluating proposed requirements. Estimate their priorities to indicate how they align with the existing requirements base so that you can choose an appropriate implementation sequence. Any actions you can take to move requirements prioritization from the political arena into an objective and analytical one will improve the project's ability to deliver the most important functionality in the most appropriate sequence.

 Next Steps

◆ Apply the prioritization model described in this chapter to ten or fifteen features or use cases from your current project. How well do the calculated priorities compare with the priorities you had assigned by some different method? How well do they compare with your intuitive sense of the proper priorities?

◆ If there is a disconnect between what the model predicts for priorities and what you think is right, analyze which part of the model is not giving sensible results. Try applying different weighting factors to benefit, penalty, cost, and risk. Adjust the model until it provides results consistent with what you expect.

◆ Once you have calibrated and adjusted the prioritization model, apply it to a new project. Incorporate the calculated priorities into the decision-making process and see if this yields results that the stakeholders find more satisfying than their previous prioritization approach.

14

Verifying Requirements Quality

Most software developers have experienced the frustration of discovering requirement problems late in the development process or after the product was delivered. Substantial effort is needed to fix requirement errors that are discovered after work based on those requirements has already been completed. Studies have shown that it costs 68 to 110 times more to correct a requirement defect found by the customer than to fix an error found during requirements development. Another study found that an error found during requirements development took an average of only 30 minutes to fix, whereas a defect found by system testing took 5 to 17 hours to correct (Kelly, Sherif, and Hops 1992). Any measures you can take to detect errors in the requirements specifications will clearly save you substantial time and money.

On many projects, including those that follow a classic waterfall life cycle, testing is a late-stage development activity. Requirements-related problems linger in the product until they are finally found through expensive and time-consuming system testing or by the customer. If you start your test planning and test-case development early in the development process, you'll detect many errors shortly after they are made. This prevents them from doing further damage and reduces your testing and maintenance costs.

Figure 14-1 illustrates the V model of software development, which shows test activities beginning in parallel with the corresponding development activities (Davis 1993). This model indicates that acceptance testing is based on the user requirements, system testing is based on the functional requirements, and integration testing is based on the system's architecture. You should begin planning your testing activities and developing preliminary test cases of each kind during the corresponding development phase. You can't actually run any tests during requirements development, because you don't have any software to execute yet. However, you can create conceptual test cases based on the requirements and use them to find errors, ambiguities, and omissions in your SRS and analysis models long before your team writes any code.

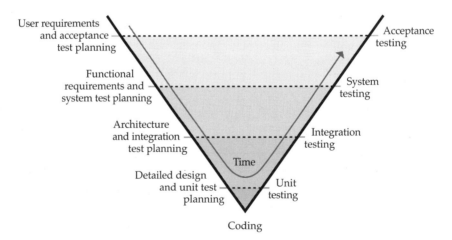

FIGURE 14-1 *V model of software development.*

Requirements verification is the fourth component (with elicitation, analysis, and specification) of requirements development.[1] Requirements verification includes activities intended to ensure the following:

◆ The SRS correctly describes the intended system behaviors and characteristics.

◆ The software requirements were correctly derived from the system requirements or other origins.

◆ The requirements are complete and of high quality.

◆ All views of the requirements are consistent.

◆ The requirements provide an adequate basis to proceed with product design, construction, and testing.

Verification ensures that the requirements conform to the characteristics of excellent requirement statements (complete, correct, feasible, necessary, prioritized, unambiguous, verifiable) and of excellent requirements specifications (complete, consistent, modifiable, traceable). Of course, you can only verify those requirements that have been documented. Unstated, implicit requirements that exist only in the minds of customers or developers cannot be verified.

Verification is not a single discrete phase that you perform after you have gathered and documented all of the requirements. Some verification activities, such as incremental reviews of the growing SRS, are threaded throughout the iterative elicitation, analysis, and specification processes. Other verification steps, such as formal inspection of the SRS, are useful as a final quality filter prior to baselining the SRS. Incorporate requirements verification activities as discrete tasks in your project plan or work breakdown structure, and plan some time for the subsequent rework that usually follows any quality control activity.

---

1. Some authors use the term "validation" for this requirements engineering step. Verification determines whether the product of a development activity meets the requirements established for it at the beginning of the activity (doing the thing right). Validation assesses whether an interim or final product actually satisfies the top-level specified requirements (doing the right thing). For software requirements, the distinction between the terms is subtle and debatable, so I've adopted the IEEE term "verification" for this requirements engineering step (Thayer and Dorfman 1997).

Project participants sometimes are reluctant to invest time in reviewing and testing an SRS. Although it seems that inserting time into the schedule to improve requirements quality would delay the planned ship date by that same amount of time, this expectation assumes a zero return on your investment in requirements verification. In reality, that investment can actually shorten the delivery schedule by reducing the rework required and by accelerating system testing. Capers Jones reports that every dollar spent to prevent defects will reduce your defect repair costs by three to ten dollars (Jones 1994). Better requirements also lead to higher product quality and greater customer satisfaction, which reduce the product's lifetime costs for maintenance, enhancement, and customer support. Investing in requirements quality almost always saves you more money than you spend.

Various techniques can help you verify the correctness and quality of your requirements (Wallace and Ippolito 1997). This chapter focuses on two of the most important verification techniques: formal and informal requirements reviews, and conceptual test cases developed from use cases and functional requirements.

REVIEWING REQUIREMENTS

Every time someone other than the author of a software work product examines the product for problems, a technical review is taking place. Reviews of requirements documents are an excellent technique for identifying ambiguous or unverifiable requirements, requirements that aren't clearly enough defined to provide as a basis for design, and "requirements" that are in fact design specifications.

Requirements reviews also provide a way for the stakeholders to agree on the seriousness of a specific issue. My colleague Barry once led an SRS review that included representatives from four user classes. One user raised an issue that turned out to be a showstopper: it would demand significant changes to the requirements. After the meeting, the requirements analyst and project manager were angry that this issue had not been raised during the past two months when they were meeting with that same user to define the requirements. After some investigation, it turned out that this user *had* raised that issue repeatedly, but she had been ignored. When several users agreed during the review that this was a serious issue, the analyst and project manager realized they couldn't ignore it any longer.

Different kinds of technical reviews go by a variety of names. Informal approaches include distribution of the work product to several peers to look over and a walkthrough in which the author describes the product and solicits comments. Informal reviews are good for educating other people about the product and getting unstructured feedback, but they typically are not systematic, thorough, or performed in a consistent way. Informal reviews do not require written records.

Whereas informal reviews are performed in an ad hoc fashion, a formal review follows a well-defined process with a prescribed sequence of steps. A formal review should result in a written report that identifies the material, the reviewers, the review team's judgment as to whether the product is complete or needs further work, and a summary of the defects found and issues raised. The members of a formal review team share responsibility for the quality of the review, although authors are ultimately responsible for the quality of the products they create (Freedman and Weinberg 1990).

The best-established type of formal technical review is called an *inspection* (Ebenau and Strauss 1994; Gilb and Graham 1993). Inspection of requirements documents is arguably the highest-leverage software quality technique available. Several companies have measured savings of ten hours of work for every hour invested in inspecting requirements documents and other software work products (Grady 1994). I know of no other software development or quality practice that can yield a 1000 percent return on investment.

If you are serious about maximizing the quality of your software, you will inspect every line of every requirements document you create. Although detailed inspection of large requirements documents is tedious and time consuming, the people I know who have adopted requirements inspections agree that every minute they spent was worthwhile. If you don't think you have time to inspect everything, use a simple risk analysis to differentiate those parts of the requirements documents that you should inspect from less critical portions for which an informal review will meet your quality objectives.

On the Chemical Tracking System, the teams representing the various user classes informally reviewed their contributions to the growing SRS after each elicitation workshop, uncovering many errors almost immediately. After elicitation was complete, one analyst combined all the SRS fragments from the different user classes into a single document of about 50 pages, plus several appendices. Two analysts, one developer, three product champions, the project manager, and a tester inspected this SRS in three two-hour inspection meetings. The inspection team found 223 additional errors, including several dozen major defects. All the inspectors agreed that the time they'd spent grinding through the SRS, one requirement at a time, during the inspection meetings saved the project team countless more hours in the long run.

THE INSPECTION PROCESS

Michael Fagan developed the inspection process at IBM in the mid-1970s (Fagan 1976), and it has since been recognized as a software industry best practice (Brown 1996). Any software work product can be inspected, including requirements and design documents, source code, test documentation, project plans, and so on. Inspection is a well-defined multistage process that involves a small team of trained participants who focus successively on portions of the work product to find defects. Inspections provide a quality gate through which the documents must pass before they are baselined. While there is some debate whether the Fagan method is the most effective and efficient form of inspection (Glass 1999), there's no question that inspections are a powerful quality technique.

Participants

The participants in an inspection should represent three perspectives:

1. *The author of the work product and perhaps peers of the author* The analyst who wrote the requirements document provides this perspective.

2. *The author of any predecessor work product or specification for the item being inspected* This might be a systems engineer or system architect who can examine the SRS for proper traceability of each requirement to a system specification. In the absence of a higher level requirements document, the inspection must include actual customers to ensure that the SRS accurately and completely describes their requirements.

3. *People who have to do work based on the document being inspected* For an SRS, you might include a developer, a tester, a project manager, and a user documentation writer, all of whose work is derived from the SRS. These inspectors will detect different kinds of problems. A tester is most likely to catch an unverifiable requirement, while a developer will spot requirements that are technically infeasible.

Try to keep the team to seven or fewer inspectors. Large teams easily get bogged down in side discussions, problem solving, and debates over whether something is really an error, thereby slowing the rate at which they cover the material during the inspection and increasing the cost of finding each defect.

Inspection Roles

Some inspection team members perform specific roles during the inspection; these roles vary a bit from one inspection process to another, but the functions performed are similar.

Author   The author created or maintains the product being inspected. The author of an SRS is usually the analyst who gathered customer requirements and wrote the specification. During informal reviews such as walkthroughs, the author often leads the discussion. However, the author takes a fairly passive role during an inspection and should not assume any of the other assigned roles—moderator, reader, or recorder. By not having an active role and parking his ego at the door, the author can listen to the comments from other inspectors, respond to—but not debate—their questions, and think. The author will often spot errors that other inspectors don't see.

Moderator   The moderator, or inspection leader, plans the inspection with the author, coordinates the activities, and facilitates the inspection meeting. The moderator distributes the materials to be inspected to the participants several days before the inspection meeting, starts the meeting on time, encourages contributions from all participants, and keeps the meeting focused on finding defects rather than resolving issues that are raised. Reporting the inspection results to management or to someone who collects data from multiple inspections is also the moderator's responsibility. A final moderator role is to follow up on proposed changes with the author, to make sure that the defects and issues arising from the inspection are addressed properly.

Reader   One inspector is assigned the role of reader. During the inspection meeting, the reader paraphrases the document under inspection one chunk at a time and allows the other participants to raise issues with his or her interpretation. For a requirements specification, the reader should present one labeled requirement or short paragraph at a time. By stating the requirement in his or her own words, the reader provides an interpretation that might differ from that held by other inspectors, which is one way to reveal ambiguity or a possible defect.

Recorder   The recorder, or scribe, documents the issues raised and defects found during the inspection meeting on standard forms. The recorder should review aloud what was written to confirm the record's accuracy. The other inspectors should help the recorder capture the essence of each issue in a cogent way that clearly communicates to the author the location and nature of the issue.

Inspection Stages

An inspection is a multistep event, as illustrated in Figure 14-2 (adapted from Ebenau and Strauss 1994). The purpose of each inspection process stage is summarized briefly below.

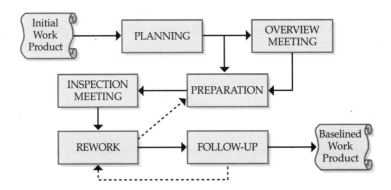

FIGURE 14-2   *Inspection process stages.*

Planning   The author and moderator plan the inspection together, determining who should participate, what materials the inspectors should receive prior to the inspection meeting, and how many inspection meetings will be needed. The inspection rate has a large impact on how many defects are found (Gilb and Graham 1993). As illustrated in Figure 14-3, proceeding through the SRS more slowly reveals the most defects. (An alternative interpretation of this frequently reported relationship is that the inspection slows down if you encounter a lot of defects.) Because no one has infinite time available for requirements inspections, select an appropriate rate based on the risk of overlooking major defects. Four to six pages per hour is a practical guideline, but adjust this rate based on the following factors:

- The amount of text on a page

- The complexity of the specification

- How critical the material being inspected is to project success

◆ Your own previous inspection data

◆ The experience level of the SRS author

Overview meeting   The overview meeting provides an opportunity to inform the inspectors about the background of the material they will be inspecting, any assumptions the author made, and the author's specific inspection objectives. You can omit this meeting if all inspectors are already adequately familiar with the items being inspected.

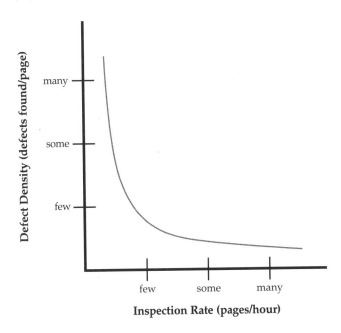

FIGURE 14-3   *Number of defects found as a function of inspection rate.*

Preparation   During preparation for the formal inspection, each inspector examines the product to identify possible defects and issues to be raised, using use the checklists of typical defects (described later in this chapter) as a guide. Up to 75 percent of the defects found by an inspection are discovered during preparation, so don't omit this step. Inadequately prepared inspectors result in ineffective inspection meetings, which can lead the team to conclude erroneously that inspections are a waste of time. Remember that the time you spend examining a colleague's work is an investment in improving the collective quality of the team's products and that other team members will be helping you improve your own products in the same way.

Inspection meeting   During the inspection meeting, the reader leads the inspection team through the SRS, paraphrasing one requirement at a time. As inspectors bring up possible defects and other issues, the recorder captures them on a form that becomes the action item list for the requirements author. The purpose of the meeting is to identify as many major defects in the requirements document as possible. It's easy for the inspectors to report only superficial and cosmetic issues, or to be sidetracked into discussing whether an issue really is a defect, debating questions of project scope, and brainstorming solutions to problems. These activities are useful, but they distract attention from the core objective of finding significant defects and improvement opportunities. The inspection meeting shouldn't last more than about two hours; if you need more time, schedule another meeting. At the meeting's conclusion, the team decides whether the requirements document is accepted as is, accepted with minor revisions, or not accepted because major revision and reinspection are needed.

Some researchers suggest that inspection meetings are too labor intensive to justify their value. However, I've found that the meetings can reveal additional defects that none of the inspectors found during their individual preparation. As with all quality activities, you must make a risk-based decision as to how much energy to devote to improving requirements quality before you proceed with design and construction.

Rework   Nearly every quality control activity I've observed found some defects. Therefore, the author should plan to spend some time reworking the document following the inspection meeting. Uncorrected requirement defects will be expensive to fix down the road, so this is the time to resolve the ambiguities, eliminate the fuzziness, and lay the foundation for a successful development project. If you don't intend to correct the defects, there's not much point in holding an inspection.

Follow-up   In this final inspection step, the moderator or a designated individual follows up on the rework that the author performed. Follow-up ensures that all open issues have been resolved and that the requirements errors were fixed correctly. Follow-up brings closure to the inspection process and enables the moderator to determine whether the inspection's exit criteria have been satisfied.

Entry and Exit Criteria

You are ready to inspect a software requirements document when it satisfies specific prerequisites. These *entry criteria* set some clear expectations for authors to follow when preparing for an inspection. They also keep the inspection team from wasting time on issues that should be resolved prior to the inspection. The moderator uses the entry criteria as a checklist before deciding to proceed with the inspection. Following are some suggested inspection entry criteria for requirements documents:

- ☐ The document conforms to the standard template.

- ☐ The document has been spell-checked and, if appropriate, grammar-checked.

- ☐ The author has visually examined the document for any layout errors.

- ☐ Any predecessor or reference documents that the inspectors will need to perform their work, such as a system requirements specification, are available.

- ☐ Line numbers are printed on the document to facilitate referring to specific locations during the inspection.

- ☐ All open issues are marked as TBD (to be determined).

- ☐ A glossary of terms used in the document is included.

Similarly, you should define the *exit criteria* that must be satisfied before the moderator declares the inspection complete. Here are some possible exit criteria for requirements document inspections:

- ☐ All issues raised by the inspection have been addressed.

- ☐ Any changes made in the document were made correctly.

- ☐ The revised document has been spell-checked and, if appropriate, grammar-checked.

- ☐ All TBDs have been resolved, or each TBD's resolution process, target date, and owner has been documented.

- ☐ The document has been checked into the project's configuration management system.

- ☐ Inspection metrics have been reported to the appropriate collection point.

Requirements Inspection Checklists

To help inspectors be on the lookout for typical kinds of errors in the products they inspect, develop a checklist for each type of requirements document your organization creates. These checklists call the inspectors' attention to historically frequent requirement problems. Figure 14-4 illustrates a checklist for inspecting an SRS, and Figure 14-5 contains a use-case inspection checklist.

No one can remember all of the items on a long checklist. Pare each list to meet your organization's needs and modify them to reflect the defects that you find most often in your own requirements. You might ask different inspectors to use different subsets of the overall checklist to look for defects. One person could check that all internal document cross-references are correct, while another determines whether the requirements can serve as the basis for design, and a third specifically evaluates verifiability. Some studies have shown that giving inspectors specific defect-detection responsibilities—providing structured thought processes or scenarios to help them hunt for particular kinds of errors—is more effective than simply handing all the inspectors a checklist (Porter, Votta, and Basili 1995).

REQUIREMENTS REVIEW CHALLENGES

Several challenges face the organization that reviews its requirements documents (Wiegers 1998). Below are some common problems, with suggestions for how to address each.

Large requirements documents   The prospect of thoroughly inspecting a several-hundred-page SRS is daunting. You might be tempted to skip the inspection entirely and just proceed with construction—not a good choice. Even with an SRS of moderate size, all inspectors might carefully examine the first part and a few stalwarts study the middle, but it's likely that no one will look at the last part. To avoid overwhelming the inspection team, don't wait to begin reviewing the SRS until you're ready to baseline it. Perform informal, incremental reviews while you're developing the SRS, prior to inspecting the completed document. Ask certain inspectors to start at different locations in the document to make certain that fresh eyes have looked at every page. If you have enough inspectors available, set up several small teams to inspect different portions of the material.

Large inspection teams   Many project participants and customers hold a stake in the requirements, so you might have a long list of potential participants for requirements inspections. However, large inspection teams make it difficult to schedule meetings, are prone to holding side conversations during inspection meetings, and have difficulty reaching agreement on issues. I once participated in an inspection with 14 inspectors. Fourteen people can't agree to leave a burning room, let alone agree on whether a particular requirement is correct. Try the following approaches to deal with a potentially large inspection team:

◆   Make sure every participant is there to find defects, not to learn what is in the SRS or to protect a political position. If education is the goal for some participants, invite them to the overview meeting but not to the inspection meeting.

◆   Understand which perspective (such as customer, developer, or tester) each inspector represents, and politely decline the participation of people who duplicate a perspective that's already covered. You might ask the people who represent a particular perspective to pool their feedback from preparation and send just one representative to the inspection meeting.

◆   Establish several small teams to inspect the SRS in parallel and combine their defect lists, removing any duplicates. Research has shown that multiple inspection teams find more defects in a requirements document than does a single large group (Martin and Tsai 1990; Schneider, Martin, and Tsai 1992; Kosman 1997). The teams tend to spot different subsets of the defects that are present, so the results of parallel inspections are primarily additive rather than redundant.

Geographic separation of inspectors   More and more development organizations are building products through the collaboration of geographically isolated teams. This separation makes requirements reviews more challenging. Videoconferencing can be an effective solution, but teleconferencing does not let you read the body language and expressions of other reviewers as effectively as you can in a face-to-face meeting. Both kinds of remote conferencing are harder to moderate than face-to-face sessions.

Requirement Checklist

ORGANIZATION AND COMPLETENESS

☐ Are all internal cross-references to other requirements correct?

☐ Are all requirements written at a consistent and appropriate level of detail?

☐ Do the requirements provide an adequate basis for design?

☐ Is the implementation priority of each requirement included?

☐ Are all external hardware, software, and communication interfaces defined?

☐ Are algorithms intrinsic to the functional requirements defined?

☐ Does the SRS include all of the known customer or system needs?

☐ Is any necessary information missing from a requirement? If so, is it identified as TBD?

☐ Is the expected behavior documented for all anticipated error conditions?

CORRECTNESS

☐ Do any requirements conflict with or duplicate other requirements?

☐ Is each requirement written in clear, concise, and unambiguous language?

☐ Is each requirement verifiable by testing, demonstration, review, or analysis?

☐ Is each requirement in scope for the project?

☐ Is each requirement free from content and grammatical errors?

☐ Can all of the requirements be implemented within known constraints?

☐ Are any specified error messages unique and meaningful?

QUALITY ATTRIBUTES

☐ Are all performance objectives properly specified?

☐ Are all security and safety considerations properly specified?

☐ Are other pertinent quality attribute goals explicitly documented and quantified, with the acceptable trade-offs specified?

FIGURE 14-4   *Inspection checklist for software requirements specifications.*   *(continued)*

Figure 14-4 *continued*

TRACEABILITY

- ☐ Is each requirement uniquely and correctly identified?
- ☐ Is each software functional requirement traced to a higher-level requirement (e.g., system requirement or use case)?

SPECIAL ISSUES

- ☐ Are all requirements actually requirements, not design or implementation solutions?
- ☐ Are the time-critical functions identified and their timing criteria specified?
- ☐ Have internationalization issues been adequately addressed?

- ☐ Is the use case a stand-alone, discrete task?
- ☐ Is the goal, or measurable value, of the use case clear?
- ☐ Is it clear which actor(s) benefit from the use case?
- ☐ Is the use case written at the essential (abstract) level, rather than as a specific scenario?
- ☐ Is the use case free of design and implementation details?
- ☐ Are all anticipated alternative courses documented?
- ☐ Are all known exception conditions documented?
- ☐ Are there any common action sequences that could be split into separate use cases?
- ☐ Is the dialog sequence for each course clearly written, unambiguous, and complete?
- ☐ Is every actor and step in the use case pertinent to performing that task?
- ☐ Is each course defined in the use case feasible?
- ☐ Is each course defined in the use case verifiable?

FIGURE 14-5   *Inspection checklist for use-case documents.*

Document reviews of an electronic file placed in a shared network folder provide an alternative to a traditional inspection meeting. In this approach, reviewers use word processor features to insert their comments in the text under review. Each reviewer's comments are labeled with his or her initials, and each reviewer can see what previous reviewers had to say. Web-based chat tools can enable real-time remote discussions, but they provide a low communication bandwidth. Web-based collaboration software embedded in tools like ReviewPro from Software Development Technologies (*http://www.sdtcorp.com*) can also help. If you choose not to hold an inspection meeting, recognize that this can reduce the inspection's effectiveness by perhaps 25 percent.

TESTING THE REQUIREMENTS

It's often hard to visualize how a system will behave under specific circumstances by reading the SRS. Test cases that are based on the functional requirements or derived from use cases help make the expected system behaviors tangible to the project participants. The simple act of designing test cases will reveal many problems with the requirements, even without executing the tests on an operational system (Beizer 1990). If you begin to develop test cases as soon as portions of the requirements stabilize, you can find problems while it's still early enough to correct them inexpensively.

Writing black-box, or functional, test cases crystallizes your vision of how the system should behave under specific conditions. Vague and ambiguous requirements will jump out at you because you won't be able to describe the expected system response. When analysts, developers, and customers walk through the test cases together, they will share a clear vision of how the product will work.

You can derive conceptual functional test cases from the use cases very early in the development process (Ambler 1995; Collard 1999). You can then use the test cases to verify textual requirements specifications and analysis models (such as dialog maps) and to evaluate prototypes. Such test cases, based on anticipated usage scenarios, can serve as the foundation for customer acceptance testing. You can also elaborate them into detailed test cases and procedures for formal system testing (Hsia, Kung, and Sell 1997). The basic question you are asking the customers to answer when they define their acceptance criteria is "How would you know if the software is really what you are looking for?" If they can't answer this question for each feature or use case, they need to clarify the requirements.

In an earlier chapter, I related a situation in which I asked our group's Unix scripting guru, Charlie, to code a simple e-mail interface extension for a commercial defect-tracking system we were using. I wrote down about a dozen requirements, which Charlie found very helpful; he had never been given requirements for a script before. Unfortunately, I waited a couple of weeks before I wrote the test cases for this e-mail function. Sure enough, I had made an error in one of the requirements. I found the mistake because my vision of how I expected the e-mail function to work, represented in about twenty test cases, was not consistent with one of the requirements. A bit chagrined, I corrected the defective requirement before Charlie had completed his implementation, and when he delivered the script, it was defect-free.

The notion of testing requirements might seem abstract to you at first. An example might illustrate this concept more clearly, so let's see how the Chemical Tracking System team tied together requirements specification, analysis modeling, and early test-case generation. Following are listed a business requirement, a use case, a functional requirement, part of a dialog map, and a test case that relate to the task of requesting a chemical.

Business requirement   One of the primary business motivations for this system was the following requirement:

> *The Chemical Tracking System will reduce chemical purchasing costs by encouraging the reuse of chemical containers that are already available within the company.*

Do Example for Ivermectin

Use case   A use case that aligns with this business requirement is "Request a Chemical," which includes a path that permits the user to request a chemical container that is already available in the chemical stockroom. Here is the use-case description (see Figure 8-3 for more details):

> *The Requester specifies the chemical to request, either by entering its chemical ID number or by importing its structure from a chemical drawing tool. The system can satisfy the request either by offering the Requester a new or used container of the chemical from the chemical stockroom or by letting the Requester place an order to an outside vendor.*

Functional requirement   Here is one bit of functionality associated with letting the user select an available chemical rather than placing a new order with a vendor:

> *If the stockroom has containers of the chemical being requested, the system shall display a list of the available containers. The user shall either select a container or ask to place an order for a new container from a vendor.*

Dialog map   Figure 14-6 illustrates a portion of the dialog map for the "Request a Chemical" use case that pertains to this function. The boxes in the dialog map represent conceptual dialog elements between the user and the system, and the arrows represent possible navigation paths from one dialog element to another.

Test case   Because this use case has several possible execution paths, you can envision quite a few test cases to address the normal course, alternative courses, and exceptions. Here is just one test case, based on the path that shows the user the available containers in the chemical stockroom. This test case was derived from both the use-case description of this user task and the dialog map in Figure 14-6:

> *At dialog box DB40, enter a valid chemical ID; the chemical stockroom has two containers of this chemical. Dialog box DB50 appears, with the two container numbers. Select the second of the two containers. DB50 closes and container 2 is added to the bottom of the Current Chemical Request List in dialog box DB70.*

Ramesh, the test lead for the Chemical Tracking System, wrote several test cases like this, based on his understanding of how the user would interact with the system to request a chemical. He mapped each test case against the corresponding functional requirements to make certain that every test case could be "executed" by the existing set of requirements and that at least one test case covered every functional requirement. Next, Ramesh traced the execution path for every test case on the dialog map with a highlighter pen. The shaded line in Figure 14-7 shows how the sample test case shown above traces onto the dialog map.

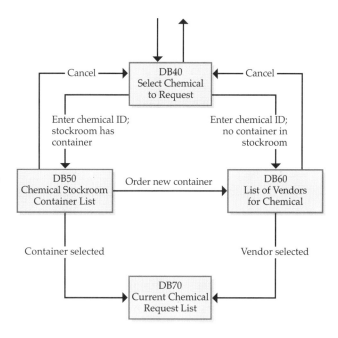

FIGURE 14-6   *Portion of the dialog map for the "Request a Chemical" use case.*

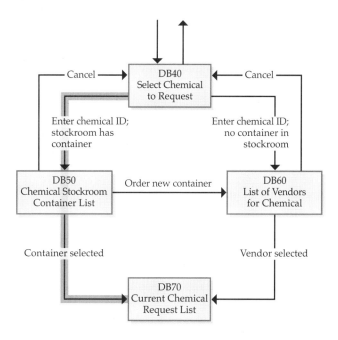

FIGURE 14-7   *Tracing a test case onto the dialog map for the "Request a Chemical" use case.*

By tracing the execution path for each test case, you can find incorrect or missing requirements, correct errors in the dialog map, and refine the test cases. For example, suppose that after "executing" all the test cases in this fashion, the dialog map navigation line labeled "Order new container" that goes from DB50 to DB60 has not been highlighted. Two interpretations are possible:

1. The navigation is not a permitted system behavior. The line must be removed from the dialog map, and if the SRS contains a requirement that specifies the transition, that requirement must also be removed.

2. The navigation is a legitimate system behavior, but the test case that demonstrates the behavior is missing.

Similarly, suppose a test case states that the user can take some action to move directly from dialog box DB40 to DB70. However, the dialog map in Figure 14-6 does not contain such a navigation line, so the test case cannot be executed with the existing requirements. Again, there are two possible interpretations, and you will need to determine which is correct:

1. The navigation from DB40 to DB70 is not a permitted system behavior, so the test case is wrong.

2. The navigation from DB40 to DB70 is a legitimate system behavior, but the dialog map and perhaps the SRS are missing the requirement that allows you to execute the test case.

In these examples, the analyst and tester combined requirements, analysis models, and test cases to detect missing, erroneous, and unnecessary requirements long before any code was written. Conceptual testing of software requirements is a powerful technique for controlling a project's cost and schedule by finding requirement errors very early in the game.

Collecting and documenting your requirements is an excellent starting point for software project success. You also need to make sure they are the right requirements and that they exhibit all of the characteristics of excellent requirement statements. If you combine early black-box test design with informal requirements reviews, SRS inspections, and other requirements verification techniques, you will build higher-quality systems in less time and at lower cost than you ever have before.

Next Steps

◆   Choose a page of functional requirements at random from your
    project's SRS. Convene a small team of people who represent
    different stakeholder perspectives and carefully examine the re-
    quirements on that page for any deviations from the character-
    istics of excellent requirement statements.

◆   If you found enough problems with the random review to make
    the reviewers nervous about the overall quality of the require-
    ments, persuade the user and development representatives to
    inspect the entire SRS. Train the team members in the inspection
    process for maximum effectiveness.

◆   Define conceptual test cases for a use case or a portion of the SRS
    that has not yet been coded. Determine whether the stakehold-
    ers agree that the test cases reflect the intended system behavior.
    Make sure you've defined all the functional requirements that
    will permit the test cases to be "executed" and that there are no
    superfluous requirements.

15

Beyond Requirements Development

Despite a rocky beginning, the Chemical Tracking System was coming along nicely. The project sponsor, Gerhard, and the chemical stockroom product champion, Roxanne, had been skeptical of the need to spend so much time gathering requirements. However, they were willing to join the development team and the other product champions at a one-day training class on software requirements. This class stressed the importance of having all the project stakeholders reach a shared understanding of the requirements before writing the software. The class exposed all the team members to the requirements terminology, concepts, and practices they would be using, and it motivated them to put some improved requirements techniques into action.

As the project progressed, Gerhard received excellent feedback from the user representatives about how well requirements development had gone. As a result, he sponsored a luncheon for the development team and product champions to celebrate reaching the significant milestone of baselined requirements for stage one of the Chemical Tracking System. At the luncheon, Gerhard enthusiastically thanked the requirements elicitation participants for their contributions and teamwork, and then continued, "Now that you have the requirements in good order, I look forward to seeing some code coming out of the development group very soon."

"We aren't quite ready to start writing the production code yet," the project manager reminded Gerhard. "We plan to release the system in stages, so we need to think about the best way to design the system to accommodate the future additions. Our prototypes gave us some good ideas about technical approaches that should work and helped us understand the interface characteristics the users would prefer. If we invest some time now in designing the software, we shouldn't encounter major problems as we add more functionality to the system over the next year."

Gerhard was a little frustrated. Again, it looked like the development group was stalling on getting down to the real work of programming. But was he jumping the gun?

Experienced project managers and developers understand how important it is to translate software requirements into robust designs and rational project plans. This chapter briefly explores some approaches for bridging the gap between requirements development and a successful product release by looking at the connections between requirements and project plans, designs, code, and tests.

FROM REQUIREMENTS TO PROJECT PLANS

Because the requirements define the project's intended outcomes, your project plans, estimates, and schedules should all be based on the software requirements.

REQUIREMENTS AND SCHEDULING

Many software projects practice "right-to-left scheduling," in which a delivery date is cast in concrete and then the product's requirements are defined. It often proves impossible for the developers to meet the specified ship date while including all the demanded functionality at the expected quality level. It is more realistic to define the software requirements *before* making detailed plans and commitments. However, a design-to-schedule strategy can also work, provided you have some latitude to negotiate what fraction of the desired requirements can fit within the schedule constraints.

For complex systems in which software is only a part of the final product, high-level schedules are generally established after the product-level (system) requirements are generated. Then the system requirements are decomposed and allocated into various software and hardware subsystems. At this point, the key delivery dates have been established and agreed on, based on input from a variety of sources, including marketing, sales, customer service, and development. If the schedule is constrained, the cross-functional development team must make the trade-off decisions about functionality, quality, and cost.

You might consider planning and funding the project in stages. The first stage, requirements exploration, will provide enough information to let you make realistic plans and estimates for one or more construction stages. Projects that have uncertain requirements can benefit from iterative or incremental software development life cycles. Defining requirement priorities allows you to determine what functionality to include in the initial release and in planned subsequent releases.

Software projects frequently fail to meet their goals because the developers and other project participants are poor planners, not because they're poor software engineers. Major planning mistakes include overlooking common project tasks, underestimating effort or time, failing to account for project risks, and not expecting to spend time on rework. Accurate project planning requires the following elements:

- Estimated product size, based on clearly understood requirements

- Known productivity of the development team, based on historical performance

- A comprehensive list of the tasks needed to completely implement and verify a feature or use case

- Effective estimation and planning processes

- Experience

REQUIREMENTS AND ESTIMATION

The first step in project estimating is to relate the requirements to the size of the software product. You can base size estimates on textual requirements, graphical analysis models, prototypes, or user interface designs. Although there is no perfect measure of software size, the following are some frequently used metrics:

◆   Function points and feature points (Jones 1996b), or 3-D function points (Whitmire 1995)

◆   The number, type, and complexity of graphical user interface (GUI) elements

◆   Lines of source code needed to implement specific requirements

◆   A count of object classes or other metrics for object-oriented systems (Whitmire 1997)

◆   The number of individually testable requirements (Wilson 1995)

All of these methods can work for estimating size, but whatever approach you choose must be based on your experience. If you don't record the actual results you achieve on your current project, compare those results to your estimates, and use that knowledge to improve your estimating ability, your estimates will forever remain guesses. It takes time to accumulate data so that you can correlate some measure of software size with actual development effort. Your objective is to develop equations or heuristics that will let you estimate the size of the completed software from its documented requirements. Another approach is to estimate the lines of code, function points, or GUI elements from the requirements and use a commercial software estimation tool to suggest feasible combinations of staffing levels and development schedules. You can get information about some of the available estimation tools from *http://www.methods-tools.com.*

Vague and uncertain requirements inevitably lead to uncertainty in your size estimates, and hence in your effort and schedule estimates. Because uncertainty about requirements is unavoidable early in the project, include contingency buffers in your schedule and budget to accommodate some requirements growth and the likely overruns. A sensible home-remodeling project includes contingencies for unanticipated developments; shouldn't you do the same for your software projects?

Plan to invest some time in determining which metrics are most appropriate for the kinds of projects you work on. Recognize that development time does not have a linear relationship to the size of the product or the size of the team. There's a complex relationship between product size, effort, development time, productivity, and staff buildup time (Putnam and Myers 1997). Understanding this relationship can keep you from being trapped into making scheduling or staffing commitments that lie in the "impossible region" where no similar project has ever been completed successfully.

FROM REQUIREMENTS TO DESIGNS AND CODE

A gray area lies between requirements and design, but try to keep your specifications as free from implementation bias as possible. Ideally, the descriptions of what the system is intended to do should not be slanted by design considerations (Jackson 1995). Requirements development and specification should concentrate on understanding and describing the intended external behaviors of the system. Include designers or developers in requirements inspections to make sure the requirements can serve as the basis for design.

A variety of software designs will usually satisfy the resulting requirements, designs that will vary in their performance, efficiency, robustness, and the technical methods employed. If you leap directly from a requirements specification into code, you're essentially designing the software on the fly, with poorly structured software as the likely result. Contemplate the most effective way to construct the system before you actually build it. Thinking about design alternatives will also help to ensure that developers respect any stated design constraints or design-related quality attribute specifications.

I once worked on a project that did a thorough job of requirements analysis, building detailed data flow diagrams that depicted a sequence of eight transformational processes simulating the behavior of a photographic system. After working so hard on analysis, we were tempted to dive right into the source code editor. Instead, we took the time to create a design model, again represented by a data flow diagram. We quickly realized that three of the steps in the model used identical computational algorithms, another three used a different set of equations, and the remaining two steps shared a third set.

The analysis models represented the customer's and development team's understanding of the problem we were solving, and the design models illustrated how we intended to build the system. By taking the time to think through the design, we simplified the core problem by about 60 percent, reducing eight sets of complex calculations to just three. Had we begun coding immediately after requirements analysis, we doubtless would have noticed the code repetition at some point during construction. However, we saved a lot of time (and therefore money) by detecting these simplifications early on. It is more efficient to rework designs than to rework code.

As with requirements, excellent designs are the result of iteration. Make multiple passes through the design to refine your initial concepts as you gain more information and get additional ideas. Shortcomings in design lead to software systems that are difficult to maintain and extend and which don't satisfy the customer's performance and reliability objectives. The time you spend translating requirements into designs is an excellent investment in building high-quality, robust software products.

A product's requirements and quality attributes determine appropriate architectural approaches to use when designing the product (Bass, Clements, and Kazman 1998). Studying and reviewing a proposed architecture is another way to illuminate the requirements and enhance their clarity. This is a kind of bottom-up approach to requirements analysis, analogous to prototyping. Both methods center around this thought process: "If I understand the requirements correctly, then this approach is a good way to satisfy them. Now that I have a preliminary architecture (or prototype) in hand, does it help me understand the requirements better?"

You don't have to develop a complete, detailed design for the entire product before you can begin implementing any portion of the requirements. However, you should design each component before you code it. Design planning is of most benefit to very difficult projects, systems with many internal component interfaces and interactions, and projects staffed with inexperienced developers (McConnell 1998). However, all projects will benefit from the following steps:

◆   Develop a solid architecture of subsystems and software components that will hold up during maintenance.

◆   Identify the object classes or functional modules you need to build, defining their interfaces, responsibilities, and collaborations with other code units.

◆ Define each code unit's intended functionality, following the sound design principles of strong cohesion, loose coupling, and information hiding.

◆ Make sure your design accommodates all of the functional requirements and does not contain unnecessary functionality.

As developers translate the requirements into designs and code, they will encounter points of ambiguity and confusion. Ideally, developers can route these issues back to the customers for resolution. If an issue cannot be resolved immediately, any assumptions, guesses, or interpretations a developer makes should be documented and reviewed with customer representatives. If you encounter many such problems, the requirements probably weren't sufficiently clear or detailed before they were passed to the developers for implementation. In this situation, a review of the remaining requirements with a developer or two is a good idea before construction continues.

FROM REQUIREMENTS TO TESTS

The specified requirements provide the foundation for system testing, which determines whether the software satisfies its requirements. You must test the completed product against what it was intended to do as documented in the SRS, not against the design or the code. System testing that is based on the code can become a self-fulfilling prophecy. The product might correctly exhibit all of the behaviors described in test cases based on the code, but that doesn't mean it correctly implements the user requirements. If you don't have well-documented requirements, you'll have to elicit them again to develop suitable test cases—an inefficient and inaccurate approach. Include testers in requirements inspections to make sure the requirements are verifiable and can serve as the basis for system testing.

As each requirement stabilizes during requirements development, the project's system testers should document how they will verify it—through testing, inspection, demonstration, or analysis. The simple act of thinking through how you will verify each requirement is itself a useful quality practice. Use analytical techniques such as cause-and-effect graphs to derive test cases based on the logic described in a requirement. This will reveal ambiguities, missing or implied "else" conditions, and other problems. Every requirement should trace to at least one test case in your system test suite, so that no expected system behavior goes unverified. You can measure testing progress in part by tracking the percentage of the requirements that have passed their tests. Skillful testers will augment purely requirements-based testing with their understanding of the product's intended functions, usage, quality characteristics, and quirks.

Specification-based testing applies several test design strategies: action driven, data driven (including boundary value analysis and equivalence class partitioning), logic driven, event driven, and state driven (Poston 1996). It's fairly easy to generate test cases automatically from formal specifications, but you'll have to develop test cases manually from the more common natural-language requirements specifications. Object models lend themselves more readily to automated test-case generation than do the various structured analysis diagrams.

As development progresses, you'll elaborate the requirements from the high level of abstraction found in use cases, through the detailed software functional requirements, and ultimately down to the specifications for individual code modules. Testing authority Boris Beizer (1999) points out that testing against requirements must be performed at every level of software construction, not just the end user level. Much of the code in an application is not directly accessed by users, but is needed for the product's infrastructure operations. Each module must satisfy its own requirements or specification, even if that module's function is invisible to the user of the overall software product. Consequently, testing the system against user requirements is a necessary, but not sufficient, condition for system testing.

FROM REQUIREMENTS TO SUCCESS

I recently encountered a project in which a new development team came on board to implement an application for which an earlier team had developed the requirements. The new team took one look at the dozen three-inch binders that contained the SRS, shuddered in horror, and began coding. They didn't refer to the SRS during their construction process; instead they built what they thought they were supposed to, based on an incomplete and inaccurate understanding of the intended system. I wasn't surprised that this project encountered a lot of problems. The prospect of trying to understand such a huge volume of requirements (which might or might not have been well written) is certainly daunting, but ignoring them is a decisive step toward project failure.

I know of a more successful project that had a practice of listing all of the requirements that were addressed by a specific code release. The project's quality assurance group evaluated each release by performing the tests for those requirements. A requirement that was not met according to its test criteria was counted as an error. If more than a predetermined number of requirements were not met, or if specific high-impact requirements were not satisfied, the release was rejected. This project was successful because it used its documented requirements as the foundation for deciding when a release was ready to ship.

The ultimate deliverable of a software development project is a software system that meets the customers' needs and expectations. The requirements are an essential step on the path from product concept to satisfied customers. If you don't base your project plans, software designs, and system tests on a foundation of high-quality requirements, you're likely to waste a great deal of effort trying to deliver an excellent product.

However, don't become a slave to your requirements processes, either. Avoid the analysis paralysis trap, in which the team spends so much time generating unnecessary documents and holding ritualized meetings and reviews that no software ever gets written and the project is canceled. Strive for a sensible balance between rigid specification and off-the-top-of-the-head coding that will reduce to an acceptable level the risk of building the wrong product.

 *Next Steps*

◆   See if you can trace all of the requirements in an implemented portion of your SRS to individual elements of your software design. These might be processes in data flow models, tables in an entity-relationship diagram, object classes or methods, or other design elements. If your developers do not routinely create software designs before they begin cutting code, perhaps they need some training in software design.

◆   Keep records of the lines of code, function points, object classes, or GUI elements that are needed to implement each product feature or use case. Also, record your estimates for the effort needed to completely implement and verify each feature or use case, as well as the actual effort required. Derive correlations between size and effort that will help you make more accurate estimates from future requirements specifications.

PART III

SOFTWARE REQUIREMENTS MANAGEMENT

16

Requirements Management Principles and Practices

Chapter 1 divided the discipline of requirements engineering into requirements development and requirements management. Requirements development involves eliciting, analyzing, specifying, and verifying a software project's requirements. Typical requirements development products include a vision and scope document, a use-case document, a software requirements specification, and associated analysis models. Once reviewed and approved, these documents define the requirements baseline for the development effort. The baseline constitutes an agreement between the customers and the development group about the functional and nonfunctional requirements for the planned product. The project likely will have additional agreements regarding deliverables, constraints, schedules, budgets, or contractual commitments, but these topics lie beyond the scope of this book.

The requirements agreement is the bridge between requirements development and requirements management. Requirements management includes all activities that maintain the integrity and accuracy of the requirements agreement as the project progresses, as Figure 16-1 shows. Requirements management emphasizes:

◆   Controlling changes to the requirements baseline

◆   Keeping project plans current with the requirements

◆   Controlling versions of both individual requirements and requirements documents

◆   Managing the relationships between requirements, and links or dependencies between individual requirements and other project deliverables

◆   Tracking the status of the requirements in the baseline

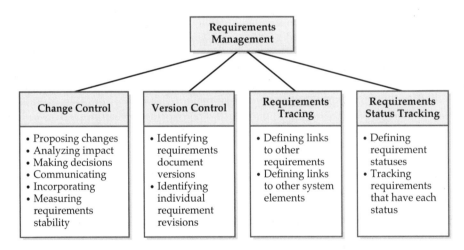

FIGURE 16-1   *Major requirements management activities.*

This chapter addresses the basic principles of requirements management. The other chapters in Part III describe specific requirements management practices in more detail, including change control (discussed in Chapter 17), requirements tracing (covered in Chapter 18), and change impact analysis (also discussed in Chapter 18). Part III concludes with a discussion of commercial tools that can help you manage your project's requirements (Chapter 19).

REQUIREMENTS MANAGEMENT AND THE CAPABILITY MATURITY MODEL

The Capability Maturity Model for Software (CMM) is a useful guide for requirements management (CMU/SEI 1995). The CMM was developed by the Software Engineering Institute, which is part of Carnegie Mellon University in Pittsburgh, Pennsylvania. The CMM is a widely used framework for guiding process improvement in a software development organization. It describes five *maturity levels* of software process capability. Organizations at Level 1 typically conduct their projects in an ad hoc and informal fashion, achieving success primarily through the heroic efforts of talented practitioners and managers. Organizations at higher maturity levels combine capable, creative, and trained people with sensible software engineering and project management processes to consistently achieve software success.

To achieve Level 2 of the CMM, an organization must demonstrate that it satisfies goals in six *key process areas* (KPAs) of software development and management. Requirements management is one of these six areas, and its goals are as follows:

1. The software requirements are controlled to establish a baseline for software engineering and management use.

2. Software plans, products, and activities are kept consistent with the software requirements.

Whether or not they know or care about the CMM, most software development organizations will benefit from achieving these two goals. The CMM identifies several prerequisites and technical practices that enable an organization to consistently achieve these goals, but it does not prescribe specific requirements management processes that the organization must follow.

The requirements management KPA does not address gathering and analyzing the project's requirements. It assumes that the software requirements have already been collected or that they were allocated from higher-level system requirements. Once the requirements are in hand and documented, the software development group and any other affected groups (such as quality assurance and testing) review them. Identified problems are resolved with the customers or other requirements sources. The software development plan is based on the approved requirements.

The development group should agree to the requirements and identify any constraints, risks, contingencies, or assumptions before making commitments to customers, the marketing department, or managers. You might be pressured to commit to requirements that are unrealistic for technical feasibility or scheduling reasons. However, you should never make commitments you know you cannot keep. No one wins in such a situation.

This KPA also recommends that requirements documents be managed through version control and change control. Version control ensures that the version of the requirements being used for development or planning is known at all times. Change control provides a way to incorporate requirements changes in a controlled and disciplined manner, based on good business and technical decisions to approve or reject proposed changes. As requirements are modified, added, or deleted during development, the software development plan should be updated to remain consistent with the new requirements. Plans that don't reflect the current reality cannot usefully guide your project.

When proposed changes in the requirements are accepted, you might not be able to meet the existing commitments to schedule and quality. In this case, you must negotiate changes to those commitments with affected managers, developers, and other related groups. The project can respond to new or changed requirements in several ways:

- ◆ Defer low-priority requirements
- ◆ Obtain additional staff
- ◆ Mandate overtime, preferably with pay, for a short period
- ◆ Slip the schedule to accommodate the new functionality
- ◆ Let quality suffer in the press to ship by the original date (Too often, this is the default reaction.)

There is no single, globally correct choice because projects differ in their flexibility of features, schedule, staff, budget, and quality (Wiegers 1996a). Base the options you select on the priorities that the key project stakeholders established during the early planning stages. No matter how you respond to changing requirements or project conditions (such as staff turnover), get in the habit of adjusting commitments when necessary. This is better than unrealistically expecting that somehow all the new features will be magically incorporated before the original delivery date without any consequences (such as budget overruns or team member burnout).

Even if you are not using the CMM to guide your software process improvements, the principles and practices outlined in the requirements management KPA make good sense. Every development organization can benefit from the thoughtful application of these approaches.

REQUIREMENTS MANAGEMENT PROCEDURES

Your organization should define the steps that project teams will perform to manage their requirements. Documenting these steps enables the members of the organization to perform essential project activities consistently and effectively. Consider addressing the following topics:

- Tools, techniques, and conventions for controlling versions of the various requirements documents or of individual requirements

- The ways that new requirements and changes to existing ones are proposed, processed, negotiated, and communicated to all affected functional areas

- How the requirements are baselined

- The requirement statuses that you will use, as well as who is permitted to change them

- Requirement status tracking and reporting procedures

- The steps to follow for analyzing the impact of proposed changes

- How changes in the requirements will be reflected in the project's plans and commitments, and under what conditions

You can include all of this information in a single document. Alternatively, you might prefer to write individual procedures for the major requirements management functions, such as a change control procedure, an impact analysis procedure, and a status tracking procedure. These procedures will probably be useful across multiple projects in your organization because they represent common functions that every project should perform.

Version Control of Requirements Specifications

"I finally finished implementing the inventory reorder report feature,"
Shari said at the project's weekly status meeting.

"Oh, the customers canceled that feature two weeks ago," the project
manager replied. "Didn't you get the revised SRS?"

If you've ever heard a conversation like this one, you know how frustrating, expensive, and demoralizing it is when team members waste time working from an obsolete requirements document. I know of one development team that received a flood of defect reports after promoting a new software release to system test. The testers had been working from an outdated SRS that did not correspond to the current product functionality, which led to the spurious defect reports. The team spent considerable time trying to identify the problem, and they spent even more time repeating the testing against the correct version of the SRS.

Version control is an essential aspect of managing your requirements. Every version of the requirements documents must be uniquely identified. Every member of the team must be able to access the current version of the requirements, and changes must be clearly documented and communicated to everyone affected. To minimize confusion, conflicts, and miscommunication, permit only designated individuals to update the requirements. These same practices apply to all your key project documents.

Each published version of the requirements documents should include a revision history that identifies the changes made, the date each change was made, the individual who made the change, and the reasons for each change. You can use standard revision marks, such as strikethrough for deletions, underscore for additions, and vertical revision bars in the margin to indicate the location of each change. Since these notations can clutter the document, word processors that support revision marks will let you view and print either the edited document or its final incarnation. Consider appending a version number to each individual requirement label, which you can increment whenever the requirement is modified.

The simplest means of version control is to manually label each revision of the SRS according to a standard convention. Schemes that try to differentiate document versions based on revision date or the date the document was printed are prone to error, so I don't recommend them. I have used a manual scheme that labels the first version of any new document "version 1.0 draft 1." The next draft is "version 1.0 draft 2," and the draft number is incremented with each iteration until the document is approved and baselined. At that time, the label is changed to "version 1.0 approved." The next version is designated either "version 1.1 draft 1" for a minor revision or "version 2.0 draft 1" for a major change. ("Major" and "minor" are rather subjective terms.) This scheme clearly distinguishes between draft and baselined document versions, but it requires manual discipline.

A more sophisticated level of version control involves storing the requirements documents in a version control tool, such as those used for controlling source code through check-in and check-out procedures. Many commercial configuration management tools are available for this purpose. I know of one project that stored several hundred use-case documents written in Microsoft Word in such a version control tool. The tool let the team members access every previous version of every use-case document, and it provided a log that described the history of changes made to each one. The project's requirements analysts had read/write access to the documents stored in the tool, while the other team members had read-only access. This version control scheme worked well for that project.

The most powerful approach to version control is to store the requirements in the database of a commercial requirements management tool, as described in Chapter 19. These tools can track and report the complete history of changes made to every requirement, which is valuable when you need to revert to an earlier version of a requirement. Comments describing the rationale behind a decision to add, change, delete, or reject a requirement are helpful if the requirement becomes a topic for discussion again in the future.

REQUIREMENT ATTRIBUTES

In addition to its text, each functional requirement should have several pieces of information, or *attributes*, associated with it. These attributes establish a context and background for each requirement that goes well beyond the description of its intended functionality. Attribute values can be stored in a spreadsheet, a database, or a requirements management tool. The commercial tools typically provide several system-generated attributes in addition to letting you define other attributes of various data types. Such tools let you filter, sort, and query the database to view selected subsets of requirements based on their attribute values.

A rich set of attributes is especially important on large, complex projects. Consider specifying attributes such as the following for each of your requirements:

- Date the requirement was created

- Version number of the requirement

- Author who created the requirement

- Person responsible for ensuring that the requirement is satisfied

- Requirement status

- Origin of the requirement or rationale behind it (or a reference to the location where this information can be found)

- Subsystem to which the requirement is allocated

- Product release to which the requirement is allocated

- Verification method to be used or acceptance test criteria

- Priority or importance to the product (specified as high, medium, or low, or you could define individual attributes for the four dimensions of priority described in Chapter 13: benefit, penalty, cost, and risk)

- Stability of the requirement (an indicator of how likely it is that changes will be made to the requirement in the future; unstable requirements might indicate that you are attempting to automate ill-defined, chaotic, or unrepeatable business processes)

Defining and updating these attribute values is part of the cost of requirements management. Select the minimum subset of attributes that will help you manage your project effectively. For example, you might not need to record both the name of the person responsible for ensuring that the requirement is satisfied and the subsystem to which the requirement is allocated. If any of this information already has been captured elsewhere, perhaps in an overall development tracking system, you should not duplicate it in the requirements database.

Tracking the status of each requirement throughout development is an important aspect of requirements management (Caputo 1998). Overall project monitoring is improved if you can periodically report the percentage of your entire requirements set that exists in each possible status category. Tracking the requirements status will work only if you establish clear expectations and define who is permitted to modify the status information and the conditions that must be satisfied for any status change. A tool can help you track the date that each status change was made.

Table 16-1 suggests several requirement statuses. Some practitioners add the status Designed (which means the design elements that address the functional requirement have been created and reviewed) or Delivered (meaning the software in which the requirement is implemented is in the hands of the users, as in a beta test). It's also valuable to keep a record of requirements that were proposed but never approved (that is, a status of Rejected) because such requirements have a way of resurfacing during development.

TABLE 16-1   SUGGESTED REQUIREMENT STATUSES

Status	Definition
Proposed	The requirement has been requested by a source who has the authority to provide requirements.
Approved	The requirement has been analyzed, its impact on the rest of the project has been estimated (including cost and interference with other parts of the product), and it has been allocated to the baseline for a specific build number or product release. The software development group has committed to implement the requirement.
Implemented	The code that implements the requirement has been designed, written, and unit tested.
Verified	The implemented requirement has been verified through the selected approach, such as testing or inspection. The requirement has been traced to pertinent test cases. The requirement is now considered complete.
Deleted	A planned requirement has been deleted from the baseline. Include an explanation of why and by whom the decision was made to delete the requirement.

Figure 16-2 illustrates a graphical way to track the status of requirements throughout the duration of a hypothetical 10-month project. It shows the percentage of all the system's requirements with their respective status values at the end of each month. Tracking the distribution by percentages doesn't show whether the number of requirements in the baseline is changing over time, but it does illustrate how you are approaching the goal of complete verification of all approved requirements.

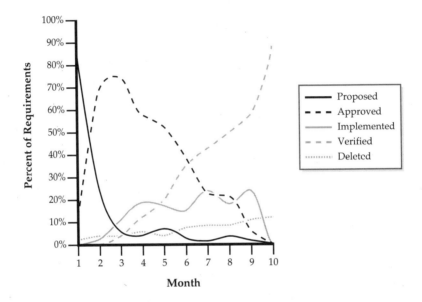

FIGURE 16-2   *Tracking the distribution of requirements status throughout a project's development cycle.*

Classifying requirements in these discrete categories is more realistic than trying to monitor the percent completion of each requirement. Software developers can be overly optimistic when they report the percentage of a task that is complete, often giving themselves considerable credit for activities they have started but not finished. This tendency to "round up" their progress leads to the all-too-common situation of software projects or major tasks being reported as "90 percent done" for a long time. You should change a requirement's status only when the specified transition conditions are satisfied. Certain status changes also lead to updating the requirements traceability matrix to indicate which design, code, and test elements addressed the requirement, as Chapter 18 will discuss.

MEASURING REQUIREMENTS MANAGEMENT EFFORT

Requirements management activities should appear as tasks in each project's work breakdown structure, with appropriate resources allocated. Measuring the cost of requirements management on your current projects is the best way to know how much effort or money to budget for requirements management in the future.

An organization that has never measured any aspect of its work usually finds it difficult to begin keeping records of how it really spends its time. Measuring actual development and project management effort requires a culture change and the individual discipline to develop a habit of recording daily work activities. However, it isn't as time-consuming as people sometimes fear, and you will gain valuable insights from knowing how your team has actually devoted its effort to various project tasks (Wiegers 1996a). Note that work effort is not the same as elapsed calendar time. Tasks can be interrupted, or they might require interactions with customers that lead to delays. The total effort for a task, in units of labor hours, doesn't necessarily change because of such factors, but the duration is longer than planned.

Tracking the actual requirements management effort also provides insight into whether your team is actually performing the intended actions to manage its requirements. Failing to carry out requirements management activities increases your project's risk of problems from uncontrolled changes, scope creep, and requirements that are inadvertently overlooked during implementation. Count the effort devoted to all the following activities as part of requirements management:

- Submitting requirements changes and proposed new requirements
- Evaluating proposed changes, including impact analysis
- Change control board activities
- Updating the requirements documents or database
- Communicating changes in the requirements to affected groups and individuals
- Tracking and reporting requirements status
- Defining and updating requirements traceability information

Managing your project's requirements helps ensure that the effort you invest in gathering, documenting, and analyzing the requirements is not squandered through neglect and the decay that can take place over time. Effective requirements management practices can help reduce the expectation gap by keeping all project participants informed about the current state of the requirements throughout the development process.

 Next Steps

◆   Select the statuses that you want to use to describe the life cycle of your functional requirements. Define the current status for each requirement in your SRS and keep them current throughout the rest of your development process.

◆   Define a version control scheme to identify your requirements documents. Document the scheme as part of your requirements management process.

◆   Write a process description of the steps your organization will perform to manage the requirements of each project. Engage several analysts to help draft, review, pilot, and approve the process activities and deliverables. Make sure the process steps you select are practical and realistic and that they add value to the project.

17

Managing Change Requests

While performing a software process assessment once, I asked the project team members how changes in the product's requirements were incorporated. One person said, "Whenever the marketing rep wants to make a change, he asks Bruce or Sandy because they always say 'yes' and the rest of us give marketing a hard time about changes." This didn't strike me as the most reasonable process for making changes. Uncontrolled change is a common source of project chaos, schedule slips, and quality problems. An organization that's serious about controlling its software projects will ensure that:

- Proposed changes are carefully evaluated.

- The appropriate individuals make decisions about changes.

◆   Changes are communicated to all affected participants.

◆   The project incorporates requirements changes in a disciplined fashion.

Unless project stakeholders control changes during development, they won't really know what will be delivered, which is certain to lead to an expectation gap. The farther into a project you get, the more resistant to change you should become because the consequences of making changes become more severe. Changes must be reflected in the project's requirements documents. Your philosophy should be that the requirements documentation will accurately describe the delivered product. If you don't keep the SRS current while the product evolves, the SRS will become less useful and the team ultimately might function as though it doesn't even have one.

When you have to make a change, start at the highest level of requirements document that is affected by the change and cascade the impact of the change downward through all other affected requirements. For example, a proposed change might affect a use case and its functional requirements but not affect any business requirements. A modified high-level system requirement could impact multiple software requirements. If you make the change only at the lowest affected level of requirement (typically a functional requirement), that requirement might become inconsistent with its parent.

CONTROLLING SCOPE CREEP

Capers Jones (1994) reports that creeping requirements pose a risk to 80 percent of management information systems projects and 70 percent of military software projects. Creeping requirements include new functionality and significant modifications that are presented after the project requirements are baselined. The problem is not only that requirements change, but that late changes have a big impact on work already performed. If every proposed change is approved, it might appear to project sponsors, participants, and customers that the project will never be completed—and indeed, it might not.

Some evolution of requirements is legitimate and unavoidable on most projects. Business processes, market opportunities, competing products, and software technologies can change during the time it takes to develop a system, and management might decide to redirect the project in response. Your project schedule should include some buffer time to accommodate such natural requirements growth. Uncontrolled scope creep, in which the project continuously incorporates new functionality without adjusting resources, schedules, or quality goals, is more insidious. A small modification here, a little enhancement there, and pretty soon the project has no hope of delivering what the customers expect on schedule and at acceptable quality.

The first step in managing scope creep is to document the vision, scope, and limitations of the new system as part of the business requirements, as described in Chapter 6. Evaluate every proposed requirement or feature against the scope and vision to see whether it really belongs in the product. Effective requirements elicitation techniques that emphasize customer involvement can reduce the number of requirements that are missed early on, only to be added to the team's workload after commitments are made and resources are allocated (Jones 1996a). Another effective technique for controlling creeping requirements is prototyping, which gives users a preview of a possible implementation to help developers and users reach a shared understanding of the actual user needs (Jones 1994).

The most effective technique for controlling scope creep is the ability to say no (Weinberg 1995). Most people don't like to say no, and developers can receive intense pressure to incorporate every proposed requirement. Philosophies such as "the customer is always right" or "we will achieve total customer satisfaction" are fine in the abstract, but you pay a price for abiding by them. Ignoring the price doesn't alter the fact that change is not free. I know of a successful commercial development company where the CEO is accustomed to suggesting a new feature and hearing the development manager say "not now." "Not now" is more palatable than a simple rejection because it holds the promise of including the feature in a subsequent release. Including every feature requested by a customer, the marketing department, management, or a developer can lead to missed commitments, slipshod quality, burned-out developers, and bloatware. Even though customers aren't always right, they do always have a point, so you should capture their ideas for possible inclusion in later development cycles.

In an ideal world, you would gather all a new system's requirements before beginning construction, and they would remain stable throughout the development effort. This is the premise behind the sequential or "waterfall" software development life cycle, but it doesn't work well in practice. Of course, at some point you must freeze the requirements for a specific release.

However, stifling change prematurely ignores the reality that sometimes customers aren't sure what they need, user needs will change, and developers want to be responsive to those changes. To cope with these realities, you need a process that will incorporate the most appropriate changes into the project in a controlled way.

THE CHANGE CONTROL PROCESS

A well-defined change control process provides stakeholders with a formal mechanism for proposing changes in requirements. This process lets the project's leaders make well-informed business decisions that will provide the greatest customer and business value while controlling the life cycle costs of the product. The change control process lets you track the status of all proposed changes, and it helps ensure that no suggested changes are lost or overlooked. Once you've baselined a set of requirements, you should follow your change control process for all proposed changes to them.

A change control process is not intended to be an obstacle to making changes. Instead, it's a funneling and filtering mechanism to ensure that the most appropriate changes are adopted and that the negative impacts on the project are minimized. Your change process should be well-documented, as simple as possible, and—above all—effective. If your change process is ineffective, cumbersome, or too complicated, people will likely revert to their old methods for making changes (and perhaps they should).

Controlling requirements changes is tied to the project's other configuration management practices. Managing requirements changes is similar to the process for tracking and making decisions about bug reports, and the same tools can support both activities. Remember, though, a tool is not a process. Using a commercial problem-tracking tool to manage proposed modifications to requirements doesn't replace a written procedure that describes the contents and processing of a change request.

CHANGE CONTROL POLICY

Project management should clearly communicate a policy that states its expectations of how proposed requirements changes will be handled. Policies are meaningful only if they are realistic, add value in some way, and are enforced. I have found the following elements of a change control policy to be helpful:

◆   All requirements changes must follow the process. If a change request is not submitted in accordance with this process, it won't be considered.

◆   No design or implementation work other than feasibility exploration will be performed on unapproved changes.

◆   Simply requesting a change doesn't guarantee that it will be made. The project's change control board (CCB) will decide which changes to implement. (We'll discuss CCBs later in the chapter.)

◆   The contents of the change database must be visible to all project stakeholders.

◆   The original text of a change request must not be modified or deleted from the database.

◆   Every incorporated requirement change must be traceable to an approved change request.

Of course, there are tiny changes that hardly affect the project at all, and there are big ones that significantly affect it. In principle, you'll handle all of these through the change control process. In practice, you might elect to leave certain detailed requirements decisions to the developers' discretion. No change affecting more than one individual should bypass your change control process though.

I know of one project with two large components, a user interface–intensive application and an internal knowledge base, but no change process. This project encountered problems when the knowledge-base developers altered some of their external interfaces but didn't communicate those changes to the application developers. On another project, developers introduced new and modified functionality that the rest of the team didn't discover until system testing, which led to rework of test procedures and user documentation. Uniform change control practices help avoid such problems and the associated frustration, development rework, and wasted testing time.

CHANGE CONTROL PROCEDURE

Figure 17-1 illustrates a template for describing a change control procedure, which can apply to requirements modifications and other project changes. The following discussion pertains primarily to how the procedure would handle requirements changes. I find it helpful to include the following four components in procedures and process descriptions, which the template in Figure 17-1 reflects:

◆   *Entry criteria*—the conditions that must be satisfied before executing the process or procedure

◆   The various *tasks* involved in the process or procedure and the project role responsible for performing each one

◆   Steps to *verify* that the tasks were completed correctly

◆   *Exit criteria*—the conditions that indicate when the process or procedure is completed

1. **Introduction**
   1.1 Purpose
   1.2 Scope
   1.3 Definitions

2. **Roles and Responsibilities**

3. **Change Request Status**

4. **Entry Criteria**

5. **Tasks**
   5.1 Create Change Request
   5.2 Evaluate Change Request
   5.3 Make Decisions
   5.4 Communicate Change

6. **Verification**

7. **Exit Criteria**

8. **Change Control Status Reporting**

Appendix: Data Items Stored

FIGURE 17-1   *Sample change control procedure template.*

1. Introduction

The introduction describes the purpose of this procedure and identifies the organizational scope to which it applies. If this procedure covers changes only in certain work products, identify them here. Also indicate whether any specific kinds of changes are exempted. For example, you might exempt changes in interim or temporary work products created during the course of a project. This section should also define any terms that are necessary for understanding the rest of the document.

2. Roles and Responsibilities

List the project team members (by role, not by name) that participate in the change control activities and describe their responsibilities. Table 17-1 suggests some pertinent roles. Adapt these roles and their responsibilities to your environment and needs, keeping the process as simple as possible while remaining effective. Different individuals don't have to fill each role; for example, the project manager might also receive submitted change requests. On a small project, several—perhaps all—roles can be filled by the same person.

TABLE 17-1   POSSIBLE PROJECT ROLES IN CHANGE MANAGEMENT ACTIVITIES

Role	Description and Responsibilities
CCB Chair	Chairperson of the change control board; generally has final decision-making authority if the CCB does not reach agreement
CCB	The group that decides to approve or reject proposed changes for a specific project
Evaluator	The person whom the project manager asks to analyze the impact of a proposed change
Modifier	The person responsible for making changes in a work product in response to an approved change request; updates the status of the request over time
Originator	Someone who submits a new change request
Project Manager	The person who asks someone to be the evaluator for each change request and someone to be the modifier for each approved change request
Request Receiver	The person to whom new change requests are submitted
Verifier	The person responsible for determining whether the change was made correctly

3. Change Request Status

A change request passes through a defined life cycle, having a different status at each stage in its life. You can represent these status changes using a state-transition diagram, as illustrated in Figure 17-2. Update a request's status only when the specified criteria are met.

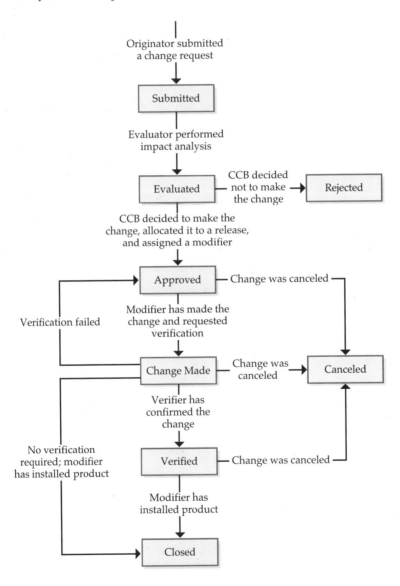

FIGURE 17-2   *State-transition diagram for a change request.*

4. Entry Criteria

The basic entry criterion for your change control procedure is:

◆ A valid change request has been received through an appropriate channel.

All potential originators should know how to submit a change request, whether it's by completing a paper or Web-based form, sending an e-mail message, or using a change control tool. Route all change requests to a single point of contact, and assign a unique identification tag to every change request.

5. Tasks

After receiving a new change request, the next step is to evaluate the proposal for technical feasibility, cost, and alignment with the project's business requirements and resource constraints. The CCB chair might ask the evaluator to perform systematic impact analysis (discussed in Chapter 18), risk analysis, hazard analysis, or other assessments. This analysis ensures that the potential consequences of accepting the change are well understood. The evaluator and the CCB should also consider the business and technical implications of rejecting the change.

The appropriate decision makers, chartered as the CCB, then elect whether to approve or reject the requested change. The CCB gives each approved change a priority level or target implementation date, or allocates it to a specific build or release. The CCB communicates the decision by updating the request's status and notifying all team members who might have to change work products, such as the SRS, a requirements database, design models, user interface components, code, test documentation, and user documentation. The modifier(s) can then update the affected work products as necessary.

6. Verification

Requirements changes are typically verified through an inspection to ensure that the updated SRS, use-case documents, and analysis models correctly reflect all aspects of the change. Use traceability information to find all parts of the system that the change touched and that therefore must be verified. (Chapter 18 will cover this topic in more detail.) Multiple team members might participate in verifying the changes made in downstream work products through testing or inspection. After verification, the modifier installs the updated work products to make them available to the rest of the team.

7. Exit Criteria

The following exit criteria must all be satisfied to properly complete an execution of your change control procedure:

◆   The status of the request is Rejected, Closed, or Canceled.

◆   All modified work products are installed into the correct locations.

◆   The originator, CCB chair, project manager, and other relevant project participants have been notified of the change details and the current status.

◆   The requirements traceability matrix has been updated (more on this in Chapter 18).

8. Change Control Status Reporting

Identify the reports and charts that you will use to summarize the contents of the change control database and the number of change requests with each status. Describe the procedures for producing the reports. The project manager will usually generate these reports to aid in tracking the project's status.

Appendix: Data Items Stored

Table 17-2 lists some data items to consider storing for each change request. When you define your own list, indicate which items are required and which are optional. Also, indicate whether the value for each item is set automatically by your change control tool or manually by one of the change management participants. You will likely revise your data item list as you gain experience, so don't commit it to an automated tool until you pilot the procedure with a simple spreadsheet or even paper forms first.

CHANGE CONTROL TOOLS

Automated tools can help your change control process operate more efficiently (Wiegers 1996a). Many teams use commercial problem- or issue-tracking tools to collect, store, and manage requirements changes. You can use these tools to generate a list of recently submitted change proposals to serve as the agenda for a CCB meeting. Problem-tracking tools can also report the number of requests with each possible change status at any given time.

TABLE 17-2   **SUGGESTED CHANGE REQUEST DATA ITEMS**

Item	Description
Change Origin	Functional area that requested the change; possible groups include marketing, management, customer, software engineering, hardware engineering, and testing
Change Request ID	Identification tag or sequence number assigned to the request
Change Type	Type of change request, such as a requirement change, proposed enhancement, or bug report
Date Submitted	Date the change request was submitted
Date Updated	Date the change request was most recently updated
Description	Free-form text description of the change being requested
Implementation Priority	The relative importance of making the change as determined by the CCB: low, medium, or high
Modifier	Name of the person who is primarily responsible for implementing the change
Originator	Name of the person who submitted this change request; you might also want to include the originator's contact information
Originator Priority	The relative importance of making the change from the originator's point of view: low, medium, or high
Planned Release	Product release or build number for which this approved change is scheduled
Project	Name of the project in which a change is being requested
Response	Free-form text of responses made to the change request; multiple responses can be made over time; do not change existing responses when entering a new one
Status	The current status of the change request, selected from the options in Figure 17-2
Title	One-line summary of the proposed change
Verifier	Name of the person who is responsible for determining whether the change was made correctly

One Web development team I worked with used a highly configurable issue-management tool to store requests for software requirements changes, bug reports, suggested product enhancements, updates to Web-site content, and requests for new development projects. Because the available tools, vendors, and features frequently change, I won't give any specific recommendations here. An excellent Web resource for links to software tool information is *http://www.methods-tools.com*. Look for the following features in a tool to support your requirements change process:

- Lets you define the data items you want included in a change request

- Lets you define a state-transition diagram for the change request life cycle

- Enforces the state-transition diagram so that authorized users can make only the permitted status changes

- Records the date of every status change and the identity of the person who made that change

- Lets you define who receives automatic e-mail notification when an Originator submits a new request or when a request's status is updated

- Allows you to generate the standard and custom reports and charts that you need

Some commercial requirements management tools (discussed in Chapter 19) have a simple change proposal system built in. These systems can link a proposed change to a specific requirement so that the individual responsible for each requirement is notified by e-mail whenever someone submits a pertinent change request.

THE CHANGE CONTROL BOARD

The change control board, or CCB (sometimes known as the configuration control board), has been identified as a best practice for software development (McConnell 1996). The CCB is the body of people, be it one individual or a diverse group, that makes binding decisions about which proposed requirement changes and suggested new product features to approve. The CCB typically also decides which reported defects to correct and in which build or release. Many projects already have some de facto group that makes change decisions; establishing a CCB formalizes this group's authority and defines its operating procedures.

In the broadest sense, a CCB reviews and approves changes to any baselined work products on a project, of which the requirements documents are only one example. Large projects can have several levels of control boards, some of which are responsible for making business decisions (such as requirements changes) and some of which make technical decisions (Sorensen 1999). Some CCBs are empowered to make decisions and simply inform management about them, while others can only make recommendations for management decision. A higher-level CCB will likely have the authority to approve changes with greater impact on the project plans than a lower-level board. On a small project, only one or two people could make all the change decisions.

To some people, the term "change control board" conjures an image of wasteful bureaucratic overhead. However, you should think of the CCB as providing a valuable structure to help you manage even a small project. This structure doesn't have to be time-consuming or cumbersome—just effective. An effective CCB will consider all proposed changes at regular intervals and make timely decisions based on analysis of the potential impacts and benefits of each proposed change. Your CCB should be no larger and no more formal than necessary to ensure that the right people make good business decisions about every request.

CCB COMPOSITION

The CCB membership should represent all groups that could be affected by a change that lies within the scope of that CCB's authority. The CCB might include representatives from several of the following areas:

- Product or program management
- Project management
- Development
- Testing or quality assurance
- Marketing or customer representatives
- User documentation
- Technical support
- Help desk or user support line
- Configuration management

The same handful of individuals will fill several of these roles on small projects, and other roles won't always be necessary. The CCB for a project with both software and hardware components might also include representatives from hardware engineering, system engineering, manufacturing, and perhaps hardware quality assurance and configuration management. When you establish a CCB, include the fewest number of people you can to provide adequate representation and decision-making authority. Large groups can have difficulty convening meetings and making decisions. Make sure the CCB members understand their responsibilities and take them seriously. You can invite other select individuals to a CCB meeting when specific proposals are discussed to ensure that the CCB has adequate technical and business information.

CCB CHARTER

The first step in establishing the CCB is to write a charter that describes the CCB's purpose, scope of authority, membership, decision-making process, and operating procedures (Sorensen 1999). The charter should state the frequency of regularly scheduled CCB meetings and the conditions that will trigger a special meeting. The scope of the CCB's authority will indicate which decisions it can make and which ones it must pass on to a higher-level CCB or manager for resolution.

Making Decisions

The decision-making process description should identify:

◆ The number of CCB members that constitutes a quorum for making decisions at a meeting or the roles that must be represented for the meeting to proceed

◆ Whether voting, consensus, or some other mechanism is used to make decisions

◆ Whether the CCB Chair is permitted to overrule the CCB's collective decision

The CCB should base its decisions on the balance between the anticipated benefit and the estimated impact of accepting the proposed change. Benefits from improving the product include financial savings or additional revenue, increased customer satisfaction, competitive advantage, and reduced time to market. The impact indicates the adverse effects that accepting the proposed change could have on the product or project. These impacts include increased development and support costs, delayed delivery schedule, degraded product quality, reduced functionality, and user dissatisfaction. If the estimated cost or schedule impact exceeds the established thresholds for this level of CCB, refer the change to management or to a higher-level CCB. Otherwise, use the CCB's decision-making process to approve or reject the proposed change and to allocate each approved change to a specific build or product release.

Communicating Status

Once the CCB makes its decision, a designated individual updates the request's status in the change database. Some tools will then automatically generate e-mail messages to communicate the new status to the individual who proposed the change and to the others affected by the change. If e-mail is not generated automatically, those affected must be informed manually so that they can fully process the change.

Renegotiating Commitments

Change always has a price. Even a rejected change consumes the resources needed to submit, evaluate, and decide to reject it. New product features have a larger impact. It's not realistic to assume that you can keep stuffing more functionality into a project with schedule, staff, budget, and quality constraints and still succeed. When your project accepts significant requirements changes, plan to renegotiate commitments with management and customers to accommodate the changes (Humphrey 1997). You might negotiate for more time or staff, to defer pending requirements of lower priority, or to compromise on quality. If you don't obtain some commitment adjustments, document the threats to success in your project's risk management plan so that no one is surprised if the project doesn't achieve the desired outcome.

MEASURING CHANGE ACTIVITY

Software measurements provide insight into your projects, products, and processes that is more accurate than subjective impressions or vague recollections of what happened in the past. The measurements you select should be motivated by the questions you or your managers are trying to answer and the goals you're trying to achieve. Measuring change activity is a way to assess the stability of the requirements and to identify opportunities for process improvement that might reduce the number of changes requested in the future. Consider measuring the following aspects of your requirements change activity (CMU/SEI 1995):

- The number of change requests received, open, and closed

- The cumulative number of changes made, including added, deleted, and modified requirements (You can also express this as a percentage of the total number of requirements in the baseline.)

- The number of change requests that originated from each source

- The number of changes proposed and made in each requirement since it was baselined

- The total effort devoted to handling changes

Start with simple measurements to begin establishing a measurement culture in your organization and to collect the key data you need to manage your projects effectively. As you gain experience, you can make your measurements as sophisticated as necessary to help your projects succeed.

Figure 17-3 illustrates a way to track the number of requirements changes your project experiences during development. This chart tracks the rate at which new requirements change proposals appear. You can track the number of approved change requests similarly. You don't need to count requirements changes made prior to baselining because you know the requirements are still evolving. However, once you've baselined the requirements, all proposed changes should follow your change control process, and you should begin to track the frequency of change (in other words, the requirements stability). This chart should trend toward zero as the project approaches its ship date. A sustained high frequency of changes implies a risk of not meeting your schedule commitments. It probably also indicates that the original baselined requirements were incomplete, suggesting that it might be a good idea to improve your requirements elicitation practices.

A project manager who is concerned that frequent requirements changes might prevent the product from shipping on schedule can gain further insight by tracking the requirements change origins. Figure 17-4 illustrates a way to represent the number of change requests that came from different sources. The project manager could discuss Figure 17-4 with the marketing representatives and point out that marketing is presenting the most requirements changes. This might lead to a fruitful discussion about what actions the team could take to reduce the number of changes that marketing requests in the future. Using data as a starting point for such discussions is more constructive than holding a confrontational meeting stimulated by frustration.

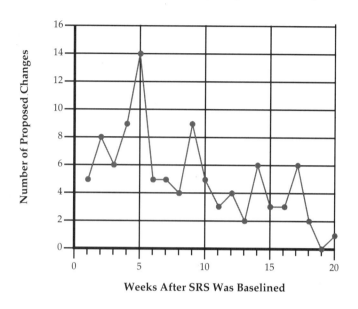

FIGURE 17-3   *Sample chart of requirements change activity.*

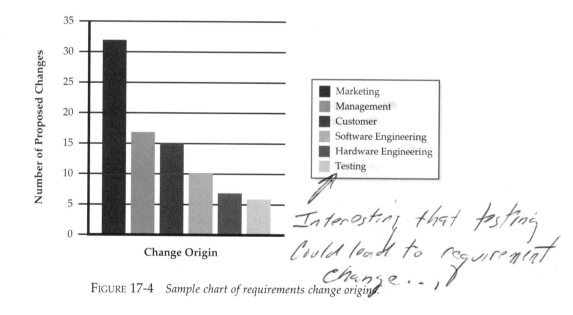

FIGURE 17-4   *Sample chart of requirements change origins.*

Interesting that testing could lead to requirement change..,

Requirements change is a reality for nearly all software projects. Disciplined change management practices can reduce the disruption that changes cause. Improved requirements development techniques can reduce the number of requirements changes with which your project must cope. Effective requirements elicitation and management practices will improve your ability to deliver on project commitments.

 Next Steps

◆ Identify the decision makers on your project and set them up as a change control board. Have the CCB write a charter to make sure everyone understands the board's purpose, composition, and decision-making process.

◆ Define a state-transition diagram for the life cycle of proposed requirements changes in your project, starting with the diagram in Figure 17-2. Write a procedure to describe how your team will handle proposed requirements changes. Use the procedure manually until you convince yourself that it is practical, effective, and as simple as you can make it.

◆ Select a commercial problem-tracking or issue-tracking tool that is compatible with your operating environment and that you can tailor to support the change control procedure you developed in the previous step.

18

Links in the Requirements Chain

"*How's your development work coming, Glenn?" asked Dave, the Chemical Tracking System project manager, during a project status review meeting.*

"*I'm not as far along as I'd planned to be," Glenn admitted. "I'm adding a new vendor catalog query function for Marcie, and it's taking a lot longer than I expected.*"

Dave was puzzled. "I don't remember discussing a new catalog query function at a change control board meeting recently. Did Marcie submit that request through the change process?"

"*No, she approached me directly with the suggestion," said Glenn. "I should have asked her to submit it as a formal change request, but it seemed pretty simple so I told her I'd work it in. It turned out not to be simple at all. Every time I think I'm done, I realize I missed a change needed in another file, so I have to fix that, rebuild the component, and test it again. I thought this would take about five hours, but I've spent almost four days on it so far. That's why I'm not done with my other scheduled tasks. I know I'm holding up the next build. Should I finish adding this query function or go back to what I was working on before?"*

A software change that appears simple and straightforward on the surface is often much more difficult and time consuming than you would expect. It's difficult to find all the parts of a system that might be affected by even a minor modification. Before you commit to accepting a proposed change in your project's requirements, make sure you know what you're getting into.

This chapter addresses the related subjects of requirements tracing and requirements change impact analysis. Requirements tracing involves documenting the dependencies and logical links between individual requirements and other system elements. These elements include other requirements, architecture and other design components, source code modules, tests, help files, and documentation. Traceability information greatly facilitates change impact analysis, which helps you identify and estimate all the work you might have to do to fully implement a proposed requirement change.

TRACING REQUIREMENTS

Traceability links allow you to follow the life of a requirement both forward and backward, from origin through implementation (Gotel and Finkelstein 1994). Chapter 1 identified traceability as one of the characteristics of excellent requirements specifications. To permit traceability, each requirement must be uniquely labeled so that you can refer to it unambiguously (Davis 1993).

Figure 18-1 illustrates four types of requirements traceability links (Jarke 1998). Customer needs are traced *forward to requirements,* so you can tell what requirements will be affected if those needs change during or after development. This also gives you confidence that the specification has addressed all stated customer needs. Conversely, you can trace *backward from requirements* to customer needs to identify the origin of each software requirement. If you represented customer needs in the form of use cases, the top half of Figure 18-1 illustrates tracing between use cases and functional requirements.

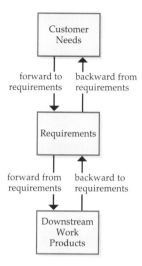

FIGURE 18-1   *Four types of requirements traceability.*

The bottom half of Figure 18-1 indicates that, as system requirements flow into software requirements, designs, code, and other artifacts during development, you can trace *forward from requirements* by defining links between individual requirements and specific product elements. This type of link assures that you have satisfied every requirement because you know which product components address each one. The fourth type of link traces specific work products *backward to requirements* so that you know why you created each item. Most applications include code that doesn't relate directly to user-specified requirements, but you should know why you write every line of code. If you can't trace a design element, code segment, or test back to a requirement, you might have an instance of gold-plating. However, if these "orphan" elements represent legitimate functionality, your specification might be missing a requirement.

Traceability links help you keep track of parentage, interconnections, and dependencies among individual requirements. This information identifies the propagation of change that can result when a specific requirement is deleted or modified. If you've mapped specific requirements into tasks in your project's work-breakdown structure, those tasks will be affected when a requirement is changed or deleted. Figure 18-2 illustrates the many kinds of direct traceability relationships that can be defined on a project. You don't necessarily need to define and manage all these traceability link types. Decide which links are pertinent to your project and can contribute the most to successful development and efficient maintenance.

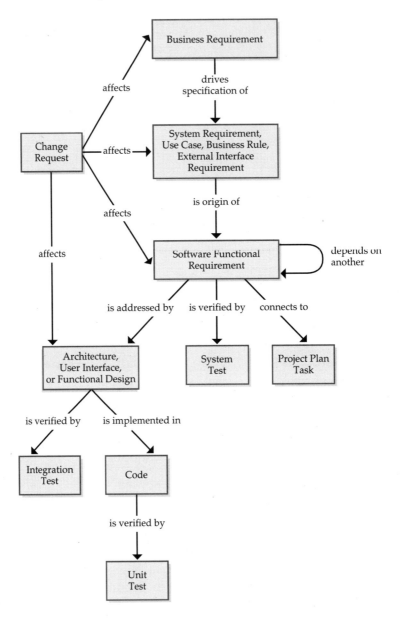

FIGURE 18-2   *Some possible requirements traceability links.*

MOTIVATIONS FOR TRACING REQUIREMENTS

I've had the embarrassing experience of writing a program and then realizing I had inadvertently omitted a requirement. I had simply missed it, so I had to go back and write additional code after I thought I was done programming. Overlooking a requirement or two is more than an embarrassment if it means that a customer isn't satisfied or a delivered product is missing a safety-critical function. At one level, requirements tracing provides a way to demonstrate compliance with a contract or specification. At a more sophisticated level, requirements tracing can improve the quality of your delivered products, reduce maintenance costs, and facilitate reuse (Ramesh 1998).

Tracing requirements is a manually intensive task that requires organizational commitment. Keeping the link information current as the system undergoes development and maintenance takes discipline. If the traceability information becomes obsolete, you'll probably never reconstruct it. Because of these realities, you should adopt requirements traceability for the right reasons (Ramesh et al. 1995). Following are some of the benefits of implementing requirements traceability on your project:

- ◆ *Certification.* Traceability information can be used for certification in safety-critical applications to demonstrate that all requirements were implemented.

- ◆ *Change impact analysis.* Without traceability information, there's a high probability of overlooking a system element that might be affected if you add, delete, or modify a particular requirement.

- ◆ *Maintenance.* Reliable traceability information facilitates making changes correctly and completely during maintenance, which improves your productivity. If you don't have traceability information for an entire system, build it one piece at a time as you perform software surgery and add enhancements. Begin by listing the requirements from the part of the system you worked on and record the traceability links from there downward.

- ◆ *Project tracking.* If you diligently record the traceability data during development, you will have an accurate record of the implementation status of planned functionality. Missing links indicate work products that have not yet been created.

◆ *Reengineering.* You can list the functions in a legacy system you're replacing and record where they were addressed in the new system's requirements and software components. Defining traceability links offers a way to capture some of what you learn through reverse engineering of an existing system.

◆ *Reuse.* Traceability information can facilitate the reuse of product components by identifying packages of related requirements, designs, code, tests, and other artifacts.

◆ *Risk reduction.* Documenting the component interconnections reduces the risk if a key team member with essential knowledge about the system leaves the project (Ambler 1999).

◆ *Testing.* The links between tests, requirements, and code point you toward likely parts of the code to examine for a bug when a test fails to yield the intended result.

Many of these are long-term benefits, reducing overall product life-cycle costs but increasing the development cost by the effort expended to accumulate and manage the traceability information. You should view requirements traceability as an investment that increases your chances of delivering a product that satisfies all the stated customer requirements and is easy to maintain. Although difficult to quantify, this investment will pay dividends anytime you have to modify, extend, or replace the product. Defining traceability links is fairly painless if you collect the information as development proceeds, but it's expensive to do on a completed system.

Requirements traceability is addressed at level 3 of the Capability Maturity Model (CMU/SEI 1995). Activity 10 of the Software Product Engineering key process area states, "Consistency is maintained across software work products, including the software plans, process descriptions, allocated requirements, software requirements, software design, code, test plans, and test procedures." Subpractices within this activity define some specific expectations of how an organization handles requirements traceability.

THE REQUIREMENTS TRACEABILITY MATRIX

The most common way to represent the links between requirements and other system elements is in a *requirements traceability matrix*. Table 18-1 illustrates a fragment of one such matrix, drawn from the Chemical Tracking System. This table shows how each functional requirement is linked backward to a specific use case, and forward to one or more design, code, and test elements. Design elements can be objects in models such as data flow diagrams, tables in a relational data model, or object classes. Code references can be methods in a class, source code filenames, or procedures or functions within the source file. You can add more columns to extend the links to other work products, such as online help documentation. Including more detail in your traceability information takes more work, but it also gives you the precise locations of the related software elements, which can save time when you perform change impact analysis and maintenance.

TABLE 18-1 ONE KIND OF REQUIREMENTS TRACEABILITY MATRIX

Use Case	Functional Requirement	Design Element	Code	Test Case
UC-28	catalog.query.sort	Class catalog	catalog.sort()	search.7 search.8
UC-29	catalog.query.import	Class catalog	catalog.import() catalog.validate()	search.8 search.13 search.14

Traceability links can define one-to-one, one-to-many, or many-to-many relationships between types of system elements. Table 18-1 accommodates these cardinalities by letting you enter several items in each table cell. Here are some examples of the possible link cardinalities:

◆ *One-to-one.* One design element is implemented in one code module.

◆ *One-to-many.* One functional requirement is verified by multiple test cases.

◆ *Many-to-many.* Each use case leads to multiple functional requirements, and certain functional requirements are common to several use cases.

Manually creating a requirements traceability matrix is a matter of habit and discipline, and it is practical for small projects. Once the use cases are baselined, you're ready to begin adding the functional requirements derived from each use case to the matrix. Continue to populate the matrix as you proceed with software design, construction, and test development.

For example, when you've completed implementing a functional requirement, you can update its design and code cells in the matrix and change the requirement's status to "implemented."

Another way to represent traceability information is through a set of matrices that define links between pairs of system elements, such as:

◆ One type of requirement to requirements of another type

◆ One type of requirement to other requirements of that same type

◆ One type of requirement to test cases

You can use these matrices to define various relationships that are possible between pairs of requirements, such as "specifies/is specified by," "depends on," "is parent of," and "constrains/is constrained by" (Sommerville and Sawyer 1997).

Table 18-2 illustrates a two-way traceability matrix. Most cells in the matrix are empty. Each cell at the intersection of two linked components is marked to indicate the connection. You can use different symbols in the cells to explicitly indicate "traced-to" and "traced-from" or other relationships. Table 18-2 uses an arrow to indicate that a functional requirement is traced from a particular use case. These matrices are more amenable to automated tool support than is the single traceability table illustrated in Table 18-1.

TABLE 18-2   REQUIREMENTS TRACEABILITY MATRIX
                    SHOWING LINKS BETWEEN USE CASES
                    AND FUNCTIONAL REQUIREMENTS

Functional Requirement	Use Case			
	UC-1	UC-2	UC-3	UC-4
FR-1	↵			
FR-2	↵			
FR-3			↵	
FR-4			↵	
FR-5		↵		↵
FR-6			↵	

Traceability links should be defined by whoever has the appropriate information. Table 18-3 identifies some typical sources of knowledge about links between various types of source and target objects. Determine the roles and individuals who can supply each type of traceability information for your project.

TABLE 18-3 LIKELY SOURCES OF TRACEABILITY LINK INFORMATION

Link Source Object Type	Link Target Object Type	Information Source
System requirement	Software requirement	System engineer
Use case	Functional requirement	Requirements analyst
Functional requirement	Functional requirement	Requirements analyst
Functional requirement	Software architecture element	Software architect
Functional requirement	Other design elements	Developer
Design element	Code	Developer
Functional requirement	Test case	Test engineer

TOOLS FOR REQUIREMENTS TRACEABILITY

Requirements traceability cannot be fully automated because the knowledge of the links originates in the minds of the development team members. However, once you've identified the links, certain tools can help you manage the vast quantity of traceability information. You can use a spreadsheet to maintain traceability matrices for a couple hundred requirements, but larger systems demand a more robust solution.

Chapter 19 describes commercial requirements management tools with strong requirements tracing capabilities. These products use the type of traceability matrix illustrated in Table 18-2. You can store requirements and other information in a tool's database and define links between the various types of stored objects, including peer links between two requirements of the same kind. Some of the tools let you differentiate "traced-to" and "traced-from" relationships, automatically defining the complementary links. That is, if you indicate that requirement R is traced to test case T, the tool will also show the symmetrical relationship in which T is traced from R. Some tools automatically flag a link as *suspect* whenever the object on either end of the link is modified. This lets you know which system elements you must examine to ensure that you have accounted for all the ripple effects of a change.

The tools also let you define cross-project or cross-subsystem links. I know of one large project that had 20 major subsystems, with certain high-level product requirements apportioned among multiple subsystems. In some cases, a requirement that was allocated to one subsystem was actually implemented through a service that another subsystem provided. This project used a commercial requirements management tool to successfully track these complex traceability relationships.

REQUIREMENTS TRACEABILITY PROCEDURE

Consider following this sequence of steps when you begin to implement requirements traceability on a project:

1. Decide what kinds of link relationships you want to define, using the possibilities shown in Figure 18-2.

2. Choose the type of traceability matrix you want to use: the single matrix shown in Table 18-1 or several of the matrices illustrated in Table 18-2.

3. Identify the parts of the product for which you want to maintain traceability information. Start with the critical core functions, the high-risk portions, or the portions you expect will undergo the most maintenance and evolution over time.

4. Modify your procedures and checklists to remind developers to update the links after implementing a requirement or an approved change.

5. Define the tagging conventions you will use to uniquely identify all system elements so that they can be linked together (Song et al. 1998). If necessary, write scripts that will parse the system files to construct and update the traceability matrices.

6. Identify the individuals who will supply each type of link information.

7. Educate the team about the concepts and importance of requirements traceability, your objectives for this activity, where the traceability data is stored, and the techniques for defining the links—for example, using the traceability features of a requirements management tool. Make sure all participants commit to their responsibilities.

8. Inform participants that the traceability data must be updated as soon as someone completes a task that creates or changes a link in the requirements chain.

9. Audit the traceability information periodically as development progresses to make sure it's being kept current. If a requirement is reported as implemented and verified yet its traceability data is incomplete or inaccurate, your traceability process isn't working as intended.

Is Requirements Traceability Feasible? Is it Necessary?

You might conclude that creating a requirements traceability matrix is more trouble than it's worth or that it's simply not realistic for your project. Consider this example: A conference attendee who worked at an aircraft manufacturer told me that the SRS for the company's latest jetliner was a stack of paper six feet thick and that it had a complete requirements traceability matrix. I've flown on that very model of airplane, and I was happy to hear that the developers had managed their software requirements so rigorously. Managing traceability on a huge product with many interrelated subsystems is a lot of work, but this aircraft manufacturer knew it was essential.

Not all companies build products that can have grave consequences if the software has problems. However, you should take requirements tracing seriously, especially for your business's core information systems. The CEO of a major corporation who was present when I described traceability at a seminar asked, "Why *wouldn't* you create a traceability matrix for your strategic business systems?" That's an excellent question. You should decide to use any improved requirements engineering practice based on both the costs of applying the technique and the risks of not using it. As with all software processes, invest your valuable time where you expect the greatest payback.

CHANGE ISN'T FREE: IMPACT ANALYSIS

Many developers have had the experience illustrated in the dialogue at the beginning of this chapter, in which an apparently simple change turns out to be far more complicated than expected. This can happen with proposed requirements modifications and when adding enhancements to an existing system. Too often, developers don't—or can't—provide realistic estimates of the cost and other ramifications of a proposed software change. The misperception that change is free is one cause of project scope creep. People make more thoughtful choices when they see price tags on the available options.

Impact analysis is an important part of responsible requirements management (Arnold and Bohner 1998). Impact analysis provides accurate understanding of the implications of a proposed change, helping you make informed business decisions about which proposals to approve. The analysis examines the context of the proposed change to identify existing components that might have to be modified or discarded, identify new work products to be created, and estimate the effort associated with each task. Your ability to perform impact analysis depends on the quality and completeness of your traceability data.

No one likes the fact that making a change costs time and money and can have other undesirable consequences. At some point in their career, most developers have been asked to add functionality without affecting the project cost or schedule. The correct response to such requests for miracles is "No," expressed in terms of negotiating trade-offs for what *can* be done within the project's time, budget, and resource constraints.

IMPACT ANALYSIS PROCEDURE

A member of the project's CCB will typically ask a knowledgeable developer to perform the impact analysis for a specific change proposal. Figure 18-3 presents a checklist of questions designed to help the impact analyst understand the implications of accepting a proposed change. A second checklist, shown in Figure 18-4, contains prompting questions to help identify all the software elements that the change might affect. As you gain experience using these checklists, modify them to fit the nature of your own projects.

☐ Do any existing requirements in the baseline conflict with the proposed change?

☐ Do any other pending requirements changes conflict with the proposed change?

☐ What are the business or technical consequences of not making the change?

☐ What are possible adverse side effects or other risks of making the proposed change?

☐ Will the proposed change adversely affect performance requirements or other quality attributes?

☐ Is the proposed change feasible within known technical constraints and current staff skills?

☐ Will the proposed change place unacceptable demands on any computer resources required for the development, test, or host environments?

☐ Must any tools be acquired to implement and test the change?

☐ How will the proposed change affect the sequence, dependencies, effort, or scheduled duration of any tasks currently in the project plan?

☐ Will prototyping or other user input be required to verify the proposed change?

☐ How much effort that has already been invested in the project will be lost if this change is accepted?

☐ Will the proposed change cause an increase in product unit cost, such as by increasing third-party product licensing fees?

☐ Will the change affect any marketing, manufacturing, training, or customer support plans?

FIGURE 18-3   *Checklist of possible implications of a proposed change.*

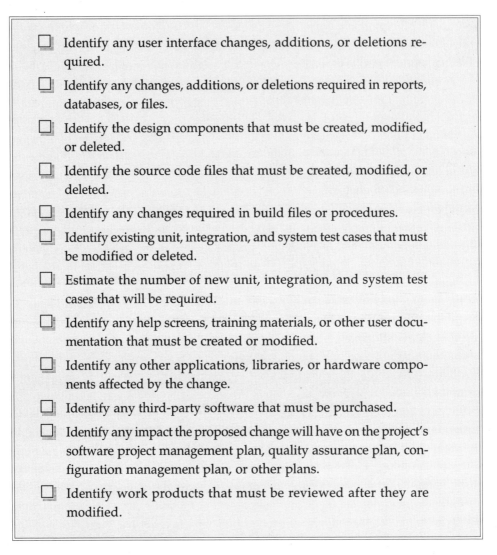

- ☐ Identify any user interface changes, additions, or deletions required.

- ☐ Identify any changes, additions, or deletions required in reports, databases, or files.

- ☐ Identify the design components that must be created, modified, or deleted.

- ☐ Identify the source code files that must be created, modified, or deleted.

- ☐ Identify any changes required in build files or procedures.

- ☐ Identify existing unit, integration, and system test cases that must be modified or deleted.

- ☐ Estimate the number of new unit, integration, and system test cases that will be required.

- ☐ Identify any help screens, training materials, or other user documentation that must be created or modified.

- ☐ Identify any other applications, libraries, or hardware components affected by the change.

- ☐ Identify any third-party software that must be purchased.

- ☐ Identify any impact the proposed change will have on the project's software project management plan, quality assurance plan, configuration management plan, or other plans.

- ☐ Identify work products that must be reviewed after they are modified.

FIGURE 18-4   *Checklist of possible software elements affected by a proposed change.*

Following is a simple procedure for evaluating the impact of a proposed requirement change. Many estimation problems arise because the estimator doesn't think of all the steps required to complete an activity. Therefore, this impact analysis approach emphasizes comprehensive task identification. For significant changes, a small team—rather than just one developer—should do the analysis and effort estimation to make sure important tasks are not overlooked.

1. Work through the checklist in Figure 18-3.

2. Work through the checklist in Figure 18-4, using available trace-ability information. Some requirements management tools include an impact analysis report that follows traceability links and finds the system elements that depend on the requirements affected by a change proposal.

3. Use the worksheet in Figure 18-5 to estimate the effort required for the anticipated tasks. Most change requests will require only a subset of the tasks on the worksheet.

4. Total the effort estimates.

5. Identify the sequence in which the tasks must be performed and how they can be interleaved with currently planned tasks.

6. Determine whether the change is on the project's critical path. If a task on the critical path slips, the project's completion date will slip. Every change consumes resources, but if you can plan a change to avoid affecting tasks that are currently on the critical path, the change won't cause the entire project to slip.

7. Estimate the impact of the proposed change on the project's schedule and cost.

8. Evaluate the change's priority by estimating the relative benefit, penalty, cost, and technical risk compared to other discretionary requirements. (For more information on this topic, see Chapter 13.)

9. Report the impact analysis results to the CCB so that they can use the information as part of the decision-making process for approving or rejecting change requests.

In most cases, this procedure shouldn't take more than an hour or two to complete. This might seem like a lot of time to a busy developer, but it's a small investment in making sure the project invests its limited resources wisely. If you can adequately assess the impact of a change without such a systematic evaluation, go right ahead; just make sure you aren't stepping into quicksand.

EFFORT (LABOR HOURS)	TASK
_____	Update the SRS or requirements database.
_____	Develop and evaluate a prototype.
_____	Create new design components.
_____	Modify existing design components.
_____	Develop new user interface components.
_____	Modify existing user interface components.
_____	Develop new user documentation and help screens.
_____	Modify existing user documentation and help screens.
_____	Develop new source code.
_____	Modify existing source code.
_____	Purchase and integrate third-party software.
_____	Modify build files.
_____	Develop new unit and integration tests.
_____	Modify existing unit and integration tests.
_____	Perform unit and integration testing after implementation.
_____	Write new system test cases.
_____	Modify existing system test cases.
_____	Modify automated test drivers.
_____	Perform regression testing.
_____	Develop new reports.
_____	Modify existing reports.
_____	Develop new database elements.
_____	Modify existing database elements.
_____	Develop new data files.
_____	Modify existing data files.
_____	Modify various project plans.
_____	Update other documentation.
_____	Update the requirements traceability matrix.
_____	Review work products.
_____	Perform rework following reviews and testing.
_____	**Total Estimated Effort**

FIGURE 18-5   *Estimating effort for a requirement change.*

IMPACT ANALYSIS REPORT TEMPLATE

Figure 18-6 suggests a template for reporting the results from analyzing the potential impact of each requirement change. Using a standard template will make it easier for the CCB members to find the information they need to make informed decisions. The people who will implement the change will need the analysis details and the effort planning worksheet, but the CCB needs only the summary of analysis results. As with all templates, try it and then adjust it to meet your project needs.

Change Request ID: _____

Title: _____

Description: _____

                      _____

Analyst: _____

Date Prepared: _____

Prioritization Estimates:

    Relative Benefit: _____ (1-9)

    Relative Penalty: _____ (1-9)

    Relative Cost: _____ (1-9)

    Relative Risk: _____ (1-9)

    Calculated Priority: _____

Estimated total effort: _____ labor hours

Estimated lost effort: _____ labor hours

Estimated schedule impact: _____ days

Additional cost impact: _____ dollars

Quality impact: _____

                             _____

Other requirements affected: _____

Other tasks affected: _____

Plans to be updated: _____

Integration issues: _____

Life-cycle cost issues: _____

Other components to examine _____

    for possible changes: _____

FIGURE 18-6   *Impact analysis report template.*

 *Next Steps*

◆ Set up a traceability matrix for 15 or 20 requirements from an important portion of the system you're currently developing. Try the approaches shown in both Tables 18-1 and 18-2. Populate the matrix as development progresses for a few weeks. Then evaluate which method seems most effective and what procedures for collecting and storing traceability information will work for your team.

◆ The next time you evaluate a requirement change request, first estimate the effort using your old method, then estimate it again using the impact analysis approach described in this chapter. If you do eventually implement the change, compare the two estimates to see which agrees more closely with the actual effort. Modify the checklists and worksheet to suit your projects based on your experience.

◆ The next time you perform maintenance on a poorly documented system, record what you learn from your reverse-engineering analysis of the part of the product you are modifying. Build a fragment of a traceability matrix for the piece of the puzzle you're manipulating so that the next time someone has to work on it they have a head start. Grow the traceability matrix as your team continues to maintain the product.

19

Tools for Requirements Management

Earlier chapters discussed the creation of a natural language SRS to contain the functional and nonfunctional requirements, in addition to writing documents that contain the business requirements and use-case descriptions. A document-based approach to storing requirements has several limitations, including the following:

- It's difficult to keep the documents current and synchronized.
- Communicating changes to all affected team members is a manual process.

◆   It's not easy to store supplementary information (attributes) about each requirement.

◆   It's hard to define links between functional requirements and the corresponding use cases, designs, code, tests, and project tasks.

◆   Tracking the status of individual requirements is cumbersome.

A requirements management tool that stores requirements-related information in a multiuser database provides a robust solution to these restrictions. Small projects can use spreadsheets or simple databases to manage their requirements, storing both the requirements text and several attributes of each requirement (Sommerville and Sawyer 1997). Larger projects will benefit from using commercial requirements management products, which include functions to let users import requirements from source documents, define attribute values, manipulate and display the database contents, export requirements in various formats, define traceability links, and connect requirements to other software development tools. Investigate the tools available commercially before you consider developing your own.

I classify these products as requirements management—not requirements development—tools. They won't help you identify your prospective users or gather the right requirements for your project. However, they will give you a lot of flexibility in managing changes to those requirements throughout development and using the requirements as the foundation for design, testing, and project management. These tools don't replace a defined process that describes how your project will elicit and manage its requirements. Use a tool when you already have an approach that works but requires greater efficiency; don't try to use a tool to compensate for a lack of process, discipline, or understanding.

This chapter presents several benefits of using a requirements management tool and identifies some general capabilities you can expect to find in such a product. Table 19-1 lists several commercial requirements management tools that include most of these features. This chapter doesn't contain a feature-by-feature tool comparison because these products are still evolving and their capabilities will change with future releases. The prices, supported platforms, and even vendors of software development tools also change frequently. Use the Web addresses in Table 19-1 to get current information about the products, recognizing that Web addresses themselves are subject to change if, say, one tool vendor acquires another. You can find detailed feature comparisons of these and several other tools on the International

Council on Systems Engineering's Web site at *http://www.incose.org/toc.html* along with guidance on how to select a requirements management tool (Jones et al. 1995).

TABLE 19-1 SOME COMMERCIAL REQUIREMENTS MANAGEMENT TOOLS

Tool	Vendor	Database- or Document-Centric
Caliber-RM	Starbase Corporation, *http://www.starbase.com*	database
DOORS	Telelogic, *http://www.telelogic.com*	database
DOORSrequireIT	Telelogic, *http://www.telelogic.com*	document
RequisitePro	Rational Software Corporation, *http://www.rational.com*	document
RTM Workshop	Integrated Chipware, Inc., *http://www.chipware.com*	database
Vital Link	Compliance Automation, Inc., *http://www.complianceautomation.com*	document

A significant distinction between the tools is whether they are database-centric or document-centric. Database-centric products (such as Caliber-RM and DOORS) store all requirements, attributes, and traceability information in a database. Depending on the product, the database is either commercial or proprietary, relational or object-oriented. Requirements can be imported from various source documents, but they then reside in the database. In most respects, the textual description of a requirement is treated simply as a required attribute. Some products let you link individual requirements to external files (Microsoft Word files, Microsoft Excel files, graphics files, and so on) that provide supplementary information augmenting the contents of the requirements repository.

The document-centric approach treats a document created using a word processing program such as Word or Adobe FrameMaker as the primary container for the requirements. RequisitePro enhances a document's capabilities by letting you select text to store as discrete requirements in a database. Once in the database, you can define attributes and traceability links, just as you can with the database-centric products. Mechanisms are provided to synchronize the database and document contents. DOORSrequireIT doesn't use a separate database; instead it inserts an attribute table into the Word document next to any text that the user identifies as a requirement. RTM Workshop straddles both paradigms, being primarily database-centric but also letting you maintain requirements in a Word document.

Other than the entry-level DOORSrequireIT, these tools aren't cheap, but the high cost of requirements-related problems can justify investing in them. Recognize that the cost of a tool is not simply what you pay for the licenses. It also includes annual maintenance fees and the costs of installing the software, performing administration, obtaining vendor support and consulting, training your users, and upgrading to new versions periodically. Your cost-benefit analysis should consider these additional expenses before you make a purchase.

BENEFITS OF USING A REQUIREMENTS MANAGEMENT TOOL

Even if you do a magnificent job gathering your project's requirements, automated assistance can help you work with these requirements as development progresses. A requirements management tool becomes most beneficial after time has passed and the team's memory of the requirements details has faded. Following are some of the tasks such a tool can help you perform.

Manage versions and changes   Your project should define a requirements baseline, which is a specific collection of requirements allocated to a particular release. A few of the requirements management tools provide flexible baselining functions. The tools automatically maintain a history of the changes made to every requirement, which is superior to any of the possible ways of maintaining revision histories manually in a document. You can record the rationale behind each change decision and revert to a previous version of a requirement if necessary. Some of the tools include a simple, built-in change-proposal system that links change requests directly to the affected requirements.

Store requirements attributes   You should store several attributes of each requirement in a central location, as discussed in Chapter 16. Everyone working on the project must be able to view the attributes, and selected individuals are permitted to update their values. Requirements management tools generate several system-defined attributes (such as the date a requirement was created and its version number), and they let you define additional attributes of various data types. You can sort, filter, or query the database to display subsets of the requirements that have specific attribute values.

Facilitate impact analysis   The tools enable requirements tracing by letting you define links between different kinds of requirements, between requirements in different subsystems, and between individual requirements and related system components—for example, designs, code, and tests. The links help you analyze the impact a proposed change will have on a specific requirement by identifying other system elements the change might affect. It's also a good idea to trace each functional requirement back to its origin or parent so that you know where every requirement came from.

Track requirements status   Collecting the requirements into a database lets you know how many discrete requirements you've specified for the product. Tracking the status of each requirement during development supports the overall status tracking of the project. A project manager has good insight into project status if he or she knows that 55 percent of the requirements approved for the next release have been verified, 28 percent have been implemented but not verified, and 17 percent have not yet been implemented.

Control access   You can define access permissions for individuals or groups of users. Most of the tools let you share requirements information with a geographically dispersed team through a Web interface to the database. The databases use requirement-level locking to permit multiple users to update the database contents concurrently.

Communicate with stakeholders   Requirements management tools typically permit team members to discuss requirements issues electronically through threaded conversations. Automatically triggered e-mail messages notify affected individuals when a new discussion entry is made or when a specific requirement is modified.

Reuse requirements   Storing requirements in a database facilitates reusing them in multiple projects or subprojects. Requirements that logically fit into multiple parts of the product description can be stored once and referenced when necessary to avoid having to store duplicate requirements.

COMMERCIAL REQUIREMENTS MANAGEMENT TOOLS

Commercial requirements management tools let you define different types of database elements, such as business requirements, use cases, functional requirements, hardware requirements, nonfunctional requirements, and tests. This lets you differentiate individual objects you want to treat as requirements from other useful information contained in the SRS. All the tools provide strong capabilities for defining attributes for each type of requirement, which is a great advantage over the typical document-based SRS approach.

Most requirements management tools integrate with Word to some degree, typically adding a tool-specific menu to the Word menu bar. Vital Link is based on FrameMaker, rather than Word. The higher-end tools support a rich variety of import and export file formats. Several of the tools let you select specific text from a document to be treated as a discrete requirement, as well as letting you add new requirements directly to the database. When you mark document text as a requirement, the tool visually highlights the requirement and inserts Word bookmarks and hidden text. The tools can also parse documents in various fashions to extract individual requirements. The parsing from a word-processed document will be imperfect unless you were diligent about using text styles or keywords such as "shall" when you wrote it.

The tools support hierarchical numeric requirement labels, in addition to maintaining a unique internal identifier for each requirement. These identifiers typically consist of a short text prefix that indicates the requirement type (such as UR for a user requirement) followed by a unique integer. The higher-end tools provide efficient Microsoft Windows Explorer–like displays to let you manipulate the hierarchical requirements tree. The requirements display in DOORS looks like a hierarchically structured SRS.

Output capabilities from the tools include the ability to generate a requirements document, either in a user-specified format or as a tabular report. Caliber-RM has a powerful Document Factory that lets you define an SRS template in Word using simple directives to indicate page layout, boilerplate text, attributes to extract from the database, and the text styles to use. The Document Factory populates this template with information it selects from the database according to user-defined query criteria to produce a customized specification document. Therefore, an SRS is essentially a report generated from selected database contents.

All the tools have robust traceability features that let you define the links between requirements and other system elements. In RTM Workshop, each project defines a class schema resembling an entity-relationship diagram for all the stored object types. Traceability is handled by defining links between objects in two classes (or within the same class), based on the class relationships defined in the schema. When a requirement is changed after you've established traceability links to or from it, several of the tools automatically follow the links and mark any other requirements or components that might be affected by the change as questionable or "suspect." This helps you analyze the impact of proposed requirements changes.

Other features include the ability to set up user groups and define permissions for selected users or groups to read, write, create, and delete projects, requirements, attributes, and attribute values. Several of the products let you incorporate nontextual objects such as Excel worksheets and graphics into the requirements repository. The tools include learning aids, such as tutorials or sample projects, to help you get up to speed.

These products show a trend toward increasing integration with other tools used in application development, such as testing, design-modeling, problem-tracking, and project management tools. When you select a requirements management product, determine whether it can exchange data with the other tools you use. Here are some examples of the tool interconnections that these products exhibit today:

- You can link requirements in RequisitePro to use cases modeled in Rational Rose and to test cases in Rational TeamTest.

- DOORS lets you trace requirements to individual design elements stored in Rational Rose.

- RequisitePro and DOORS can connect individual requirements to project tasks in Microsoft Project.

- Caliber-RM has a central communications framework that lets you link requirements to use-case, class, or process design elements stored in Select Software Tools' Select Enterprise and to test entities stored in Mercury Interactive's TestDirector. You can then access those linked elements directly from the requirements in Caliber-RM's database.

Implementing Requirements Management Automation

Any of these products will move your requirements management practices to a higher plane of sophistication and capability. However, the diligence of the users is a critical success factor. Dedicated, disciplined, and knowledgeable people will make progress even with mediocre tools, while the best tools won't pay for themselves in the hands of unmotivated or ill-trained users. Don't write a check for a requirements management tool unless you're willing to respect the learning curve and make the time investment. Because you can't expect an instantaneous return on your investment, don't base a major project's success on a tool that you are using for the first time. Gain some experience working with the tool on a pilot project before you employ it on a high-stakes project.

Select a tool based on the platform, pricing, access modes, and requirements paradigm—document-centric or database-centric—that best fits your development environment. The following procedure can help you select the right tool:

1. Define your project's requirements for a requirements management tool. Identify the capabilities that are most significant to you, the other tools to which you'd like the product to connect, and whether issues such as remote data access through the Web are important. Decide whether you want to continue using documents to contain some of your requirements information or whether you prefer to store all the information in a database.

2. List 10 to 15 factors that will influence your selection decision. Include subjective categories such as tailorability as well as the efficiency and effectiveness of the GUI.

3. Distribute 100 points among the selection factors you listed in step 2, giving more points to the more important factors.

4. Obtain current information about the available requirements management tools, and rate the candidates against each of your selection factors. Scores for the subjective factors will have to wait until you can actually work with each tool. A vendor demonstration can fill in some of the blanks, but the demo likely will be biased toward the tool's strengths and isn't a substitute for using the product yourself for several hours.

5. Calculate the score for each candidate based on the weight you gave each factor to see which products appear to best fit your needs.

6. Solicit experience reports from other users of each candidate product, perhaps by posting queries in online discussion forums, to supplement your own evaluation and the vendor's literature and sales pitch.

7. Obtain evaluation copies from vendors of your two or three top-rated tools. Define an evaluation process before you install the candidates to make sure you get the information you need to make a good decision.

8. Evaluate the tools using a real project, not just the tutorial project that comes with the product. After completing your evaluations, adjust your rating scores if necessary and see which tool ranks highest.

9. To make a decision, combine the ratings, licensing costs, and ongoing costs with information on vendor support, input from current users, and your team's subjective impressions of the products.

Recognize that it will take effort to load a project's requirements into the database, define attributes, set the traceability links, keep the database's contents current, define security groups and privileges, and train users. Make an organization-wide commitment to actually use the product you select, instead of letting it become expensive shelfware. Avoid the temptation to develop your own requirements management tool or to cobble together general-purpose office automation products in an attempt to mimic the commercial products. This approach initially looks like an easy solution, but it can quickly grow into an effort much too large for a team that doesn't have the resources to build the tool right.

Provided you remember that a tool cannot overcome process deficiencies, you're likely to find that commercial requirements management tools enhance the control you have over your software requirements. Once you've made a requirements database work for you, you'll never go back to plain paper.

Next Steps

◆ Analyze shortcomings in your current requirements management process to see whether a commercial requirements management tool is likely to provide sufficient value to justify the investment. Make sure you understand the causes of your current shortcomings, rather than simply assuming a tool will correct them.

◆ Before launching a comparative evaluation, assess your team's readiness for adopting a tool. Reflect on previous attempts to incorporate new tools into your development process to understand why they succeeded or failed so that you can position yourselves for success.

Epilogue

Nothing is more important to the success of a software project than understanding what problem you need to solve and what you intend to build to
solve it. The project's requirements provide the foundation for that success.
If the development team and its customers don't agree on the product's
capabilities and characteristics, the most likely outcome is one of those unpleasant software surprises that we'd all prefer to avoid. If your current
requirements practices are not giving you the results you need, selectively
and thoughtfully apply some of the many techniques presented in this book.
Key themes of effective software requirements engineering include:

♦ Involving customer representatives early and extensively

♦ Developing requirements iteratively and incrementally

- Representing the requirements in several ways to make sure every-one understands them

- Assuring the requirements' completeness and correctness with all concerned groups

- Controlling the way requirements changes are made

Changing the way a software development organization works is difficult. It's hard to acknowledge that your current approaches aren't working as well as you would like and to figure out what to try next. It's hard to find the time to learn about new techniques, develop improved processes, pilot and adjust them, and roll them out to the whole project team or organization. It can be difficult to convince the team members and other stakeholders that change is needed. However, if you don't change the way you work, you have no reason to believe that the current project will go any better than the last project.

Success in software process improvement depends on:

- Addressing clear points of pain in the organization

- Focusing on a few improvement areas at a time

- Setting clear goals and defining action plans for your improvement activities

- Addressing the human and cultural factors associated with organizational change

- Persuading senior managers to view process improvement as a strategic investment in business success

Keep these process improvement principles in mind as you define a roadmap to improved requirements engineering practice and commence your journey. Stay grounded in practical approaches that are appropriate for your organization and team. If you actively apply known good practices and rely on common sense, you can significantly improve how you handle your project's requirements, with all the advantages that brings. And remember that without excellent requirements, software is like a box of chocolates: you never know what you're going to get.

Appendix

Current Requirements Practice Self-Assessment

This Appendix contains twenty questions you can use to calibrate your current requirements engineering practices and identify areas to reinforce. Select from the four possible responses for each question the one that most closely describes the way you currently deal with that software requirements issue. If you wish to quantify the self-assessment, give yourself zero points for each "a" response, 1 point for each "b," 3 points for each "c," and 5 points for each "d" response. The maximum possible score is 100 points. However, don't focus so much on a high score as on using this self-assessment to spot opportunities to apply new practices that might benefit your organization. Each question refers you to the chapter that addresses the topic addressed by the question.

Some of the questions might not pertain to the kind of software your organization develops. Situations are different; your project might not need the most comprehensive, sophisticated approaches. For example, highly innovative products with no precedent in the marketplace will likely have volatile requirements evolving from a general product concept. Recognize, though, that informal approaches to requirements increase the likelihood of doing extensive rework. Most organizations will benefit from following the practices at the high end of the scale.

1. How is the project's scope defined, communicated, and used? [Chapter 6]

   a. The person who conceives the product communicates telepathically with the development group.

   b. There is a written project vision statement somewhere.

   c. We use a standard vision and scope document template, and all project members have access to the vision and scope document.

   d. All proposed features and requirement changes are evaluated to see whether they lie within the documented vision and scope.

2. How are the customer communities for the product identified and characterized? [Chapter 7]

   a. We aren't sure who our customers might be.

   b. Marketing probably knows who the customers are.

   c. Target customers are identified by management, from marketing surveys, and from our existing customer base.

   d. Marketing, management, and key customer representatives identify distinct user classes, whose characteristics are summarized in the SRS.

3. How do you obtain voice-of-the-customer input? [Chapter 7]

   a. Development already knows what to build.

   b. Marketing feels they can provide the user perspective.

   c. Focus groups of typical users are surveyed or interviewed.

    d.   Specific individuals who represent different user classes participate on the project, with agreed-upon responsibilities and authority.

4.   How well trained and how experienced are your requirements analysts? [Chapter 2]

    a.   They have little experience and no specific training in developing requirements; they would rather write code.

    b.   The analysts are developers who have taken a one- or two-day class on software requirements and have interacted with users before.

    c.   They've had several days of training and considerable experience in interviewing techniques and facilitating group sessions.

    d.   We have professional business or systems analysts with extensive experience in collaborating with users. They understand both the application domain and the software development process.

5.   How are the system requirements allocated to the software portions of the product? [Chapter 7]

    a.   Software is expected to compensate for any deficiencies in the hardware.

    b.   Software and hardware engineers discuss which subsystem should perform which functions.

    c.   A system engineer analyzes the system requirements and allocates some of them to software.

    d.   Portions of the system requirements are allocated to software subsystems and traced into specific software requirements. Subsystem interfaces are explicitly defined and documented.

6.   What techniques are used to analyze the customer's problem? [Chapter 8]

    a.   Our developers are smart; they understand the problem fine.

    b.   We ask users what they want, write it down, and then build it.

    c.   We talk with users about their business needs and their current systems and write an SRS.

    d.   We observe users doing their current tasks, model their current workflow processes, and learn what they need the new system to do. This shows us how parts of their process might be automated, and gives us ideas about what software features would be most valuable.

7.   What approaches are used to identify all specific software requirements? [Chapter 8]

    a.   We begin with a general understanding, write some code, and modify the code until we're done.

    b.   Management or marketing provides a product concept, and the developers write the requirements. Marketing tells development if they've missed anything, and sometimes marketing remembers to tell development if the product concept changes.

    c.   Marketing or customer representatives tell us what features and functions the product should contain.

    d.   We hold structured interviews or workshops with representatives from the different user classes for the product. We employ use cases to understand the user tasks, and we derive functional requirements from the use cases.

8.   How are the software requirements documented? [Chapters 9 and 10]

    a.   We piece together oral history, e-mail messages, voice-mail messages, interview notes, and meeting notes.

    b.   We write unstructured narrative textual documents, or we draw structured or object-oriented analysis models.

    c.   We write requirements in structured natural language at a consistent level of detail according to a standard SRS template, combined with some graphical analysis models using standard notations.

    d.   We store our requirements in a database or a commercial requirements management tool and our analysis models in a CASE tool. Several attributes are stored along with each requirement.

9.   How are nonfunctional requirements, such as software quality attributes, elicited and documented? [Chapter 11]

    a.   What are "software quality attributes"?

    b.   We do beta testing of the user interface to get feedback about what the users prefer.

    c.   Certain attributes, such as performance and security requirements, are documented.

    d.   We talk to customers to identify the important quality attributes for each product, and then we document them in a precise and verifiable way in the SRS.

10.   How are the individual requirements labeled? [Chapter 9]

    a.   We use paragraphs of narrative text; specific requirements are not discretely identified.

    b.   We use bulleted and numbered lists.

    c.   We use a hierarchical numbering scheme, such as "3.1.2.4."

    d.   Every discrete requirement has a unique, meaningful label that is not disrupted when other requirements are added, moved, or deleted.

11.   How are priorities for individual features or requirements established? [Chapter 13]

    a.   All of them are important, or we wouldn't have written them down in the first place.

    b.   The customers tell us which requirements are most important to them.

    c.   All requirements are labeled as high, medium, or low priority by customer consensus.

    d.   We use an analytical process to evaluate the value, cost, and risk associated with each use case, feature, or functional requirement to help us make priority decisions.

12. What techniques are used to prepare a partial solution and verify a mutual understanding of the problem? [Chapter 12]

    a. None; we just build the system.

    b. We build some simple prototypes and ask users for feedback. Sometimes we're forced to deliver prototype code.

    c. We create prototypes for both user interface mock-ups and technical proofs-of-concept when appropriate.

    d. We plan to create throwaway paper and electronic prototypes to help us refine the requirements. Sometimes we build evolutionary prototypes. We use structured evaluation scripts to obtain customer feedback on our prototypes.

13. How is the quality of the documented requirements evaluated? [Chapter 14]

    a. We think our requirements are pretty good.

    b. We pass the requirements documents around for feedback.

    c. The analyst and some developers hold informal reviews.

    d. We formally inspect our SRS and analysis models, with participants that include customers, developers, and testers. We write test cases against the requirements and use them to validate the SRS and models.

14. How are different versions of the requirements documents distinguished? [Chapter 16]

    a. The date the document is printed is generated automatically.

    b. We use a sequence number such as 1.0, 1.1, and so on for each document version.

    c. We have an identification scheme that distinguishes draft versions from baselined versions and major revisions from minor revisions.

    d. The requirements documents are stored under version control in a configuration management system, or requirements are stored in a commercial requirements management tool that maintains a revision history of each requirement.

15. How are software requirements traced back to their origin? [Chapter 18]

    a. They aren't.

    b. We know where many of the requirements came from.

    c. All requirements have an identified origin.

    d. We have full two-way tracing between every software requirement and some voice-of-the-customer statement, system requirement, use case, standard, regulation, architectural need, or other origin.

16. How are requirements used as the basis for developing project plans? [Chapter 15]

    a. The ship date is set before we begin gathering requirements. We can't change either the schedule or the requirements.

    b. We go through a rapid descoping phase to drop features just before the delivery date.

    c. The first iteration of the project plan addresses the schedule needed to gather requirements, and the rest of the project plan is developed after we have the requirements. However, we can't change the plan thereafter.

    d. We estimate the product size from the requirements, and base the schedules and plans on the estimated effort needed to implement the required functionality. Plans and commitments are updated through negotiation if the requirements change or the schedule slips.

17. How are the requirements used as a basis for design? [Chapter 15]

    a. We don't explicitly do design.

    b. If we have documented requirements, we might refer to them during programming.

    c. The requirements documents include the user interface design and other aspects of the solution we intend to implement.

    d. Designers inspect the SRS to make sure it can be used as the basis for design. We have full two-way traceability between individual functional requirements and design elements.

18. How are the requirements used as the basis for testing? [Chapter 15]

    a. There is no direct connection between requirements and testing.

    b. The testers test against what the developers said they built.

    c. We write system test cases against the use cases and functional requirements.

    d. Testers inspect the SRS to make sure the requirements are verifiable and to begin planning the testing process. We trace system tests back to specific functional requirements. Testing progress is measured in part by requirements coverage.

19. How is a software requirements baseline defined and managed for each project? [Chapter 16]

    a. What's a "baseline"?

    b. The customers and managers sign off on the requirements, but we still get a lot of changes and customer complaints.

    c. We define a requirements baseline, but it's not always kept current as changes are made over time.

    d. The requirements are stored in a database when an initial baseline is defined. The database and SRS are updated as requirements changes are approved. We maintain a change history for each requirement once it is baselined.

20. How are changes to the requirements managed? [Chapter 17]

    a. Uncontrolled changes creep into the project regularly.

    b. Change is discouraged by freezing the requirements after the requirements phase is complete.

    c. We use a standard form for submitting change requests to a central submission point. The project manager decides which changes to incorporate.

    d. Changes are made according to a defined change control process that uses a tool to collect, store, and communicate change requests. The impact of each change is evaluated before deciding whether to approve it, and a change control board makes those decisions.

References

Ambler, Scott. 1995. "Reduce Development Costs with Use-Case Scenario Testing." *Software Development* 3(7):53–61.

———.1999. "Trace Your Design." *Software Development* 7(4):48–55.

Andriole, Stephen J. 1996. *Managing Systems Requirements: Methods, Tools, and Cases*. New York: McGraw-Hill.

Arlow, Jim. 1998. "Use Cases, UML Visual Modeling and the Trivialisation of Business Requirements." *Requirements Engineering* 3(2):150–152.

Arnold, Robert S., and Shawn A. Bohner. 1998. *Software Change Impact Analysis*. Los Alamitos, CA: IEEE Computer Society Press.

Bass, Len, Paul Clements, and Rick Kazman. 1998. *Software Architecture in Practice*. Reading, MA: Addison-Wesley.

Beizer, Boris. 1990. *Software Testing Techniques*, 2d ed. New York: Van Nostrand Reinhold.

———. 1999. "Best and Worst Testing Practices: A Baker's Dozen." *Cutter IT Journal* 12(2):32–38.

Beyer, Hugh, and Karen Holtzblatt. 1998. *Contextual Design: Defining Customer-Centered Systems*. San Francisco: Morgan Kaufmann Publishers, Inc.

Boehm, Barry W. 1981. *Software Engineering Economics*. Englewood Cliffs, NJ: Prentice-Hall.

———. 1988. "A Spiral Model of Software Development and Enhancement," *IEEE Computer* 21(5):61–72.

Boehm, Barry, et al. 1976. "Quantitative Evaluation of Software Quality," *Second IEEE International Conference on Software Engineering*. Los Alamitos, CA: IEEE Computer Society Press.

Booch, Grady, James Rumbaugh, and Ivar Jacobson. 1999. *The Unified Modeling Language User Guide*. Reading, MA: Addison-Wesley.

Brooks, Frederick P., Jr. 1987. "No Silver Bullet: Essence and Accidents of Software Engineering," *Computer* 20(4):10–19.

Brown, Norm. 1996. "Industrial-Strength Management Strategies," *IEEE Software* 13(4):94–103.

Caputo, Kim. 1998. *CMM Implementation Guide: Choreographing Software Process Improvement*. Reading, MA: Addison-Wesley.

Carnegie Mellon University/Software Engineering Institute. 1995. *The Capability Maturity Model: Guidelines for Improving the Software Process*. Reading, MA: Addison-Wesley.

Carr, Marvin J., Suresh L. Konda, Ira Monarch, F. Carol Ulrich, and Clay F. Walker. 1993. *Taxonomy-Based Risk Identification* (CMU/SEI-93-TR-6). Pittsburgh, PA: Software Engineering Institute, Carnegie Mellon University.

Charette, Robert N. 1990. *Applications Strategies for Risk Analysis*. New York: McGraw-Hill.

Christel, Michael G., and Kyo C. Kang. 1992. *Issues in Requirements Elicitation* (CMU/SEI-92-TR-12). Pittsburgh, PA: Software Engineering Institute, Carnegie Mellon University.

Cockburn, Alistair. 1997a. "Goals and Use Cases." *J. Object-Oriented Programming* 10(5):35–40.

———. 1997b "Using Goal-Based Use Cases." *J. Object-Oriented Programming* 10(6):56–62.

Cohen, Lou. 1995. *Quality Function Deployment: How to Make QFD Work for You.* Reading, MA: Addison-Wesley.

Collard, Ross. 1999. "Test Design." *Software Testing and Quality Engineering* 1(4):30–37.

Constantine, Larry. 1998. "Prototyping from the User's Viewpoint." *Software Development* 6(11):51–57.

Davis, Alan M. 1993. *Software Requirements: Objects, Functions, and States.* Englewood Cliffs, NJ: PTR Prentice Hall.

———. 1995. *201 Principles of Software Development.* New York: McGraw-Hill.

DeGrace, Peter, and Leslie Hulet Stahl. 1993. *The Olduvai Imperative: CASE and the State of Software Engineering Practice.* Englewood Cliffs, NJ: Yourdon Press/Prentice-Hall.

DeMarco, Tom. 1979. *Structured Analysis and System Specification.* Englewood Cliffs, NJ: Prentice-Hall.

Dorfman, Merlin, and Richard H. Thayer. 1990. *Standards, Guidelines, and Examples on System and Software Requirements Engineering.* Los Alamitos, CA: IEEE Computer Society Press.

Ebenau, Robert G., and Susan H. Strauss. 1994. *Software Inspection Process.* New York: McGraw-Hill.

Fagan, Michael E. 1976. "Design and Code Inspections to Reduce Errors in Program Development." *IBM Systems Journal* 15(3):182–211.

Freedman, Daniel P., and Gerald M. Weinberg. 1990. *Handbook of Walkthroughs, Inspections, and Technical Reviews: Evaluating Programs, Projects, and Products,* 3d ed. New York: Dorset House Publishing.

Gause, Donald C., and Brian Lawrence. 1999. "User-Driven Design." *Software Testing & Quality Engineering* 1(1):22–28.

Gause, Donald C., and Gerald M. Weinberg. 1989. *Exploring Requirements: Quality Before Design.* New York: Dorset House Publishing.

Gilb, Tom. 1988. *Principles of Software Engineering Management.* Harlow, England: Addison Wesley Longman Ltd.

Gilb, Tom, and Dorothy Graham. 1993. *Software Inspection.* Wokingham, England: Addison-Wesley.

Glass, Robert L. 1992. *Building Quality Software.* Englewood Cliffs, NJ: Prentice-Hall.

———. 1999 "Inspections—Some Surprising Findings." *Communications of the ACM* 42(4):17–19.

Gotel, O., and A. Finkelstein. 1994. "An Analysis of the Requirements Traceability Problem." In *Proceedings of the First International Conference on Requirements Engineering,* 91–104. Los Alamitos, CA: IEEE Computer Society Press.

Grady, Robert B., and Tom Van Slack. 1994. "Key Lessons in Achieving Widespread Inspection Use." *IEEE Software* 11(4):46–57.

Ham, Gary A. 1998. "Four Roads to Use Case Discovery: There Is a Use (and a Case) for Each One." *CrossTalk* 11(12): 17–19.

Hohmann, Luke. 1997. "Managing Highly Usable Graphical User Interface Development Efforts." http://members.aol.com/lhohmann/papers.htm

Hsia, Pei, David Kung, and Chris Sell. 1997. "Software Requirements and Acceptance Testing," in *Annals of Software Engineering,* Nancy R. Mead, ed. 3:291–317.

Humphrey, Watts S. 1997. *Managing Technical People: Innovation, Teamwork, and the Software Process.* Reading, MA: Addison-Wesley.

References

IEEE. 1992. IEEE Std 1061-1992: "IEEE Standard for a Software Quality Metrics Methodology," Los Alamitos, CA: IEEE Computer Society Press.

———. 1997. *IEEE Software Engineering Standards Collection.* Los Alamitos, CA: IEEE Computer Society Press.

———. 1998. IEEE Std 830-1998: "IEEE Recommended Practice for Software Requirements Specifications." Los Alamitos, CA: IEEE Computer Society Press.

International Function Point Users Group. 1999. *Function Point Counting Practices Manual, Version 4.1.* Westerville, OH: International Function Point Users Group.

Jackson, Michael. 1995. *Software Requirements & Specifications: A Lexicon of Practice, Principles, and Prejudices.* Harlow, England: Addison-Wesley.

Jacobson, Ivar, Magnus Christerson, Patrik Jonsson, and Gunnar Övergaard. 1992. *Object-Oriented Software Engineering: A Use Case Driven Approach.* Harlow, England: Addison Wesley Longman Ltd.

Jarke, Matthias. 1998. "Requirements Tracing." *Communications of the ACM* 41(12):32–36.

Jones, Capers. 1994. *Assessment and Control of Software Risks.* Englewood Cliffs, NJ: PTR Prentice Hall.

———. 1996a. "Strategies for Managing Requirements Creep." *IEEE Computer* 29(7):92–94.

———. 1996b. *Applied Software Measurement*, 2d ed. New York: McGraw-Hill.

Jones, David A., Donald M. York, John F. Nallon, and Joseph Simpson. 1995. "Factors Influencing Requirement Management Toolset Selection." *Proceedings of the Fifth Annual Symposium of the National Council on Systems Engineering,* Volume II. Seattle, WA: International Council on Systems Engineering.

Jung, Ho-Won. 1998. "Optimizing Value and Cost in Requirements Analysis." *IEEE Software* 15(4):74–78.

Karlsson, Joachim, and Kevin Ryan. 1997. "A Cost-Value Approach for Prioritizing Requirements." *IEEE Software* 14(5):67–74.

Keil, Mark, and Erran Carmel. 1995. "Customer-Developer Links in Software Development." *Communications of the ACM* 38(5):33–44.

Kelly, John C., Joseph S. Sherif, and Jonathon Hops. 1992. "An Analysis of Defect Densities Found During Software Inspections." *Journal of Systems and Software* 17(2):111–117.

Kosman, Robert J. 1997. "A Two-Step Methodology to Reduce Requirement Defects." In *Annals of Software Engineering,* Nancy R. Mead, ed. 3:477–494.

Kovitz, Benjamin L. 1999. *Practical Software Requirements: A Manual of Content and Style.* Greenwich, CT: Manning Publications Co.

Kruchten, Philippe. 1996. "A Rational Development Process" *CrossTalk* 9(7):11–16.

Larman, Craig. 1998. "The Use Case Model: What Are the Processes?" *Java Report* 3(8):62–72.

Lawrence, Brian. 1996. "Unresolved Ambiguity." *American Programmer* 9(5):17–22.

———. "Designers Must Do the Modeling." *IEEE Software* 15(2):31, 33.

Leffingwell, Dean. 1997. "Calculating the Return on Investment from More Effective Requirements Management." *American Programmer* 10(4):13–16.

Martin, Johnny, and W. T. Tsai. 1990. "N-fold Inspection: A Requirements Analysis Technique." *Communications of the ACM* 33(2):225–232.

McCabe, Thomas J. 1982. *Structured Testing: A Software Testing Methodology Using the Cyclomatic Complexity Metric.* National Bureau of Standards Special Publication 500-99.

McConnell, Steve. 1996. *Rapid Development: Taming Wild Software Schedules.* Redmond, WA: Microsoft Press.

———. 1998. *Software Project Survival Guide.* Redmond, WA: Microsoft Press.

McGraw, Karen L., and Karan Harbison. 1997. *User-Centered Requirements: The Scenario-Based Engineering Process.* Mahwah, NJ: Lawrence Erlbaum Associates.

Musa, John, Anthony Iannino, and Kazuhira Okumoto. 1987. *Software Reliability: Measurement, Prediction, Application.* New York: McGraw-Hill.

Nelsen, E. Dale. 1990. "System Engineering and Requirement Allocation." In Thayer, Richard H., and Merlin Dorfman, *System and Software Requirements Engineering.* Los Alamitos, CA: IEEE Computer Society Press.

Pardee, William J. 1996. *To Satisfy & Delight Your Customer: How to Manage for Customer Value.* New York: Dorset House Publishing.

Porter, Adam A., Lawrence G. Votta, Jr., and Victor R. Basili. 1995. "Comparing Detection Methods for Software Requirements Inspections: A Replicated Experiment." *IEEE Transactions on Software Engineering* 21(6):563–575.

Poston, Robert M. 1996. *Automating Specification-Based Software Testing.* Los Alamitos, CA: IEEE Computer Society Press.

Putnam, Lawrence H., and Ware Myers. 1997. *Industrial Strength Software: Effective Management Using Measurement.* Los Alamitos, CA: IEEE Computer Society Press.

Ramesh, Bala, Curtis Stubbs, Timothy Powers, and Michael Edwards. 1995. "Lessons Learned from Implementing Requirements Traceability." *CrossTalk* 8(4):11–15, 20.

Ramesh, Balasubramaniam. 1998. "Factors Influencing Requirements Traceability Practice." *Communications of the ACM* 41(12):37–44.

Regnell, Björn, Kristofer Kimbler, and Anders Wesslén. 1995. "Improving the Use Case Driven Approach to Requirements Engineering." *Proceedings of the Second IEEE International Symposium on Requirements Engineering,* pp. 40–47. Los Alamitos, CA: IEEE Computer Society Press.

Rettig, Marc. 1994. "Prototyping for Tiny Fingers." *Communications of the ACM* 37(4):21–27.

Robertson, James and Suzanne Robertson. 1994. *Complete Systems Analysis: The Workbook, The Textbook, The Answers.* New York: Dorset House Publishing.

————. 1997. "Requirements: Made to Measure," *American Programmer* 10(8):27–32.

Robertson, Suzanne, and James Robertson. 1999. *Mastering the Requirements Process.* Harlow, England: Addison-Wesley.

Rubin, Howard. 1999. "The *1999 Worldwide Benchmark Report*: Software Engineering and IT Findings for 1998 and 1999, Part II." *IT Metrics Strategies* 5(3): 1-13.

Rumbaugh, James. 1994. "Getting Started: Using Use Cases to Capture Requirements." *J. Object-Oriented Programming* 7(5):1–12, 23.

Schneider, G. Michael, Johnny Martin, and W. T. Tsai. 1992. "An Experimental Study of Fault Detection in User Requirements." *ACM Transactions on Software Engineering and Methodology* 1(2):188–204.

Smith, Craig. 1998. "Using a Quality Model Framework to Strengthen the Requirements Bridge." *Proceedings of the Third International Conference on Requirements Engineering,* pp. 118–125. Los Alamitos, CA: IEEE Computer Society Press.

Sommerville, Ian, and Pete Sawyer. 1997. *Requirements Engineering: A Good Practice Guide.* Chichester, England: John Wiley & Sons.

Song, Xiping, Bill Hasling, Gaurav Mangla, and Bill Sherman. 1998. "Lessons Learned from Building a Web-Based Requirements Tracing System." *Proceedings of the Third International Conference on Requirements Engineering,* pp. 41–50. Los Alamitos, CA: IEEE Computer Society Press.

Sorensen, Reed. 1999. "CCB—An Acronym for 'Chocolate Chip Brownies'? A Tutorial on Control Boards," *CrossTalk* 12(3):3–6.

Thayer, Richard H., and Merlin Dorfman, eds. 1997. *Software Requirements Engineering*, 2d ed. Los Alamitos, CA: IEEE Computer Society Press.

The Standish Group. 1995. *The CHAOS Report*. Dennis, MA: The Standish Group International, Inc.

Thompson, Bruce, and Karl Wiegers. 1995. "Creative Client/Server for Evolving Enterprises." *Software Development* 3(2):34–44.

Voas, Jeffrey. 1999. "Protecting Against What? The Achilles Heel of Information Assurance." *IEEE Software* 16(1):28–29.

Wallace, Dolores R., and Laura M. Ippolito. 1997. "Verifying and Validating Software Requirements Specifications." In Thayer, Richard H., and Merlin Dorfman, eds., *Software Requirements Engineering*, 2d ed., pp. 389–404. Los Alamitos, CA: IEEE Computer Society Press.

Weinberg, Gerald M. 1995. "Just Say No! Improving the Requirements Process." *American Programmer* 8(10):19–23.

Whitmire, Scott A. 1995. "An Introduction to 3D Function Points." *Software Development* 3(4):43–53.

———. 1997. *Object-Oriented Design Measurement*. New York: John Wiley & Sons.

Wiegers, Karl E. 1996a. *Creating a Software Engineering Culture*. New York: Dorset House Publishing.

———. 1996b. "Reducing Maintenance with Design Abstraction." *Software Development* 4(4):47–50.

———. 1998. "The Seven Deadly Sins of Software Reviews." *Software Development* 6(3):44–47.

Wieringa, R. J. 1996. *Requirements Engineering: Frameworks for Understanding*. Chichester, England: John Wiley & Sons.

Williams, Ray C., Julie A. Walker, and Audrey J. Dorofee. 1997. "Putting Risk Management into Practice." *IEEE Software* 14(3):75–82.

Wilson, Peter B. 1995. "Testable Requirements—An Alternative Sizing Measure." *The Journal of the Quality Assurance Institute* 9(4):3–11.

Wood, David P., and Kyo C. Kang. 1992. *A Classification and Bibliography of Software Prototyping* (CMU/SEI-92-TR-13). Pittsburgh, PA: Software Engineering Institute, Carnegie Mellon University.

Wood, Jane, and Denise Silver. 1995. *Joint Application Development*, 2d ed. New York: John Wiley & Sons.

Zultner, Richard E. 1993. "TQM for Technical Teams." *Communications of the ACM* 36(10):79–91.

INDEX

Page numbers in italics refer to tables, figures, or illustrations.

V

W

KARL E. WIEGERS

Karl E. Wiegers is principal consultant at Process Impact, a software process consulting and education company based in Portland, Oregon. He has consulted and presented training seminars at dozens of companies throughout North America. Previously, Karl spent 18 years at Eastman Kodak Company, where he held positions as a photographic research scientist, software developer, software manager, and software process and quality improvement leader. Karl received a B.S. in chemistry from Boise State College, and an M.S. and a Ph.D. in organic chemistry from the University of Illinois. He is a member of the IEEE, IEEE Computer Society, and ACM.

Karl is the author of the *Software Development* Productivity Award–winning book *Creating a Software Engineering Culture* (Dorset House, 1996), as well as more than 135 articles on many aspects of computing, chemistry, and military history. He is a contributing editor for *Software Development* magazine and a member of the editorial board for *IEEE Software* magazine.

When he isn't in front of the computer or the classroom, Karl enjoys playing his Gibson Les Paul guitar, riding his Suzuki VX800 motorcycle, studying military history, cooking, and sipping wine with his wife, Chris Zambito, and their black cat, Gremlin.

The manuscript for this book was prepared and submitted to Microsoft Press in electronic form. Text files were prepared using Microsoft Word 2000. Pages were composed by Microsoft Press using Adobe PageMaker 6.52 for Windows, with text and display type in Palatino. Composed pages were delivered to the printer as electronic prepress files.

Cover Design
Greg Hickman

Cover Illustration
Todd Daman

Interior Graphics
Rob Nance

Composition
Paula Gorelick

Index
Richard Genova

Best practices
for real-world software development

Now you can apply the industry's best software engineering practices to your own development projects with the BEST PRACTICES series from Microsoft Press. Written by some of the most knowledgeable and articulate practitioners in the business, these award-winning books take a pragmatic approach to managing the people, processes, and principles of software development. Use them to learn how to:

- Get high-pressure development schedules under control

- Energize software teams to work effectively
- Communicate delivery and quality expectations across the team and to management
- Keep costs down
- Deliver the best possible product to customers

Packed with practical, field-tested tools and tactics, BEST PRACTICES books offer candid accounts of what works and what doesn't, straight from the real-world experiences of the leading software vendors. Get them—and you get the inside track to everyday software excellence.

Code Complete	Debugging the Development Process	Dynamics of Software Development	Managing the Testing Process	Rapid Development	Writing Solid Code	Software Project Survival Guide
ISBN: 1-55615-484-4	ISBN: 1-55615-650-2	ISBN: 1-55615-823-8	ISBN: 0-7356-0584-X	ISBN: 1-55615-900-5	ISBN: 1-55615-551-4	ISBN: 1-57231-621-7
U.S.A. $35.00	U.S.A. $24.95	U.S.A. $24.95	U.S.A. $39.99	U.S.A. $35.00	U.S.A. $24.95	U.S.A. $24.99
UK £29.95	UK £22.99	UK £22.99	UK £37.49 [V.A.T. included]	UK £32.49	UK £22.99	UK £22.49
Canada $44.95	Canada $32.95	Canada $33.95	Canada $59.99	Canada $46.95	Canada $32.95	Canada $34.99

Microsoft®

mspress.microsoft.com

Get a **Free**
e-mail newsletter, updates,
special offers, links to related books,
and more when you

register on line!

Register your Microsoft Press® title on our Web site and you'll get a FREE subscription to our e-mail newsletter, *Microsoft Press Book Connections.* You'll find out about newly released and upcoming books and learning tools, online events, software downloads, special offers and coupons for Microsoft Press customers, and information about major Microsoft® product releases. You can also read useful additional information about all the titles we publish, such as detailed book descriptions, tables of contents and indexes, sample chapters, links to related books and book series, author biographies, and reviews by other customers.

Registration is easy. Just visit this Web page and fill in your information:

http://www.microsoft.com/mspress/register

Microsoft®

- -